Moranthology

ALSO BY CAITLIN MORAN

How to Be a Woman

Moranthology

CAITLIN MORAN

HARPER  PERENNIAL

NEW YORK • LONDON • TORONTO • SYDNEY • NEW DELHI • AUCKLAND

HARPER ● PERENNIAL

First published in Great Britain in 2012 by Ebury Press, an imprint of Ebury Publishing, A Random House Group Company.

HarperCollins books may be purchased for educational, business, or sales promotional use. For information please write: Special Markets Department, HarperCollins Publishers, 10 East 53rd Street, New York, NY 10022.

FIRST U.S. EDITION

Library of Congress Cataloging-in-Publication Data is available upon request.

ISBN 978-0-06-225853-3

12 13 14 15 16 OV/RRD 10 9 8 7 6 5 4 3 2 1

To the bit in Bottom *where Rik Mayall and Adrian Edmondson hit the gas man with a frying pan forty-two times. I learned so much from you.*

Contents

Moranthology

Introduction

or: I Try to Be Good

WHEN I BECAME JOURNALIST at the age of fifteen, it was a matter of simple expediency.

Having been homeschooled for the previous five years, I had no academic qualifications whatsoever. As a resident of a housing project in Wolverhampton, this seemed to leave me with a grand total of three future employment options:

1) prostitution,
2) working the check-out at the Gateway supermarket, Warstones Drive, or,
3) becoming a writer: an option I only knew of because that was what Jo March in *Little Women*, and Mother in *The Railway Children*, had done when they also fell upon hard times.

Considering all the options, I immediately eliminated Gateway, on the basis that their tabards were of a green hue—which gave my ruddy skin tone a particularly bilious tinge.

The prostitution, meanwhile, also got the ixnay—primarily in acknowledgment that I was, at the time, sharing a bunk-bed with my sister Caz. As she put it, quite reasonably, "I don't want to listen to you being ridden like a show-pony three feet from my face. Plus, I think your Johns might hit their head on the Paddington Bear lampshade."

So, writing it was. It's a choice I've never regretted—although I do have the odd, panging moment when I consider just how useful a 40-percent discount on anything from the Gateway deli counter might have been. That is a lot of cheap Black Forest ham.

I began writing. I had a list of words and phrases I loved: a collection like others might collect records, or badges. Jaguary. Lilac. Catholic. Uxurious. Jubilee. Isosoles. Leopardskin. Mimosa. Shagreen. Iodine. Collodial mercury. Ardent. Attar of Roses. Corybantic. Viola. These would, surely, be useful. I knew I wanted to write intense things—write until I'd written myself new shoes and new hair and new friends, and a new life away from the inexorably compacting walls of our house. Words can be weapons, or love-spells, or just motorcars you can drive across county borders.

But what I didn't know was what to write intensely *about,* or how to write about it. I had no subject. I had no subjectivity. I was just a bundle of sprawling words.

As a bundle of sprawling words, I entered writing competitions, and, at 15, won one—*The Observer*'s "Young Reporter of the Year." In the letter announcing that I'd won, they offered me a chance to visit their offices, in London.

This was—clearly—my chance to pitch for a job. They had no teenagers working on the paper—ipso facto, if I went down there and made the right impression, that job was mine. I was going to pitch my ass off at these guys. I was not coming home until I had a promise of further work from them in the bag.

I spent the evening before preparing for my first ever job interview in the best way I knew how.

"People like people who bring cake!" I said to myself, at 11 PM. I was creaming butter and sugar in a bowl. The sideboard was covered in zested lemons.

"A lovely lemon and cream sponge! By bringing cake, I will become associated in their minds with cake, and they will think favorably of me, re: future employ!"

At the time, I was heavily under the influence of the autobiographies of actress, comedian and writer Maureen Lipman (imagine a Carol Burnett who spent most of her life telling amusing anecdotes on NPR). Lipman seems to spend all her time giving her friends and colleagues in the media gifts—engraved lockets, bunches of flowers, thoughtful chocolate selections.

We didn't have any kind of cake box or cake tin, for transportation down to London, so I put the sponge into a small, red suitcase I had recently bought from a tag sale, and went to bed.

The production and transportation of the lemon cream sponge—done in order to secure the job at *The Observer*—had taken maybe seven hours, in total. This was six hours and fifty-eight minutes more than I had spent thinking about the actual job. Indeed, to be more specific, it was six hours and fifty-eight minutes more than I had ever considered what I would actually ever write.

SO HERE I AM, the next day, in London. Getting off the coach at Victoria Station wearing a gigantic hat—to make me look thinner—and carrying a lemon sponge in a suitcase. If I carry the suitcase by the handle, the cake will tip on the side—so I am carrying it flat, like a tray, in both hands. The time is 11:15 AM. I am due at the *Observer* offices, in Battersea, at 12:30 PM.

"Just enough time to go to the British Museum and Buckingham Palace!" I think, having looked at the tiny map of London I have in my pocket. I am keen that this journey to London will mix business with pleasure—perhaps to creature a new thing, "Plizness."

I set off, carrying my suitcase out in front of me, like a crown on a pillow.

THREE HOURS LATER, AND I finally turn up at the *Observer* offices. I am trying very, very hard not to cry. All the skin has been flayed off my heels—it turns out that wearing white pixie-boots and no socks is a poor idea if you're going to walk for three hours. I am soaked in sweat, utterly mortified, and newly enlightened as to the scale of capital cities.

When I woke that morning, I had no idea things were so far apart in London. In Wolverhampton, if you had a reasonable jogging pace, you could touch every single remarkable building in the town in under ten minutes. Fuck it—to be honest, if you sat next to the Man on the Horse statue in Queen's Square with a tennis ball, you could bounce it off every institute of note without moving. Even the McDonald's.

London, on the other hand, seems to have endless amounts of wide, gray, straight roads, which stretch on forever, and never have the British Museum, or Buckingham Palace, or—anxiously, from 12:17 PM onwards—the *Observer* offices at the end of them. I have been lost in a park, and round the back of Trafalgar Square. At one point, I tried to hail a taxi—but was holding the cake-suitcase in both hands at the time, and so looked like someone doing an impression of the wise old monkey in the Lion King holding up a newly-born Simba for veneration, instead. The taxi just drove past.

The kindly folk at *The Observer* have, understandably, been very worried. A fifteen-year-old girl has been missing in London for three hours—then turns up weeping and limping. They sit me down in a conference room, and prepare to ask me if I've been sexually assaulted.

"I really wanted to see the British Museum's collection of cuneiform tablets!" I say, trying to satirize the idea of someone being so nerdy they kept the deputy editor of the *The Observer* waiting for a job interview.

Unfortunately, they think I'm being totally truthful, and try to make me feel better by talking about their favorite exhibits—a conversation I can't join in on, as, obviously, I never made it to the British Museum. The only museum I've ever been in is the one at Bantock House in Wolverhampton, where they have a castle made of foil candy wrappers. It is a very good castle. Shiny. I tell them about the castle. They agree it sounds very special.

But still—still! Extrordinarily, after all of this, when I've drunk three glasses of water, quickly dashed a tear from my eye under the guise of adjusting my hat, and had everyone, very kindly, say, "London really IS easy to get lost in" one hundred times—there comes the moment where the deputy editor says, "So! Now we've finally got you here, ho ho ho, would you like to work for us?"

Unfortunately, at the time, I am going through a phase of not wanting to say the right thing, or the nice thing—but the *legendary* thing. I imagine whole days' worth of conversations in my head, and then analyze them afterwards, from the vantage point of others, on their legendaryness-potential.

In the "being offered a job to write three columns in a national newspaper" scenario, which I've run through 300 times, I've finally decided that the legendary response—spoken of in awe for years to come ("And then she said—hahah, oh it was brilliant . . .") is the one I bring out now:

"Work for you? Oh I'd love to. I'd really, really love to."

I pause—then pick up a paper napkin, dip it in my glass of water, and then make as if to go and wash the walls.

"First I'll do the walls," I say, "then the floors—that way, if I drip . . ."

It's a line from *Annie*—the scene where Daddy Warbucks asks her to live with him, and Annie initially misunderstands, and thinks he wants her to be his maid. When I imagined delivering this line, I imagine everyone laughing. "We offered her a job—as a columnist—but she parodied her working-class background and obsession with musicals by pretending that we'd offered her a job as an office cleaner, instead! Legendary!"

There is no way everyone in this room won't have seen *Annie*. This line is going to be a killer.

Everyone in this room has not seen *Annie*.

There is another awkward pause.

"Would you like to write some columns for us?" the deputy editor asks, eventually, getting things back on track by pretending what I've just said never happened. "During the summer holidays? I think we'd be very interested to hear what you have to say about life—and cuneiform tablets! And tin-foil castles, ho ho ho!"

"Yes please," I say, in a very simple way. I've decided to keep everything very simple from now on.

"So," the features editor says. She's really lovely. Glossy-haired. A nice lady. "What would you like to write for us?"

I stare at her.

"What kind of ideas have you got?" she asks, again.

I keep staring. It had literally never occurred to me that I'd have to think of something to write. I thought you just turned up, said something legendary, and then they told you what to write. Like school. Papers are just . . . paid homework, surely? The grown-ups—a shadowy agglomoration who, in my mind, I presume to be politicians, Daddy Warbucks the billionaire and possibly John Craven from *Newsround*—decide what goes in the papers, and then farm it out to the writers. You don't have to . . . journalists don't . . . surely . . .

". . . could do a list of the things you feel most passionately about; issues that affect you," the deputy editor is saying. I have got nothing here. I am all out on a conversation like this. I am going to have to pull the ripcord on this situation.

"I made you a cake!" I say, brightly. "To have with your afternoon tea. A lemon sponge!"

I carefully place the suitcase on the table—having kept it, diligently, horizontal all day. Even when I sat in that "out of order" bus stop and cried—and open it up. People like people who bring cake! By bringing cake, I will become associated in their minds with cake, and they will think favorably of me, re: future employ!

In the punishing August heat, during a three-hour walk around London, all the lemon cream inside the cake has split, and gone rancid. An uneasy smell of vomit-cake fills the room. Everyone looks at me. In my head, I type out the sentence, "Write about this?"

BACK IN WOLVERHAMPTON, ON the phone, my new editors suggest that I "read the papers, watch the news—see if there's something you want to write about."

I assiduously research every high-profile current affairs story in the media for two weeks straight—then write 600 words about my brother getting lost on Ynylas beach last year. The week after, I file 600 words about going to the library with my brothers and sisters ("We are in the 'Books So Boring They Should Have Won the Booker Prize' section."). My third, and last, piece is about the family going on a picnic.

And then that's it. That was all *The Observer* offered me, and it's finished. I'm unemployed again. I'm going to have to try and find some work.

SIX MONTHS LATER, I'M on the phone, pitching ideas to *The Guardian*. I know they want "teenage-y" things, so I'm doing my best, but I don't really know much about teenagers, to be honest: being homeschooled, the only teenager I know, apart from myself, is my sister Caz, and she's currently not speaking to me.

When I go into her room, she makes me stand in the corner, facing away from her, while I talk. Years later, I see the serial killer doing exactly the same thing to his victims in *The Blair Witch Project*.

"I could write about, erm, keeping a diary, or, erm, fashions," I say, dubiously. "Or, erm, buses?"

I spend a lot of time on the bus. I've noticed a pecking-order in the seating arrangements, and am keen to share my theory that the true visionaries always sit top deck, front left, because that's the position Dan Ackroyd assumes in the car in *The Blues Brothers,* and he is my favorite Brother. I have a lot of bus-observation ready to roll.

"You can be as hard-hitting as you like," the editor says, kindly, as the word "buses" still hovers in the air. Buses.

"Errrrr . . ." I say—the commission slipping away from me. I need to say something. I need to say something ear-catchy. In a panic, I blurt: "Anorexia?"

"Yes!" she says, instantly.

It's funny because, at the time, I spend most of my free time eating cream crackers covered with Shippam's Chicken & Ham paste. I am so in love with food that I get excited when the paste squirts up through the tiny holes in the crackers, like worm-casts. If I've ever had anorexia, it lasted less than forty-five minutes. I've not been very committed to it.

"I'd love to!" I say, before modulating down into my "issues" voice. "It's a terrible disease, and I can't believe I'm watching my generation being laid to waste by it."

I know nothing about anorexia. But now I've got 500 words to fill by 5 PM so I do what anyone would do: just make up any old shit.

"Lolita didn't diet. But today, children twelve or younger are conscious of the width of their hips, the length of their legs, even the slight curve of their stomachs," I started, cheerfully, although God knows why—I hadn't actually read *Lolita*. She was the only twelve-year-old I could think of, I suspect; apart from Laura Ingalls, who wouldn't really have been appropriate in this context. I just knew Lolita was generally "victim-y," so chucked her in here. This is what you do, when you know absolutely fucking nothing.

"I had a mini-skirt like Julia Roberts. I thought I should have the legs to go with it," said Eloise, who I'd just totally made up.

I'd also seen an episode of *Casualty* where a ballerina eats toilet paper, so I put that in there, too.

The piece ran in March 1992, and astonishingly did not change anyone's views on anorexia—not even the quote from "a GP" (who I'd made up) going, "These nineteen-year-olds come in here and ask to be put on the Pill, and I'm inclined to pat them on the head and give them Smarties, instead," which is obviously what I, deep down, thought would cure anorexia at the time. Smarties.

Or here's another piece I managed to blag at *The Observer*, around the same time—1993—entitled "We've Never Had It So Bad."

"What's so great about being a teenager in the material world of the nineties?" asks Caitlin Moran.

This really was a symphonic piece of bullshit. In the piece—600 words long—I lamented that I and my friend ("She's sixteen—six and ten years on the planet, four leap years—and says her life terrifies her because it seems so long until she'll die.") were being culturally crushed by the Baby Boomers.

"Sometimes we climb up onto the five-story parking garage, and throw bits of gravel at the people below, and my friend will shout 'WHO AM I?'

and I laugh until I cry because no one can hear us, and no one can tell her."

It's specious nonesense from beginning to end: for starters, you can't get access to the roof of any five-story parking garage in Wolverhampton: they're all completely sealed off, clearly to prevent health & safety issues exactly like the one I'm lying about here. And I honestly don't think any teenager has ever shouted "WHO AM I????" to the sky, except on dramas on Channel 4, which is exactly where I'd got this from.

"She has no identity, save that which advertisers sell her," I continue piously, castigating the whole advertising industry; wholly ignoring the fact that I love the song from the Bran Flakes ad ("They're tasty/Tasty/Very very tasty/They're very tasty!") and am quite emotionally invested in the romantic plotline to the Gold Blend couple.

I'D LIKE TO QUOTE you more of the terrible pieces I wrote around this time—thrashing around, desperately, for something, anything to write about—but I can't, because this is where my Fleet Street career ground to a halt for a while. A sum total of five pieces before everyone realized—including, finally, me—that I had absolutely nothing to write about. Or, more truthfully, that I did—but I just didn't know what it was yet.

I went underground (back to bed) and tried to work out how I could get a job writing when I knew—and I'm being generous here—absolutely nothing about the world. It took a while, but by the time I was sixteen, I had a plan.

So I'd finally figured out I couldn't write about my own life, because I haven't done anything. I was going to have to write about other, older people, who've actually done stuff, instead. I was going to become a rock critic—because I read *NME* and *Melody Maker,* and they are publications where writers will use words like "jaguary" and "jubilee" and "shagreen" while describing why they do or don't like U2, and I think this is probably something I could have a go at.

I write test reviews of my five favorite albums—*Hats* by Blue Nile, *Pills'n'Thrills'n'Bellyaches* by Happy Mondays, *High Land, Hard Rain* by Aztec Camera, *Reading, Writing & Arithmetic* by the Sundays, and

Nothing's Shocking by Jane's Addiction—and send them to the reviews editor, in an envelope that I carefully scent with Lemon Essence from the kitchen cupboard, to act in lieu of a lemon sponge in a suitcase. I am still working on the presumption that people will only give me work if they somehow associate me with baked goods. Perhaps it's this kind of erroneous assumption you get educated out of you at Oxbridge.

The reviews editor calls me the next day and asks me to do a test review of a local gig. When it's printed, I get £28.42, and become the freelance stringer for the Midlands area: Birmingham, Wolverhampton, Dudley and Derby. If there's a band who've sold around 2,000 records playing in the backroom of a pub within twenty miles of Spaghetti Junction, I am all over it. I am now, vaguely, in charge of indie in West Mercia.

After I had been working at *Melody Maker* for just seven months—working my patch, filing my reviews, stacking up those £28.42s—I wrote a review of Ned's Atomic Dustbin's new album, entitled *522*.

In the hipster pecking order of the time, Ned's—as their fans called them—were pretty much the lowest of the low: a group of lads from Stourbridge—the Midlands! My patch!—barely in their twenties, who made amiable, slightly slack-jawed, very white rackets for amiable, slightly slack-jawed, very white youths to leap around to. In terms of funk, or glamor, they rated level with Bovril, or the clog. Additionally, their career was past its best. They were on the wane.

Nonetheless, a lack of funk, hotness or success is not, and never has been, a crime. It's not even against park by-laws. Therefore, the thermo-nuclear savaging I proceeded to give that album, over 480 words, was as unnecessary and unprovoked as Chewbacca strafing the local duck pond with the *Millennium Falcon*.

Actually, I wasn't using weaponry a quarter as sophisticated as the *Millennium Falcon*. It was more like Chewbacca falling out of the *Millennium Falcon*, then wading into the duck pond and kicking the ducks, then stamping on the ducks, then punching the ducks—alarmed, innocent ducks, now all quacking as the Wookiee flailed at them, wholly unprovoked, and who didn't leave the pond until the water was covered in tail-feathers.

"Hello, boys," I opened—addressing the band directly. "Funerals are a bummer, aren't they? Career in a coffin, all we have to do is chuck a bit of earth around, and troop through a thick grey gauze of rain to the wake, and get pissed. I have been chosen to stand, blearily, at the wake, and say a few words at the passing of your ability to ever sell records again. What can I say? The words of one of the great poets—Liam from Flowered Up— seem appropriate: "FUCK OFF! FUCK OFF AND DIE!"

Eighteen years later, and I am still so mortified by what I wrote, I can only look at the middle section through my fingers: "Putrid . . . anthems to nothing . . . stink . . . dirges . . . nasty scribbles . . . no-one gives a flying fuck . . ."

I accused them of being sexless, tuneless, fuckless, revolting: responsible for a musical climate where bands crawled on their bellies with three chords, rather than flying with the aspirations of gods. I was a total wanker.

I ended with: "1994 was the year we waved goodbye to Kurt Cobain and That Bloke Out of Doctor Feelgood. Feel like making it a hat-trick, Jonn(nnnnnnnnn)?"

Yes, that's right—I ended an album review by wishing death on the lead singer, either by the methodology of Kurt Cobain, who'd shot himself in April, or the lead singer of Doctor Feelgood, who'd died of cancer in August. And spelt his name "sarcastically," to boot.

The review itself was sub-headlined, "Jesus, Caitlin—there are gonna be repercussions about this one." As if the magazine itself was alarmed by what I'd written.

Looking back now, I can see what I was doing. I was a seventeen-year-old, working in an office otherwise full of adults. I was a cub, savaging some prey, and bringing back the carcass to the pack elders, to impress them. I wanted to make my mark.

However, even the most cursory examination of the situation shows us that I was not bringing back a mighty Arctic fox. I had just come back with a couple of sad, surprised ducks instead.

And of course, we can also see that I was not a white-toothed wolf-cub, either—but a puffin, or a penguin, or a giant hen: some perambulatory creature not built for pugilism. I would never go up to someone at a party and be horrible to their face—so why was I doing it in a magazine? I was just thinking of what I wrote as "some copy"—some space filled on a page, with whatever came into my head at the time.

But of course, it's not just "copy." There's no such thing as "copy." Putting things on paper doesn't make it matter less. Putting things on paper makes it matter *more*.

The bottom line is, I believed I was a nice person—the kind of person who brought a lemon sponge cake to *The Observer*, and would pick worms off the road, and put them onto the grass with a cheerful "There you go, mate"—but I appeared to be pretending to be a cunt. Why was I doing that? There are enough cunts in the world already. We don't need any more. The only kind of person who would *pretend* to be a cunt probably *is* a cunt. This faux-cuntiness was a cunt's game. I decide I was going to stop.

I'D LIKE TO PRETEND I worked all this out myself, in the weeks after the Ned's Atomic Dustbin review was printed. That I quietly figured out what my principles were, and who I wanted to be, in a determined, intellectual re-imagining of myself: a rebirth through philosophy, and reason.

In reality, the man who was to eventually be my husband took me to one side at a gig a week later and said, in his mild way, "That review was a bit . . . off."

And that was when I realized—in a huge, anxious rush—that I couldn't do what so many of the writers I enjoyed—A. A. Gill, Julie Burchill and Hunter S. Thompson—did. That gleeful arson, those cool assassinations. I was not, like them, crouched behind my typewriter, picking off marauders with a pearl-handled pistol. I couldn't manage the daily rages of the columnists who despaired over the parking restrictions, and their tax bills, and the immigrants, and the gay dads, and the BBC, and women's fat arses in the wrong dresses, and the health and safety regulations. I couldn't handle the grief.

What I was built for, I felt, was something a bit more . . . herbivore. As I started to reassess my writing style, I thought about what I liked doing—what gave me satisfaction—and realized the primary one was just . . .

pointing at things. Pointing out things I liked, and showing them to other people—like a mum shouting, "Look! Moo-cows!" as a train rushes past a farm. I liked pointing at things, and I liked being reasonable and polite about stuff. Or silly. Silly was very, very good. No one ever got hurt by silly.

Best of all was being pointedly silly about serious things: politics, repression, bigotry. Too many commentators are quick to accuse their enemies of being evil. It's far, far more effective to point out that they're acting like idiots, instead. I was up for idiot-revealing.

"I am just going to be polite and silly, and point at cool things," I decided. "When I started writing, I would have killed to have one thing to write about. Now, I have three. Politeness *and* silliness, *and* pointing. That's enough."

SO, YES. IF THIS collection is anything, it is, I hope, either silly, or polite, or pointing at something cool. There is some vaguely serious stuff in here—recently, I have enjoyed taking to my writing bureau, and writing about poverty, benefit reform and the coalition government in the manner of a shit Dickins, or Orwell, but with tits.

The fifteen-year-old wannabe journalist in Wolverhampton, who was desperately looking for something to write *about*, actually had a million things to write about, all around her: housing projects, and life on benefits, and the wholly altered state that is being grindingly, decades-long poor—too broke to travel to another town, or escape from lingering, low-level dampness, fear and boredom.

But—perhaps in reaction to all this—my underlying, abiding belief is that the world is, still, despite everything, a flat-out amazing place. This book is a collection of instances of how brilliant the world often is—written by a lifelong fan of existence, and the Earth. Yes, there might still be speed bumps; and paperwork; this world can be irksome, and even I—essentially Pollyanna, with a C-section scar—have had a couple of rants in here. I will be honest with you: there is not much in here to increase the pride levels of Nazis, internet trolls, or Lola from *Charlie and Lola*. That crayoned harpy must die. And I will actually stand by that death wish. Unlike the one I lev-elled at poor John from Ned's Atomic Dustbin, to whom I now—eighteen years later—apologize to, while lying on my belly in abject prostration and mortification. I am so, so sorry. Tell your mum I'm sorry, too. She must have been dead upset.

But, generally, this is a manifesto for joy. When I got my second chance at being a journalist—being taken on by *The Times* as a columnist when I was eighteen, in my new persona as the "pointing cheerful person"—I determined to use the opportunity to racket around as many exhilarating things as possible. As a consequence, in this collection, I go to a sex-club with Lady Gaga; smoke fags with Keith Richards; walk twenty-six miles in the rain, eating cake; become an internet dwarf called "Scottbaio," then accidentally die, on air, on the *Richard & Judy* show; and confess to, once, having trapped a wasp under a glass, then got it stoned.

The motto I have penned on my knuckles is that this is the best world we have—because it's the only world we have. It's the simplest math ever. However many terrible, rankling, peeve-inducing things may occur, there are always libraries. And rain-falling-on-sea. And the moon. And love. There is always something to look back on, with satisfaction, or forward to, with joy. There is always a moment where you boggle at the world—at yourself—at the whole, unlikely, precarious business of being alive—and then start laughing.

And that's usually when I make a cup of tea, and start typing.*

---

*Actually, it's not. I usually leave it for at least another three hours of pissing around on the Topshop website, attacking in-growing hairs on my leg with tweezers, and looking at dream apartments in New York, before panicking, and beginning to hammer at stuff a scanty hour and thirty-seven minutes before deadline—but that's not as an inspiring sentence to end on. It kind of ruins things, tbh.

Part **One**

Caffeine, *Ghostbusters*, and Marijuana

In which I explain why Ghostbusters *is the greatest film in the world, watch Michael Jackson's memorial service in a state of some astonishment, and keep the Prime Minister waiting. But I start where I always end: in bed, confusing my husband.*

I thought long and hard about what the first piece should be in what is the nearest I will ever get to releasing a The Beatles Blue Album, *or* The Beatles Red Album. *Some incredibly righteous piece about the welfare system? A rhapsodic eulogy to how much I want to bang Sherlock in* Sherlock? *Or a carefully-weighed take-down of trans-phobia, sexism and homophobia, as mediated through the unlikely, yet ultimately fitting, imagery of the Moon Landings? Don't worry—they're all in here. Especially the Sherlock thing. There's a lot of Sherlock love in here. In many ways, this book might as well be called "Deduce THIS, Sexlock Holmes!" with a picture of me licking his meerschaum, cross-eyed and screaming.*

However, in the end, I ignored the more worthwhile, culturally valid and heart-felt stuff in favor of a ratty, decades-long, rumbling semi-feud with my husband instead.

Call Me Puffin

12:17 AM. WE ARE just going to sleep. I can hear Pete's breathing is modulating into REM. In the loft, the boiler powers down into standby mode. The duvet is perfectly snugged in. The day is done.

"I love you, Bear," I say.

"Mvv mmo too," he replies. There is a silence. It is followed by a second silence. Then:

Me: "Bear. It's funny, isn't it? Bear. I call you Bear."

Pete: "Mmrg."

Me: "But you . . . you have no nickname for me. It would be nice if you had a nickname for me."

Pete: "Marrrp."

Me: "Because, you know, it's been sixteen years now. I've had lots of slightly noisome nicknames for you—Bear, Pie, Mr. Poo, The Wurbles—but you've never had a nickname for me."

Pete: "Mrrrrrb."

Me: "I mean, a nickname arises out of a need, doesn't it? To rename something in order to display ownership; or indicate that you see in some-one an aspect that no one else can, and which demands unique acknowledg-ment. So not having a nickname for me kind of suggests you would quite happily let me be stolen by tinkers; or that you can't really tell the difference between me, my sisters and Moira Stuart."

Pete, unhappily: "Mrrrrrp."

Me: "Seriously: I think I really would quite like a nickname. It would make me feel more loved. I would feel a lot more loved if you could come up with a nickname for me. Now. Do it now."

Pete, turning over in bed: "I'm asleep."

Me: "I'll help you brainstorm. It needs to be playful—yet tender."

Pete, disbelievingly: "Playful yet tender. Is this actually happening?"

Me: "Yes. And, ideally, it would be reflective of the unique insight you have into me, after all those years. What comes to mind when you think of me?"

Pete: "The word 'me.' "

Me: "Do it properly!"

Pete: "Seriously. The word 'me.' You say it a lot. That, and 'serum.' But I don't really know what that means."

Me: "Not what *I say*—It's got to be what *you think*. WHY DO YOU LOVE ME?"

Pete, vaguely: "You're a woman?"

Me, firmly: "My nickname can't be 'Woman.' All my feminist friends will write a petition against me. What else is springing to mind?"

Pete: "You're wholly unaware of how much work I have to do tomor-row."

Me, helpfully: "I'm unexpectedly practical, aren't I? Like, I mended the stereo on that rental car that time. Something along the lines of 'Mac-Gyver,' or 'John McClane'—that's the character Bruce Willis plays in *Die*

Hard. But with a sexy twist. Maybe 'Bare Grylls.' But that only really works on paper. We need something more . . . aural."

Pete: "You should call a friend to talk about this. One of those chatty gays. They'd love something like this."

Me: "What loveable quirks do you notice about me?"

Pete, despairingly, after a minute: ". . . you eat a lot of yogurt."

Me: "I eat a lot of yogurt?"

Pete: "You eat a lot of yogurt. I could call you 'Yog.'"

Me, indignant: "Yog? You can't call me Yog—that's George Michael's nickname. You can't give me a nickname that's already being used by a celebrity. You might as well call me 'Brangelina,' or 'The Pelvis.' You're not really trying here, are you?"

Pete: "I'm so very unhappy."

Me: "What about 'Puffin'? It is my favorite bird—a small, round, gothic bird with a large nose. Plus it punningly acknowledges my stoner years, proving you knew me right back in the day, when I still thought there were eight days in the week, because of the Beatles. Puffin."

Pete: "Puffin! That is good. That is very, very good. Yes. You are Puffin to me now, forever. The matter is settled to mutual satisfaction. I am wholly joyous. Do I sound sarcastic?"

Me, happily: "No. I am happy now. Bear and Puffin. That is us. We are Bear and Puffin. Goodnight, Bear."

Pete: "Goodnight."

Small, angry silence.

Me, eventually: "Puffin."

Pete: "What?"

Me: "Goodnight, Puffin. Say, 'Goodnight, Puffin.'"

Pete: "Goodnight, Puffin. You demented fucking bitch."

As you can see, my domestic life now is one of joyous fulfilment. Should you ask me how this has come to be, I would quote the words of one of The Muppet Show's *greatest acts, Marvin Suggs & The Muppaphone. As Suggs plays "Witch Doctor" on the Muppaphone—a living xylophone made of Muppets, which he repeatedly bashes with small hammers, eliciting screams—he talks about the public reaction to his act.*

"People ask me—what is your secret with the Muppaphone?" he says, in his strangulated, high-pitched voice. "And I say—MUTUAL LOVE AND RE-SPECT."

For me and Pete, it has been much the same. And so we sail on in the deep blue bliss of marriage. But it has not always been like this. I came from a radi-cally different background. In many, many ways, my early life resembles An-gela's Ashes, *or* A Child Called It. *This searing account of what it was like to reach adulthood having never had a cup of tea amply illustrates the deep mental scars I still bare, bravely, today.*

Note how the piece dates from a time when one still paid for the Evening Standard, *and how accurate my assessment of its future proved to be. I am like some kind of media scrying bowl.*

Caffeine—Lifeblood of the Twenty-first Century

AS I WRITE THIS, I'm sipping at a lovely cup of tea. Obviously, in many ways, this is the least print-worthy sentence of the week. A brew is not news. Everyone drinks tea. Of course they do.

Except, until recently, me.

Yes—until last summer, I had had three cups of coffee, and maybe ten cups of tea, in my life. My whole life. I know. I *know*. Reading my words must be like reading the musings of a Moon Man from Mars. But what can I say—hot drinks never really happened for me. I guess I never met the right person to introduce me to tea. Or perhaps I never really felt confident enough in myself to believe anyone would want to make tea for me.

Last summer, however, we had a new kitchen put in, and as the kitchen is also where I work, I had to decamp for five weeks to the coffee shops of Crouch End with my laptop. Being sensitive, I noticed that it was the custom of these places not to ask for "a big cup of tap water, please," but to drink their expensively vended tea, or coffee, instead. Within two weeks, I had gone from a caffeine virgin to someone who could easily knock back four lattes and as many teas in an afternoon, and I tell you this: it made me see everything in a whole new light.

Friends, we live in a caffeine world. We think in a caffeine way and we live caffeine lives. Our problems are the problems of people addled with popular hot beverages, and our thoughts are half our own, half the product of our cups. So many aspects of modern life I'd never understood before—things that had completely baffled me about society—suddenly became obvious, once I'd spent a month off my face on tea.

Take, for instance, headaches. Until I became a tea addict, I presumed that people saying "I have a headache" was simply a euphemism for wanting to opt out of an impending activity—like my father saying "I can't—I've got a bone in my leg," when I was little, and wanted him to play hide and seek.

Enter the world of caffeine, however, and you live in a world where your skull suddenly becomes very weak and porous, into which vexing low-level pain can seep at any minute.

Likewise, insomnia. Usually, my average span between "lights off" and dreaming of *Doctor Who* was under five minutes. Late at night after a busy day = going to sleep. It seemed quite basic. Now in the post-tea world, however, any cup after 4 PM provokes an unwelcome wakefulness in the center of the brain, present long after the non-caffeinated would be woozily stumbling to bed. When found in conjunction with caffeine problem three—low-level anxiety and restlessness—and what Thom Yorke of Radiohead once so accurately described as the "unborn chicken voices in my head" can cluck on until 1 or 2 AM. Just from tea! I tell you, it's put me right off the idea of crack.

The main thing I've noticed, however, is how unreasonable, self-absorbed and permanently outraged caffeine has made me. The bottom line is, hot drinks turn people into pigs. Simply walking along with a take-out coffee in your hand turns you into a belligerent fantasist. You really feel like you're a vital cast member of *Sex and the City* or *The West Wing*—when, of course, really, you're just a schmoo with a brew heading for H&M. Knowing all this doesn't make me any more pleasant. In the last few months, I have started arguing with people in my head.

Instance: yesterday, at Oxford Circus, I wanted to buy an *Evening Standard*, but only had coins. As I hovered to the side, counting my change, I had an absolutely apoplectic row with the newspaper man— but wholly and solely in my mind.

"What you giving me all this brahn money for?" he asked me, in his cockney way, in my imagination. "I've got a wallet—not a sack."

"This is exactly why *The Standard* is going out of business!" I shouted back, as interior monologue. "This is fifty brown pennies more than I'm paying for *The Metro*, or the *London Paper*. I *work* for a newspaper! I *know* which way the wind's blowing! It'll all be online in three years' time, treacle, and you'll be in a cardboard box being wee'd on by foxes! Screw you, man. SCREW YOU!"

This furious spat was cut short by, in the actual physical world, me giving the *Evening Standard* man 50p in loose change, and him saying "Cheers, love," and giving me my paper.

I had had three lattes before 11 AM.

There is a plus side to caffeine, of course. I've lost over ten pounds, can write a blog entry in nine minutes flat, and feel a previously undiscovered connection with the world, simply by being able to say "I could murder a brew. Tea, anyone?" to a room full of nodding people. Indeed, I would say that this feeling of finally being like everyone else is the most attractive aspect of having become a caffeine drinker. Irritable, tired, anxious and sporadically unable to see out of one eye due to migraine, I finally feel normal.

Having three columns a week in a national newspaper is a bit like having three children: you're exhausted and grumpy all the time, can't lose that final fifteen pounds, and you don't understand why they can't just crack on with it on their own and get out of your FACE.

Haha, not really! I don't mean that! What I really *mean* is that it's hard to decide which one you love the best.

The TV review allows me to have a good old natter about what we all saw on telly that week—one of the great pleasures of living on a small island that still generally tends to watch one of four channels. The magazine column, meanwhile, allows me the kind of monologue that one might deliver, in a slightly slurred yet impassioned way, to a minicab driver who is doing their best to ignore you, and turn up "Alone" by Heart on Magic FM at 3 AM.

"The thing about my hupsand, right, is that his never, never gived me a nickname, razzer plazzer mazzer fazzer TWO CHILDREN AND SEVEN-TEEN STITCHES!!! I've gotten a little sick on the seatbelt but it's fine don't worry I've got a hanky, I'm just WIPING it away. Don't look."

Sometimes, however, despite trying to be impartial, I think that my Friday column on celebrities—the innovatively named "Celebrity Watch"—might be my favorite. It's essentially a weekly stand-up routine about the contents of OK! magazine. It is the alternative career as a comedian I could have forged, had I not had such grave "sweating" issues that my damp underarms are visible from over fifty feet away within seconds of talking in front of more than nine people. Really, I'm just like Lenny Bruce, but shy.

This "Celebrity Watch" was devoted entirely to the outright honking clown-car insanity of the memorial service for the late Michael Jackson—an extraordinary event which, for all who saw it, will live on in their unhappy, gibbering minds forever. For those who haven't read "Celebrity Watch" before—a massive demographic that includes my mother and at least one senior management figure at The Times, who refers to it as "that number thing"—it takes the format of a Top Ten countdown, simply because it requires far less structure and skill to write something as a Top Ten countdown. And I refer to *myself throughout in the third person as "CW"—short for "Celebrity Watch"—because I like giving the impression of being a mysterious, powerful celebrity-judging organization ratifying all this stuff in a scientific manner, rather than the reality: someone in their bathrobe typing away while eating endless amounts of Miniature Celebrations. Snickers are my preference. The nuts are like a healthy protein.*

Celebrity Watch Special:
Michael Jackson's Memorial

TEN. UP. The Jackson Four. It was the first suggestion that not only was this going to be an unusual memorial service, but one so gigantic, random and barking that the viewer at home would often have to touch their legs, say, or look at a kettle—saying, "These are the normal things. I must remember what the normal things are."

Michael Jackson's $15,000 golden casket was carried into the arena, on the shoulders of Jackson's brothers, as a choir sang—perhaps ominously, in view of the open-casket funeral tradition—"We Will See the King." Jackson's brothers, you couldn't help but note, were all wearing a single, white, rhinestone-studded glove—Jackson's signature accessory-motif, aside from a full-face mask, and/or enraged chimp. To put this into context, it's a bit like if all the pallbearers at Elvis's funeral had all been wearing big plastic quiffs and doing that wobbly thing Elvis did with his legs. Amazing.

NINE. DOWN. Congresswoman Sheila Jackson Lee. In the ultimate "Good luck with that!" moment of 2009 so far, Congresswoman Lee took it upon herself to be the one who would mention both Jackson's $22m out-of-court settlement to Jordy Chandler, *and* 2005's seven counts of child sexual abuse, and two counts of administering an intoxicating agent in order to commit the felony. *But in a good way.*

"As a representative of Congress, we understand the constitution. We know that people are innocent until proved otherwise!" Lee said, trying to sort out that whole "persistent pedophile rumors" thing in a couple of breezy sentences, in front of Jackson's children.

Personally, CW would have played it marginally safer, and done a nice reading of "Stop All the Clocks" instead.

EIGHT. UP. Kentucky Fried Chicken. Magic Johnson—helpfully described to we Limey viewers by Paul Gambacini as "playing for the Lakers, the Manchester United of America"—appeared to walk up to the podium with two agendas: 1) To respectfully honor the life and times of the late Michael Jackson. 2) To try and mention Kentucky Fried Chicken in a positive manner as many times as possible.

"I went to Michael's house—and the chef brought Michael out a bucket of Kentucky Fried Chicken. I was like Michael—you have Kentucky Fried Chicken! That was the greatest moment of my life . . . we had such a great time, sitting on the floor, eating that bucket of Kentucky Fried Chicken. God bless you Michael!"

SEVEN. DOWN. P. Diddy. P. Diddy—who some of we more old-fashioned types may insist on still referring to as "Puff Daddy," his original, stupid made-up name—also attended the memorial. Being a man of the twenty first century, Diddy [@iamdiddy] keeps Twitter up to date with his movements at all times. The entry for the day before the funeral read, "I haven't been to sleep yet! LOL. I'm still at the after-party from last night! No sign of quitting!" There was a quick tone change with the subsequent two Tweets: "I'm at the memorial. RIP Michael Jackson," and "Just left the funeral. So sad!! RIP MJ!!!!" The next day, however, it was very much back business as usual, with the—presumably lunch-inspired—"I love sweet tarts!!!"

Interesting Diddy point: both "sweet tarts," and the burial of the King of Pop, warranted three exclamation marks.

SIX. DOWN. Brooke Shields. Giving a weeping testimonial that appeared to go on for nearly three days, Shields's aim was to try and convey to the audience what the man she had known was like. Unfortunately, the man she had known was Michael Jackson, and every anecdote she had sounded like a cross between the kind of dream you have when you've got chickenpox, and something she was making up in order to get him into even more trouble.

A case in point was the story of how, the night before Elizabeth Taylor's wedding, she and Jackson broke into Taylor's room as she slept, to look at the wedding dress, as Michael—a thirty-three-year-old black, straight man—was too excited to wait until the morning. The next day, at the wedding, Shields and Jackson "pretended to be the mother and father of [Elizabeth Taylor]. It sounds weird," Shields concluded, looking rather wild-eyed, "but we made it real!"

You think? Like CW has said once before today—good luck with that!

FIVE. UP. Diana Ross and Elizabeth Taylor. Both the pivotal gay icons in Jackson's life were absent from the memorial service—preferring to issue personal statements on the day instead.

Taylor commented that she did not want to be part of the "Whoopla"—an important coining of a new word, given that mankind did not previously have a term for "Memorial service where the corpse's daughter will 'close the show' by being herded onto a stage, weeping, while her uncles comfort her by stroking her with rhinestone gloves."

Ross, meanwhile, had different fish to fry. Following the unexpected revelation that Jackson had wanted custody of his children to go to her—inspiring thoughts of some screwball Motown version of *Baby Boom*, with Ross as Diane Keaton—it seemed as if Ross's message made her position on the matter very clear.

"I will be here [in her own home, not at the funeral, very far away from everything, particularly the children] whenever they need me [to lend them $20s, or give them advice on floor-length, fish-tail cocktail dresses and backcombing]" Ross clarified.

FOUR. UP. Paul Gambaccini and Trevor Nelson. As the BBC's commentators for the memorial service, Gambo and Nelson were put in a slightly invidious position—given that what they were commenting on did, more often than not, prompt the simple, straight-forward reaction, "Holy moly, have I really just seen an 'In Memoriam' photo-montage where a shot of Michael Jackson shaking hands with Nelson Mandela was immediately followed by a picture of Michael Jackson shaking hands with Kermit the Frog?"

In the event, Gambaccini and Nelson managed quite well—even filling the half-hour technical difficulties with this peerless piece of speculation on which celebrity would cry first: "Either Jennifer Hudson [who recently had three members of her family murdered by her estranged brother-in-law], or Usher. He's very *young*," Gambaccini said, wisely.

THREE. DOWN. Usher. Well, Paul Gambacini turned out to be a veritable Nostradamus of celebrity grief: Usher *did* cry during his version of "Gone Too Soon." Usher—who, ironically, was not cast as an usher during the event—appeared to have some manner of odd, compulsive moment during his number: leaving the stage, he walked down to Jackson's coffin, and touched the side of it briefly, before, in some manner of trance, he kind of *jiggled the lid* a bit. Almost as if he were checking the quality of the hinges.

Ironically, Celebrity Watch can imagine Usher using "Jiggle the Lid" as the title of his next album. It has a tone of urban suggestiveness.

TWO. UP. *The Mirror*. In a week where the entire media went, "Right, he's dead now, and none of his relatives have the time, money or inclination left to sue us, so we can just print absolutely anything that comes into our minds. Any old crazy s**t. Chimps, sperm, drugs, ghosts. The lot. Woot!"—*The Mirror* won a close-fought battle for "Most wholly unnecessary and ancillary bullet-point."

Relaying how Jackson was to be buried without his brain, due to the requirements of the autopsy, *The Mirror* spared no detail—including, with no little relish, the phrase, "The brain will be placed in a plastic bucket."

At the end, on a separate line, the report concluded: "Michael Jackson starred in the 1978 musical *The Wiz* as the Scarecrow—playing the character without a brain."

ONE. DOWN. Shaheen Jafargholi. If Michael Jackson died "of" anything, it was—and I think we're all in agreement here—a combination of being treated as a cross between a sideshow and a demi-god for possessing such unearthly talent; working an adult career from the age of six onwards; fetishishing his own ruined childhood to the point where it drove him insane, and then having that insanity in a media spotlight so remorseless, there are entire wars that have been given less coverage than the changing colors of Michael Jackson's skin.

If there was *one single thing* we could learn from the life of Michael Jackson, it would seem—other than that sequin-appliquéd military-wear dates unexpectedly well—it is that child stardom is a terrible idea.

So at Michael Jackson's memorial on Tuesday, it was interesting to see that one of the twelve live performances came from Shaheen Jafargholi—the Welsh, twelve-year-old semi-finalist from this year's *Britain's Got Talent*.

Introduced on stage by Smokey Robinson to sing "Who's Lovin' You?"—a song which, as Robinson helpfully pointed out, a nine-year-old Jackson had sung with "such knowingness and pain." HELLO! THERE'S A CLUE THERE!—Jafargholi had to face down a worldwide audience of millions and, right in front of him, the entire Jackson family, Stevie Wonder, Mariah Carey, and Michael Jackson, dead, ten feet away from him. So no pressure or crippling emotional resonance there then.

It's impossible to think of a single aspect of it that wasn't dazzlingly inappropriate. It was a supernova of wrongness. It's almost the next evolutionary stage in incorrect action. Performing children at Michael Jackson's funeral?

The next day, chat-show host Larry King said that, when he'd asked

Motown founder Berry Gordy who Shaheen was, Gordy replied, "I have no cotton pickin' idea—but if I were still in the business, I would sign him tomorrow."

Of course he would. Because while Michael Jackson might have been lying before him in a coffin, dead at fifty, it was in front of an audience of *millions*. And that's the bottom line.

Of course, the late Michael Jackson wasn't the only person to have had a problem with drug abuse. I, too, had a dark past of substance abuse that I wished to confess to Times *readers—prompted by the 2009 press hoo-ha over Julie Meyerson's controversial book,* The Lost Boy: A True Story, *in which she explained she'd kicked her teenage son out of her house when he refused to give up smoking dope. (This book caused one of those brief media flaps in 2009 that allowed the fifty craziest columnists to write regular pieces about how, basically, all women are awful and should never be allowed to do anything, particularly have children.)*

As I explained in the following piece, during my stoner years, I should have kicked myself out of my own house, except I was too stoned.

I Am Caitlin Moran, and I Was a Skunk Addict

I WAS ADDICTED TO skunk weed for four years. That it's taken me three weeks of shouty headlines about Julie Myerson's son to remember this tells you pretty much everything you need to know about dope-smokers.

But then again, "addicted" is quite an extreme word, isn't it? It's quite . . . *final.* Was I "addicted"? Yes, I smoked every day, twice as much on weekends, could neither watch TV, listen to records or have my tea without a "bifter spritzer," made a bong out of a Coke can, then another one out of an old fishtank, had three dealers, didn't really have any friends that weren't stoners, chose which bands I was going to interview on the basis of whether I could get stoned with them or not, and, once, gave a wasp a blow-back. But is that really "addiction"? You could just say that I liked it a lot. To be honest, I behaved almost identically when I first got into couscous. That stuff is so fluffy.

This, of course, is another problem with dope smokers. They can't really take a strong line on anything—because everything's relative, their mouth's too dry to argue, and their synapses look like an Upside-Down Pudding that's been smashed about with a stick.

I want to make it clear that I don't smoke now. I haven't taken anything since I was twenty-two because, and I will be honest with you here, I eventually went stark raving mad, and ended up riding a bicycle up and down Holloway Road, trying to "sweat the poison out." At the time, I was so fat from a stoner diet of deep-fried crispy beef and Mango Soleros that I had bought the bicycle—the chunkiest, most industrial mountain bike in the shop—on the basis that it made me look "thinner" than all the other, smaller, more aerodynamic bicycles available. As a consequence, I could scarcely pedal it more than fifty yards without having to lie down in someone's front yard for a rest. I was operating on some pretty exciting and innovative logic at the time.

I started smoking weed when I was seventeen, because that is just what you do if you like the Beatles. If this were America, I could probably now sue Paul McCartney, wholly on this basis.

From the very start, I was a terrible stoner. Not in any sense of being hardcore, and wild, like some crazy-eyed loner on a voyage to Valhalla. I mean literally terrible. Every time I smoked I passed out. I once got so stoned interviewing Radiohead that I had to be put to bed in the bass player's spare bedroom. Except I was so stoned I missed the door to the spare bedroom, kept walking up the stairs, and went and slept in the loft, instead—where a wasps' nest had been recently fumigated, and the floor was covered in crunchy, dead wasps. In the morning, my lovely millionaire genius host was distraught.

"You slept in the waspy loft!" he horrored.

"Oh it's ok," I said, cheerfully. "I was stoned!"

I did a kind of "We *all* know what it's like when you're so stoned you interview the biggest band in the world by just nodding at them, then break into their loft and sleep on some insect's" face. He just stared at me like I was mad.

Of course, it's a miracle I had a job at all. Work-rate wise, a ferocious skunk habit suits someone who can survive on the proceeds of six, maybe seven hours of work a week, tops. You're looking at musicians "between albums," housewives, pre-school children, royalty, etc. Despite Michael Phelps's admirable efforts in this area, it is not really the ideal drug for Olympic athletes—or, indeed, anyone who really needs to get a jiggy on in furthering their life. Everything grinds to a halt when you start smoking. In the four years I was chonged off my num-nuts, there was one, sole innovation in my life: the invention of the Shoe Wall—a wall in the hall where I banged in twenty nails, in dispiritingly uneven lines, and then hung up all my shoes. Needless to say, when I finally did stop smoking, I remodelled the entire house, lost sixty pounds, took down the Shoe Wall and quadrupled my work rate in six months flat.

Towards the end of my four-year skunk-in, signs of the End of Days started to accumulate. A friend who had been smoking since he was thirteen totally wigged out, and developed schizophrenia. Although sympathetic, my main reaction was to think, "Some people can handle it, and some people can't," and then smugly light up a big fat jay. I was also starting to notice that it was taking huge amounts of skunk to get half as wasted as before—necessitating the invention of first the Coke can bong, and then the fishtank bong, as my smoking took on a borderline industrial intensity. Paranoid I was being ripped off, I "tested" the potency of the skunk on a wasp by trapping it under a glass and giving it a blow-back. The wasp just lay on the floor, clearly considering buying a chunky bicycle, so I knew that, sadly, it must all be down to me.

It was as I was doing bongs out of my fishtank, while watching *Later . . . with Jools Holland*, that the end came. For some reason, as soon as the Beautiful South came on stage, I just went mad. Not in a "Hurrah! Amazing! The Beautiful South!" way—but in a way that meant, within an hour I was hysterical, holding onto the kettle, and screaming, "This is normal! This is normal!" at myself over and over again.

It turned out that it was "just" a panic attack—the first of a solid eighteen months of them—but however much I tried to calm myself down with a fishtank full of rabidly psycho-active cannabis, bafflingly, it just seemed to make the situation worse. Eventually, even I had to acknowledge that my stoner days were over, and I quit.

Do I regret spending four years off my face? No, not really—but only because I can't really remember any of it. I'm not being facetious. My memory's shot to bits. Apparently, we went to Montpelier once, for a week. I have absolute no recall of this.

Did I, then, learn anything, from four years of wandering through the rabbit holes of my mind, like Alice in Wonderland? To that, at least, I can say "yes." I learned that wasps buzz four notes lower when they're wasted. And that I am a terrible, terrible stoner.

In 2009, I interviewed the then-Prime Minister, Gordon Brown. It would be wrong to say it was as a long-game tactic to get in contact with Obama. Very wrong. Not only did Gordon—who was lovely—singularly fail to hook me up with Obama, but I nearly never got to Downing Street in the first place. It was a VERY vexatious day.

I Am Late to Interview the Prime Minister

OF COURSE I'M NOT going to be late to interview Gordon Brown. Don't be ridiculous. He's the Prime Minister of Great Britain, for goodness sake. I'm going to leave the house at 11:30 AM.

"11:30?" my husband says. He looks alarmed. He is, in general, an anxious man—he keeps packets of Heinz Ketchup in his wallet, unable to bear the possibility of being boxed into a situation where Daddies' Tomato Sauce might be the only option. "The interview's 12:30 PM! Order the cab for 10:15 AM!"

I am not going to take a cab to Downing Street. In the event of Gordon Brown asking me how I arrived, I want to say, "I travelled on the Underground transportation system of London, England, like *the people* do." I'm not quite sure what point I would be making by saying this, but it feels like it might be an important one. Something I could score highly for.

At 11:15 AM, I go up to my office to print out my sixty-two, carefully planned questions. I approach the printer with great serenity. In the past, the printer and I have had an enmity that has stretched back over generations. I ended its grandmother when the cartridge jammed halfway through printing out a map. Its mother was abandoned to Freecycle, after every functionality save b&w photocopying failed. But this HP Photosmart

C480 will not let me down. It's like Britain and France. We have finally come to an understanding. There will be antagonism and murder between us no more.

Nineteen minutes later, I am pulling every wire out of the back of the motherf***ing Goddamn betraying piece of shit, and screaming.

"What do you MEAN, the 'cartridge alignment sheet has not been detected'? What does that MEAN? I'm supposed to be interviewing THE PRIME MINISTER!"

I've missed my train. I've ordered a cab. Already it's very, very clear that when the controller said, "Yes—we have cars free!" what he meant was, "Yes—we have cars free! Free—to do *whatever they like!* Play in the sun; drive round and round the park really slowly. Sit and enjoy the sheer joy of North London."

I go and stand out in the street. It is now forty minutes until I start talking to Gordon Brown. I am in a totally deserted residential area. When a student driver crawls down the road in her silver AA Driving School vehicle, I think, "I am interviewing the Prime Minister. That probably means I'm legally entitled to flag down that car, and get her to drive me to Archway tube."

When the cab finally pulls up, it is an old, battered minivan. I realize with horror that it very closely resembles the van the Iranian terrorists shoot Doc from in *Back to the Future*. It has curtains inside, which are drawn. It looks like an Acme suicide bomb. It does *not* look like the kind of thing the policemen on the gates at Downing Street will feel relaxed about.

As we screech off towards town, the cab driver and I quickly come to an understanding. I am the delusional, sweaty woman who keeps saying, "I have to interview the Prime Minister in thirty-eight minutes!" He is the man who will cause my death when he says, "I don't know where Downing Street is."

This is, I admit, difficult information for me to process. One the one hand, I am alarmed that the cab driver doesn't know where 10 Downing Street—one of the most famous addresses in the world—is. On the other hand, I don't either, really. Is it quite near the Strand?

I have terrible, anxious cottonmouth. There is a liter of water in my handbag. I drink it. Emotionally, the template I am relating to in this situation is the 1986 film *Clockwise* starring John Cleese, who plays a man battling to reach an appointment on time, despite a series of strokes of ill fortune.

This alternates from being "useful" to "not useful." On the one hand, Cleese did, eventually, make that appointment on time. On the other, he arrived cut and bruised, in a monk's habit, with only one shoe, having had his speech eaten by a goat. It's not really a possibility I want to consider.

I abandon the cab at Euston, and run onto the Victoria line, onto the Jubilee line, then down Whitehall. It's 12:28 PM. By now, the liter of water I drank in the cab is having its unfortunate yet inevitable consequence. I have to ask myself—is the Pulitzer enough recompense for turning up at Downing Street having wet myself? It is not. I downgrade my running to a fraught trot.

Of course, when I finally get there, Gordon Brown is running twenty minutes late. My cardigan is, I realize, soaked with sweat. I am still stuffing it into my handbag when finally he comes into the room.

"Prime Minister!" I say, standing up. "Good afternoon! Thank you for agreeing to this interview!"

That evening, I hand-wash the cardigan. As I pull it out of the bag, I notice it smells odd. Intense.

"This is the smell of fear," I think to myself, holding it up to my nose. "This is the smell humans emit when they are at the limits of their terror."

Then I look into my handbag, and realize that it is not the smell of fear—it is actually the smell of a burst free sample of Fructis hair serum. I still don't really know what the smell of fear is.

You can see how badly I travel. Downing Street is seven miles from my house, and getting there nearly induced a conniptive fit. It is why all my holidays are to places as nearby as possible: Brighton. Aberystwyth. Sometimes, Bath. You'll notice, as you go through this book, that there aren't many exotic journeys to far-distant places. That's because I don't really hold with "abroad." I think the only time I venture out of the country this entire book is to go to Berlin to interview Lady Gaga—something my subconscious is clearly so disgruntled about that I passive-aggressively miss my flight, and make her wait three hours for me. Yes, Gaga—I punished you for not being in Leicester. How DARE you be in another country.

I'm not a natural passport-profferer.

What I Learned up a Mountain This Summer

A WISE MAN ONCE said that on a journey, it is not where you go, but who you *become* that really matters. Aside from the fact that this reveals that he clearly left his wife— or, possibly, mum—in charge of small, "non-mattering" journey issues like tickets, accommodations, packing, researching which restaurants will accept a 6:30 PM booking for a party with three children and an egg allergy, and where and when it would be expedient to stop and go to the toilet, it is obvious what journeys he *really* meant: vacations. In the absence of partition and mass migration, they're the only big journeys we ever undertake these days. The premise is that when we go on vacation, it should—if it's a good vacation—change us a little. It should improve us. We should acquire both the reddened, sun-damaged complexion of a bumpkin *and* some knowledge. In short, we should return from our holidays *cleverer*.

Well I'm afraid that this is not a sentiment I can hold by. I don't want to get cleverer on my vacations. I want to get stupider. Once I'm off the clock, I don't want to have to think at all. If I have to have more than one thought a day—preferably the thought "Yes, I think I *would* like to eat a cheese sandwich in the bath, while reading *Cosmo*"—then I have, clearly, failed to book the right vacation. On the right vacation, nice things would just happen to me for six days, and on the seventh, I would be put into a coma, and posted back to London, first class.

By the time I come home, I want my brain to have totally calcified through extreme lack of use. I want to be as dumb as a bag of hair, covered in sand I'm too listless and witless to brush off, and so relaxed I stand in the middle of the front room, staring at my own feet and going "Wha?" for an hour and a half.

So you can imagine, then, my disappointment when I realized that, over the course of my summer vacations, I actually *had* learned a few things. Thankfully, nearly all of them were stupid.

1. **You can make a child climb a mountain, if it thinks there's a Disney Store at the top.** Obviously you can't stand at the bottom of Stac Pollaidh and outright say, "There is a Disney Store at the top of that mountain. Those are not clouds up there—that is Disney Magic!" No—the trick is simply not to say that there isn't one up there. Imply that one would normally expect there to be one on top of a Highland mountain—but that the only way of really knowing is to spray that midge repellent all over your face, get your rain poncho on, and ship up 2,000 feet. Of course, when you get to the top, and the kids wail, "But there is no Disney Store here!," then you must bring in the second half of the Mountain Climbing for Recalcitrant Children Plan. You must say: "JESUS! It has CLOSED DOWN! This recession has hit the retail sector HARD!" Then re-motivate the children for the climb back down by not saying, but certainly kind of implying that there might be a fire sale going on in the parking lot below, with High School Musical figurines at half-price. But only if they hurry.

2. **When it comes to sleeper trains, there are two types of people in this world.** The first delight in the dollhouse-like neatness of the cabins. They adore the blankety bunk beds, and are soothed into sleep by the night-long rattle of the locomotive's trundle. The second give the stink eye as soon as they step inside, spend all night sighing, and ruin the morning croissant-in-a-bag breakfast by wailing, "That was like spending all night in the video to the Cure's 'Close To Me'! I am glad I am not going in one of those again—oh I am, in seven days. Maybe I will mention how fatally dispirited about this I am EVERY TEN MINUTES FOR THE REST OF THE VACATION."

3. **These days, everyone gets in trouble for smoking.** The last time I got caught having a sneaky fag by one of my kids, I was able to reply—with James Bond-like, ninja-swiftness—"This isn't mine, darling! I'm just holding it for Uncle Nathan!" Unfortunately, when I repeated the maneuver this summer, I didn't know that 'Uncle Nathan' was supposed to have given up six months ago, and that I'd just ratted him up in front of his kids. Who immediately started crying about him getting cancer, and wailing that they didn't want to be half-orphans, and had to be placated with having virtually all of that day's gin-fund spent on ice cream, and bubble-swords. It looks like I'm going to have to revert to the excuse of their earlier years: "It's not a cigarette, darlings—it's Sooty's wand! A naughty boy set fire to it, and mummy was trying to put it out."

4. **Scottish people do actually notice if you're Scottish or not.** If you're ludicrously impressionable/borderline human clay/me, after a couple of hours in a region with a strong accent, it can be easy to find yourself "catching" "being local." You can convince yourself it's both a friendly, and a beautiful, thing, to start throwing in "lassie" here, and a "pet" there, and that the locals will presume that you talk like this all the time at home. The reality is, of course, that they are thinking, "Why is this idiot moon-faced London woman talking like the Russ Abbott character C U Jimmy, the noo?" This August, I triumphantly smashed all my previous accent-slip records. Usually,

it takes a couple of hours, and a couple of whiskies, for the idiomatic "monkey see, monkey do" reflex to kick in. This year, I got off the London-Edinburgh train at 8 AM, and walked over to the taxi line. "Taxi?" the driver said. "Aye," I replied. My husband turned and walked away, mortified.

5. **Foxes eschew board games.** If a 2 AM, al-fresco game of Scrabble should end up being abandoned, due to excessive "wobbly tiredness," do bring it back indoors again. Leaving it on the lawn is apparently some manner of provocation to urban foxes, who will snittishly do a plop on it—as if saying "Here is my disdain for your dandy self-satisfied middle-class Viognier-fueled word-games. And it's on a double word score."

At The Times, *they love making me do stupid stuff. It's why I love working for them. Who would not wish to be rung up at 9 AM and asked if they want to dress up as Kate Middleton/meet Keith Richards on International Talk Like a Pirate Day/learn to do the "Single Ladies"-by-Beyoncé dance?*

In this instance, the 9 AM phonecall from the office was asking me if I'd like to be an imaginary dwarf, playing the gaming phenomenon that is World of Warcraft. Obviously, I said "Yes"—once I'd looked up what the Dwarven is for "Yes" ("Ai," apparently).

A week later—because of this feature—I was invited on the Richard & Judy *show to talk about World of Warcraft, as some manner of "expert." As I'm sure this feature insinuates, I really was not that. Still, in order to illustrate what we were discussing, they suggested that I play the game, live on air, so that the viewers could get a flavor of life in an online fantasy world. Panicking, the second we got on air, I pressed the wrong button, and steered my dwarf off a platform and under the Deep Run train to Stormwind City, where he died instantly.*

"Well," Richard Madeley said, after a second. "The life of a dwarf really is nasty, brutish and short, isn't it?"

I Am a Dwarf Called "Scottbaio"

WHEN KEITH AT THE office gives me World of Warcraft, bidding me to "spend a bit of time with it—it's really addictive," I do that special thing that women can do where you roll your eyes inside your head, secretly, to show that you know more than the men. Yeah *right*, I'm going to get addicted to World of Warcraft. Yeah *right*, I'm going to join a worldwide, online community of over eight million people, running around a gigantic and complex fantasy world, engaged on a series of quests.

I'll tell you right now, in my head, Keith: it's all highly unlikely. I'm not into pixie cobblers. I like real life. If I *had* to marry one of the cast of *Lord of the Rings*, it would be Sam Gamgee—the only completely prosaic, normal, non-magic one, who comes across like the owner of a garage in Cricklewood having a particularly bad day, what with this vexatious epic quest, and all.

In a nutshell: dragons embarrass me.

The box containing the game software didn't quite fit into my handbag, and I was slightly self-conscious about people spotting it as I caught the tube. The last time I felt so embarrassed about the visible contents of my handbag was last spring, when I was carrying around a gigantic book on the history of the Ku Klux Klan. For two long months, that book made me want to shout, "I'm reading this because I know they were bad—not to get tips!" to any halfway full train. Similarly, a visible copy of World of Warcraft makes me want to shout, "I don't seek to nullify my rampant sexual dysfunctions by pretending to be a Paladin called Thrusthammer Orcbash! IT'S FOR WORK!"

Of course, the person I want to shout this to the most is myself. I am the judgmental one here. By and large, my theory runs, people into goblins and wizards are people for whom the utopian sexual and racial equality offered by, say, sci-fi, is alarming. All those black chicks in lycra jumpsuits philosophizing about the fallible nature of humanity, and able to vote? Brrrr!

In short, the entire fantasy genre is the domain of the sweaty, white, non-intellectual Herbert, and has very little to offer me—a sassy, metropolitan, militant feminist with an aversion to a) items of clothing made of skinned Gnoll hide and b) swinging at someone with a two-headed axe.

Imagine my surprise, then, on being able to write the following sentence: on the first day I had World of Warcraft, I stayed up and played it until 2 AM. I got into bed at 10 PM, switched on the electric blanket, and opened my laptop, with the simple objective of "Getting my bearings" for twenty minutes. Three hours later, I was trying to retrieve the stolen journals of Grelin Whitebeard from a cave full of Rockjaw Troggs, while running a very lucrative trade in killing and skinning boars on the side. Then I accidentally got on the Deeprun Tram to Stormwind City, and had to bale out when I realized I was far too poor to be in a city where "Heavy Mithril Pants" are twenty-seven pieces of silver. 2 AM! I was so engrossed, I forgot to take out my contact lenses, and fell asleep with them glued to my eyes.

Although I am pathologically, fatally prone to exaggeration, it would be a simple statement of fact to say that World of Warcraft is approximately as addictive as methadone. Indeed, when Robbie Williams recently went into rehab with the ostensibly risible addictions of Red Bull and espresso, I thought, "It's just as well you have never been on Coldridge Pass trying to deliver a package of Kobold reports to Senir Whitebeard. Then, my friend, you would know true craving."

As with all good drugs, World of Warcraft has turned my perceptions of the world upside down. Take, for instance, the very beginning of the game, when you decide on the character you will play. Personally, I've never created a character to play a game with before—hey, I have to do that in front of the closet every morning for real, and I think all the ladies will know what I'm saying here. But when it's for an inconsequential internet diversion, and you have almost infinite choice of what you will become—good, evil, male, female, human, weird minotaur thing with problem hair—it brings to the fore several profound self-realizations. My inner self, it turns out, is a beefy ginger dwarf—one with a huge beard. He is who I want to be. He is secret Caitlin. Discovering this is the kind of thing troubled celebrities pay Dr. Drew a small fortune to discover. I had done it in seven minutes, and with a choice of beard stylings, to boot.

I named him "Scottbaio"—you remember: Chachi in *Happy Days*. The obvious ginger dwarf name—and launched him out into the world. Still, at this point, deeply skeptical about the game, I had pre-formulated a plan to make the whole experience tolerable. Whereas the ultimate purpose of most participants is to overcome the evil Horde through a serious of pitched battles and strategic quests, I had come up with something a little more subtle. I thought the best way to quell the Horde would be to gradually gentrify the Killing Fields, starting by opening a deli, and selling speciality cheese. After all, the lure of endless, sensual evil is nothing compared to a good, spoonable Vacherin. Those demons would be capitulating, buying a Victorian townhouse and coming over to the Alliance in no time.

However, as a new émigré to the realm of Sha'tar, I knew the deli was something I'd have to work up to slowly. I spent an hour tootling around a very pretty snowy mountain running a few errands—delivering parcels, relaying messages, buying nicer boots, earning a bob or two. Already, the addictive part of WoW was becoming apparent—through a cunning combination of small, quick tasks and longer, more complex ones that can be chipped away at over time—there's always something you could "pop in" and do, or just spend "ten minutes more" "knocking off." And—contrary to all perceptions of online gaming being a lonely, solitary pursuit for, ahem, "bachelors"—I found WoW to be an excellent and rewarding family pastime. My two daughters—six and three—were thrilled to sit next to me, watching mummy kill the pigs, and jump over fences.

Indeed, I was marveling at how female-friendly and "untestosteroney" it was, compared to what I expected, when a member of the Horde called "Hellfist" started stoving my head in from behind. Having no idea what to do, I fall back on my old playground technique—I try to talk my way out of it.

"Please don't smite me—I'm having an asthma attack!" I type. "I've come on a quest by accident, and if you hit me, it'll be murder!"

Hellfist makes a clucking chicken sound, to highlight my cowardice, and hits me until I die. When I resurrect in a nearby graveyard, a dwarf warrior called Cadisfael is sitting next to me.

"I ownz you, n00b," he says.

"I'm afraid I'm thirty-one, and don't have a clue what you're on about," I say, as primly as a ginger dwarf named after the over-emotional one from *Happy Days* can.

"That means that you are a newbie, and I own you. You are my bitch," Cadisfael explains, patiently.

"Buzz off, you Herbert," I say, trying to jump over a fence.

"Cait it's me, Joe," Cadisfael says, jumping over the fence with ease, and then executing an impressive Russian dance. It's my fourteen-year-old math genius brother, Joe! He's tracked me down online! Jesus!

"I've had to regenerate with a new character here," he explains, rather crossly, as we walk up a mountain. "I don't usually come to this realm. Sha'tar is for newbie losers. I'm usually in Hellscream, with the hardcore. Over there, I'm a Level 66 mage, with an Epix mount."

"I'm in a much higher tax bracket than you," I counter, trying to smash him with my giant dwarven hammer. He easily dodges the blow.

I'd like to pretend that Joe and I then spent the next week or so bonding in our fantastical realm—going on a serious of daring raids on the goblin mines together, before drinking a flagon of hot Rhapsody Malt back at the Scarlet Raven tavern. In actual fact, Joe is so repulsed by the easiness of my realm that he logs off after an hour, with a cheery farewell of "I ownz you, n00b! Pwnz!," which he then has to log back on to explain means a kind of "zapping sound that you make when you hit someone."

Still, he's given me some good tips: find a trainer who will teach me new smiting spells, earn money skinning boars, spend the money on armor, and don't try and chat to people too much—they find it weird.

I flagrantly disregard this last rule ten minutes later, in a bar at Anvilmar, where I try to start a conversation with a room of saturnine-looking dwarven warriors.

"They need a jukebox in here," I suggest, to kick start the debate. "Some Queen, bit of classic Bowie. Guns N' Roses. And maybe one of those frozen margarita machines. Razz the place up a bit."

A couple of implacable pugilists issue a polite "LOL" but then go back to buying huge and fatal swords from the weapons vendor. One small gnome girl called Flopsey, however, sidles over.

"Yeah— maybe a pub quiz, or a meat raffle?" she suggests. We sit down at the table, and spend the next twenty minutes discussing what we'd like to see in WoW to cater to the female palate. We'd like the option to work as prostitutes, we decide—it would be a very quick way of earning money. We'd like to be able to conceive and raise children—seeing if they look like the father, teaching them our spells. We'd like a bigger range of wardrobe and hair styles, and the ability to gain points simply by being amusing, or wise. Or pulling off a good outfit.

Indeed, it's turning out to be a thoroughly enjoyable conversation, when

Flopsey's character suddenly issues the message "flirting," and comes over to my side of the table. Of course! She thinks I'm a buff ginger warrior-priest—called Scottbaio! All this conversation about virtual prostitution has an entirely different spin from her side of the table! She wants my hot dwarf ass!

So here I am, a thirty-one-year-old mother of two, at 2 AM, sitting in bed in my Bliss Spa Socks—and having some polymorphous cybersexual frisson with a fifteen-year-old gnome called Flopsey, who lives in Antwerp.

Really, the modern age is a marvel.

I do a lot for charity, but I don't like to talk about it, apart from in this column, first published in 2009, and then obviously in this book, where I reprint it, desperate not to go on about how much I do for charity. PLEASE don't use the phrase "She cares too much" about me. It would EMBARRASS mememememe.

I Do a Lot for Charity, but I Would Never Mention It

WALKING A MARATHON IS eeeeeasy, compared to running it. That's just obvious. That's why I agreed to walk a marathon—the Moonwalk, in May.

Apparently, it's all in aid of a charity—but I wasn't really listening to the details, to be honest. All I heard was my friends Dent, Hughes and Kennedy saying how, once they'd finished the Moonwalk, they were going for "a massive champagne breakfast at Claridge's!"

In my head, what I could see was a giant sausage—about twenty-six miles long—and a very short stroll—around five and a half inches, and on a plate, next to some hash browns. A twenty-six-mile-walk seemed like a fairly minor consideration, really, in order to have a breakfast like that. Walking? Toddlers do it! Old people! Hens! How hard can it be?

"Sign me up for the bacon—I mean the walk!" I said, cheerfully. "What are we all wearing? Does one dress up for breakfast? 8 AM seems a little early for heels and a dress—but then, it *is* Claridge's."

"You won't care what you're wearing," Kennedy said, with an abrupt grimness. Kennedy has done marathons before. She refused to say any more. I felt my sausage get a little smaller.

The next week, Kennedy sent through an email with our training schedule on it. The email was entitled "THE TALK OF DOOM." Reading through, it was hard to argue with the declaration. It involved phrases like "You're going to lose some toenails—get used to it," and, "If you don't train, I can guarantee you the marathon is going to be one of the most miserable experiences of your life. Fact."

As my previous high-water mark of "miserable experiences" was attending a rave in Warrington where CS gas was released by an angry bouncer, and I ended up having it washed out of my eyes, with milk, by a man off his face on Ecstasy, who kept calling my teeth his "pearls," I was keen not to add to the pantheon. I went on a training walk the next day.

Fifteen miles seemed like a reasonable target. Three miles in, I realized that lacy tights are basically the midway point between "exfoliating linen facecloth" and "cilice belt."

Four miles in, I realized that my iPhone pedometer app—although free, and, also, pretty—wouldn't let me listen to music or make phone calls. This meant that, at a pace of 4mph, I was going to spend the next three hours doing nothing but walking in total silence.

There is something deeply meditative about simply putting one foot in front of the other. The Aborgines walked the Songlines across Australia. Pilgrimages to Mecca, Knock, Lourdes or the Ganges trigger powerful connections between an ostensibly idling brain, and a constantly perambulating body. I, too, felt this deep, primal connection between body and landscape, from the top of Camden Road to the bottom of it. Then I felt so bored I could have punched a bird off a tree.

To pass the time—of which I had plenty—I tried to work out the last time I'd faced so many hours of unavoidable tedium. I concluded that it would have been in 1988, when I was thirteen, with no cable, internet or iPod, and hadn't yet learned how to masturbate. In those days—which I remember as a solid year of Sundays—I would pass the hours by lying on my bed, and seeing how long I could stare at the telegraph pole outside my window without blinking.

My mother would regularly come in and find me lying on the bed, tears pouring down my face.

"What's the matter?" she would ask.

"Two minutes fifty-one seconds!" I would say—high on how much my eyes hurt.

It started to rain, hard. I trudged over Waterloo Bridge as buses neatly transferred whole puddles across my right hand side. On the South Bank, I went into Eat to get a coffee. The barrista looked scared. When I saw myself in the mirror, I could see why. My fake leopardskin coat was soaked. My hair ran with water. My sneakers didn't just squelch when I walked—they glugged. The barrista had looked at all the evidence, and concluded that I must have just failed to commit suicide by jumping in the Thames—and that now I was having a coffee, while I waited for the tide to rise a little higher.

When I went to pay for the coffee, he gave me a free brownie. I translated this brownie as the message, "Don't jump again." It was 486 calories of humanity.

When I finally got home, it was dark. I'd been walking for five hours. I was wet, bloodied and almost sub-human with boredom. I'd seen so many dull, half-empty rain-ruined streets that I'd started to believe they might actually affect my personality, and make me permanently dolorous. I lay down on the sofa, barely conscious. My brother was over for a visit.

"I'm training for the marathon," I said, by way of explanation.

"The marathon?" he said, impressed. "Blimey. Well done, Paula Radcliffe."

"It's not the running marathon," I said. "It's the Moonwalk. A walking marathon."

"Ha!" he said. "That's not really a marathon, then, is it? That's just a walk."

It was then that I realized the truth: walking a marathon is much, much, *much* harder than running one. Because everyone thinks it's easy.

Another one of my noble campaigns to make humanity a better place: this time, arguing for international recognition of the supremacy of Ghostbusters *above all other films. I have a long-standing pact with my sister that, if we ever get nominated for an Oscar, we will eschew ballgowns, diamonds and £20,000 make-overs to go up the red carpet dressed as Venkman and Spengler from* Ghostbusters—*each with a REAL unlicensed nuclear accelator on our backs. For us, there is no more glamorous look. These are our sex-clothes.*

Ghostbusters Is the Greatest Film of All Time. Please Do Not Argue with Me.

LAST WEEK, ITUNES ANNOUNCED that they were celebrating the twenty-fifth anniversary of the release of *Ghostbusters*. This they did by renting it out at 99p, as their "Film of The Week."

I had two, quite intense and simultaneous, responses to this news.

The first was somber. It was, if I may be frank, bordering on maudlin.

"Twenty-five years? *Twenty-five years*? My God, this is worse than when I realized it was ten years since 'Vogue' by Madonna was Number One. I never *used* to be able to remember things from twenty-five years ago. I am beginning to have the memory span—the reminiscing capabilities—of an old woman."

The second response was, thankfully, much brisker. It was: "99p! For the best film ever made? That's an INSULT! It's like iTunes saying you can have sex with the Queen for a pound! It won't stand, by God! IT WON'T STAND!"

But—on reflection—in many ways, the two responses kind of merged together in the middle. For the simple truth of the matter is that *Ghostbusters is* the greatest film ever made—and yet, currently, the world is too scared to admit this. In 2009, if you stood up at a party and spoke factually—"*Ghostbusters* should still be nominated for an Oscar every year, even now—that's how good it is"—you would probably experience great feelings of squirminess, and embarrassment.

And that is because the generation before us have done an excellent propaganda job installing *Star Wars* as the best film ever made, and we—their younger brothers and sisters—never realized how late in the day it was getting. If we'd realized that twenty-five bleeding years had passed a little sooner, we would have got a hustle on with shooting George Lucas's over-rated, po-faced bundle of space-tat out of the water. As it is, I think we all still thought it was, like, 1992 or something, and there was plenty of time to make the case for *Ghostbusters*, after we'd got over how good this new Blur album was.

So with the startling jolt of the quarter-century anniversary, the urgency of the task is now revealed. The Great Ghostbusters Campaign must start today. Here. Starting with this inarguable, scientific fact: *Ghostbusters* is still the most successful comedy film of all time, with a 1984 box-office of $229.2m. But this, of course, in turn, makes it the most successful film OF ALL TIME, FULL STOP—given that comedy is the supreme genre, and rules over every other format, such as "serious," "foreign" or "black & white."

Of course, there are those who will argue that comedy *isn't* the greatest genre. "What art should be about," they will say, "is revealing exquisite and resonant truths about the human condition."

Well, to be honest—no it shouldn't. I mean, it can *occasionally*, if it wants to; but really, how many penetrating insights into human nature do you need in one lifetime? Two? Three? Once you've realized that no one else has a clue what they're doing, either, and that love can be totally pointless, any further insights into human nature just start getting depressing, really.

On the other hand, what humans *do* need is "things to say." They need a huge supply of them. Amusing, essentially inconsequential things, which will make as many people in the room feel as relaxed and cordial as possible.

In this respect, *Ghostbusters* reveals itself, once again, as the greatest film ever made. When I mentioned this column on Twitter, I had over fifty suggestions as to what the best line in the film is—nearly all of them useful in everyday life.

"Back off man—I'm a scientist" is the one I find myself using the most often; most recently when the logic in opening a bottle of warm rosé at 3 AM was brought into question. "Listen—do you smell something?" is equally handy. "I think he can hear you, Ray," can be utilized whenever you think an indiscreet conversation has been overheard, but also when a large animal suddenly looks up, as if it might run towards you, and attack you. Whenever you buy takeout, it is traditional to nix all conversation about future plans with the line, "This magnificent feast represents the *last* of the petty cash." And there is no more succinct way of explaining why certain table placements would be ill-advised than, "Don't cross the streams." There are literally twenty more great lines; but one of them involves a piano, and another needs someone to mention sponges before you can use it.

By comparison, what has *Star Wars* got? "Luke—I am your father." I tell you what—you *never* get to wedge that into conversation.

Because if this is the start of the campaign to rightfully install *Ghostbusters* as the best film of all time, *Star Wars* is the one that has to be beaten. It is Connors to *Ghostbusters*'s Borg.

To those who still deludedly think they prefer *Star Wars* over *Ghostbusters*, all I need to do is ask you is this: You don't really *want* to be a Jedi, do you? In a greige cowl, getting off with your sister, without a single gag across *three* films? I think if you thought about it a little while longer, you'd realize that you'd far rather be a Ghostbuster: a nerd in New York with an unlicensed nuclear accelerator on your back, and a one-in-four chance of being Bill Murray.

I urge the world to greatly accelerate their acknowledgment of *Ghostbusters*'s true canonical placing—for, in this period of uncertainty, terrible things are happening. Last week, the twenty-fifth anniversary of the film was marked by a celebrity party, attended by, in descending order of fame: Dizzee Rascal, Nikki Grahame from Big Brother 7, DJ Ironik, Dave Berry and Rick Edwards. I know. I'm not trying to be rude but, really, if you're at that level of fame and someone invites you to a party in honor of something you love, the most effective way to show you care is to stay away.

For the rest of us—the ones who have realized the Great Truth about the Greatest Movie Ever Made—the serious campaigning must start *now*. Let's go show this prehistoric bitch how we do things downtown.

And then, a couple of months later, I interviewed Keith Richards. At the time I was going insane writing How to Be a Woman, *and working seven-day weeks for months on end—but couldn't let pass the opportunity to meet the man who, more than any other on Earth, could claim to be rock' n' roll on two, very thin, legs. I mean, really thin legs. It's like two bits of string covered in denim.*

This was another time I was attempting to give up smoking, but was derailed by someone legendary offering a fag. The next time I tried to give it up, it was when Benedict Cumberbatch, dressed as Sherlock, offered me a Marlie outside 221b Baker Street. WHO WOULD EVER SAY NO TO THESE CIGARETTES?

Keith—Noddy Holder Says You Wear a Wig

I MEET KEITH RICHARDS on International Talk Like a Pirate Day. It feels only right to inform him of this.

"International Talk Like a Pirate Day?" Keith says, with his wolfy grin, wholly amused. "ARRRGHH! ARRRHHH! Oh, I can't do it with without the eyepatch," he sighs, mock-petulantly. "I can't speak like a pirate without an eyepatch. Or being pissed—HARGH! HARGH!"

But of course, he can: to be frank, everything Keith Richards says is in the cadence of Pirate. With his black eyes, bandana and earring, even at sixty-seven, he has the air of a rakish gentleman forced to steal a frigate and abscond from polite society—due to some regrettable misunderstanding about a virgin daughter, a treasure map and a now-smoldering Admiralty building. You can see why he was the inspiration for Johnny Depp's Captain Jack Sparrow in *Pirates of the Caribbean*. Richards apparently taught Depp how to walk around a corner, drunk: "You keep your back to the wall at all times."

Today, Richards is a pirate in onshore mode. The mood is tavernish. Even though we are in the Royal Suite of Claridge's, which has a grand piano ("Shall I have a go? You can bootleg it—HARGH HARGH HARGH."), and so many rooms we never even go in half of them, Richards still brings an air of a man who's left his parrot, cutlass and Smee in the hallway—lest he need to make a quick getaway. On walking into the room he spots me, and does a double-take.

"I had no idea I was going to talk to a *lady*," he says, ordering a vodka and orange. "I need a drink when I do that."

Spotting a pack of Marlboros on the table, he eschews them, and brings out his own supplies.

"*Those* are the ones that say they'll kill you," he says, pointing at the pack on the table, with their large "SMOKING KILLS" label. "They are English, and they *would* kill you; they're bloody awful."

"Are they different from American ones?" I ask.

"Oh yes. You take them apart, if you're going to roll a hash joint, and there's bits of stalk and crap in there. It's *unacceptable* to a smoker."

He takes one of his own out of his pocket, and lights it. The smell of the smoke mingles with his cologne.

"What have you got on?" I inquire.

"I've got a hard-on—I didn't know you could smell it," he says—and then starts laughing again, in a fug of smoke. "That's a rock 'n' roll joke—one of Jerry Lee Lewis's," he explains, almost apologetically. "We're at the Rock 'n' Roll Hall of Fame, and Jerry's got his rig on—frilly shirt and tuxedo—and he's coming down the steps and this chick rushed out and was like, 'You smell great—what have you got on?' And Jerry says, 'I've got a hard-on—I didn't know you could smell it.' Pure rock 'n' roll."

Keith takes another drag on his fag, beaming.

"'Ere," he says, suddenly concerned, looking at the cigarette smoke. "I hope you're not . . . allergic."

Apologizing for a hard-on joke, and worrying that a journalist might develop a tickly cough from passive smoking, is a long way from Richards' interviews in his outlaw heyday—he once spent forty sleepless hours with the *NME* journalist Nick Kent "pinballing" around London in a Ferarri and consuming ferocious quantities of cocaine and heroin—a cocktail quaintly referred to by Richards as "the breakfast of champions."

But then, Richards has mellowed considerably over the years—possibly out of necessity, if one considers how difficult it would be to parallel park in modern-day London on a 1.5mg speedball. Giving up heroin in 1978, after his fifth bust, Richards reveals today that he's finally given up cocaine, too—in 2006, after he fell from a tree in Fiji, and had to have brain surgery.

"Yeah—that was cocaine I had to give up for that," he says, with an equinanimous sigh. "You're like—'I've got the message, oh Lord.'" He raps on the metal plate in his head. It makes a dull, thonking sound.

"I've given up everything now—which is a trip in itself," he says, with the kind of Robert Newton-esque eye-roll that indicates how interesting merely getting out of bed sober can be after forty years of caning it. Not that Richards is disapproving of getting high, of course:

"I'm just waiting for them to invent something more interesting, hahaha," he says. "I'm all ready to road test it, when they do."

Richards' image is of the last man standing at the long party that was the sixties—and the man who'd invited everyone over in the first place, anyway. During his junkie years, Richards spent over a decade on the "People Most Likely to Die" list—"I used to read it, check I was still on there. I was on it longer than anyone else. Badge of honor, hur hur."

But having spent from 1968 to 1978 with everyone expecting him to keel over in a hotel (the classic Richards quote: "Which I never did: it's the height of impoliteness to turn blue in someone else's bathroom."), Richards has now, ironically, gone on to be one of those people we now think will just . . . live forever. His tough, leathery, indestructible air gives the suggestion that heroin, whisky and cocaine, when taken in large enough quantities, have a kind of . . . *preservative* quality. Richards has been cured in a marinade of pharmaceuticals. He both gives off the aura of, and bears an undeniable physical resemblance to, to the air-dried Inca mummies of Chachapoya.

"Well, I'm not putting death on the agenda," he says, with another grin. "I don't want to see my old friend Lucifer just yet, hurgh hurgh. He's the guy I'm gonna see, isn't it—I'm not going to The Other Place, let's face it, HARGH!"

We're here today because—having resolutely, persistently and, in many ways, unfeasibly—not died, Richards has finally published his autobiography, *Life*. When Richards announced the project, he was subject to a massive bidding war that ended with Richards getting a £4.8m advance—acknowledgment of the fact that, barring Bowie or McCartney deciding to write their stories, Richards' was the motherlode, in terms of understanding that most incredible of decades—the sixties—from the inside; recounted by one of the very people pinballing the psychedelic charabanc off the bounds of "decent" society.

"Have you read it?" he asks—trying to look casual, but unable to suppress an incongruous note of eagerness.

"Oh God, yes," I say. "Oh man, it's a total hoot. Really, really amazing."

"Oh good," he says, relaxing. "You know, you start off thinking you can spin a few yarns—and by the time you get to the end of it, it's turned into something much more. One memory triggers another, and before you know it, there's 600 rounds per second coming out."

"Did you want to write your version because other books on you, and the Stones, had got it wrong?" I ask.

"I read Bill Wyman's book, but after three or four chapters—where he's going [assumes dull, priggish Wyman monotone], 'And by that point, I only had £600 left in Barclays Bank'—I was like, 'Oh, Bill.' You know what I mean? You're far more interesting than that; do me a favor. And Mick attempted it once, and ended up giving the money back. It was ten, fifteen years ago, and he'd keep ringing up and going [does Mick impression], "ere, what were we doing on August 15th nineteen-sixty-somefink?' I'd be like 'Mick, *you're* writing it. I can't remember.' And knowing Mick, there would have been a *morass* of blank chapters—because there would have been a lot of stuff he would have wanted to put to one side, hur hur."

Richards is dismissive of Stones books written by non-Stones—claiming the authors would have been 'too scared' to write the truth: "Who's really going to put Mick Jagger, or Keith Richards, up against a wall and say, 'I demand you answer this'?" he says, eyes suddenly flashing black.

"Because, you know . . ." he takes a drag on his fag. "You end up dead like that."

The reason *Life* attracted such a bidding war is because the life of Keith Richards and the Stones is one that—even in today's modern, anything-goes pop-cultural climate—takes in a still-astonishing amount of, for wont of a better word, scandal. "Would You Let Your Daughter Marry a Rolling Stone?", the Redlands bust, Marianne Faithfull in her fur rug, "Who Breaks a Butterfly on a Wheel?", the still-controversial death of Brian Jones, the Hell's Angels running amok at Altamont, the Marianne Faithfull/Mick Jagger/Anita Pallenberg/Richards four-way love-rectangle; numerous arrests, heroin, cocaine, acid, whisky, infidelity, groupies, Margaret Trudeau, riots, billions of dollars, and four decades of sweaty fans, screaming without end.

And, at the center of it all, arguably the greatest rock 'n' roll band that ever existed. "Gimme Shelter," "Jumpin' Jack Flash," "You Can't Always Get What You Want," "Wild Horses," "Brown Sugar," "Start Me Up," "Sympathy for the Devil," "Satisfaction"—each one with the ability to alone answer the question, "Mummy—what is rock 'n' roll?," and, when taken *en masse,* the reason why Keith Richards is referred to, almost factually, as "The Living Riff."

For those expecting an explosive story, *Life* certainly doesn't disappoint: it opens in 1975, with Richards in a diner in Fordyce, Arkansas, about to be busted for the fourth time. Written like a *Fear and Loathing in Las Vegas* with infinitely more resources for getting wasted—Richards is driving to the next gig because he's "bored" of the Stones' private jet—it joins Richards at the highpoint of his caner years.

As Richards describes it, he is the sole long-haired man in a room full of rednecks, and is basically wearing a hat made of drugs ("There was a flap at the side in which I'd stowed hash, Tuinals and coke"), and driving a car made of drugs ("I'd spent hours packing the side-panel with coke, grass, peyote and mescaline.").

High on cocaine ("Merck cocaine—the fluffy, pharmaceutical blow" as he describes it, lovingly), Richards is arrested, dragged to the courthouse, and becomes the center of an international news incident ("There were 5,000 Stones fans outside the courthouse")—until Mick Jagger sweet-talks the local governor, and bails him out.

"Mick was always good with the locals," Richards writes, half-admiringly, half-condescendingly—like a pirate captain commending a handsome cabin boy who has the ability to "talk posh" to the gentry.

The following 620 pages scarcely let up from there. Although things tail off in the mid-eighties—as they invariably do in the stories of sixties icons. By then, they are retired from the heart of the storm to their mansions, and are merely watching Madonna from the sidelines, puzzled—the first half of *Life*, up until 1984, is in a league of its own. As rock memoirs go, only Bob Dylan's imperial, awe-inspiring *Chronicles* can beat it.

Sitting in Richards' agent's office, reading it—the secrecy around it is immense; I have to sign confidentiality agreements before I can even see the manuscript—was like getting into a Tardis, and being witness to events only ever previously recounted by hearsay.

One of the first stories is one of the most amazing—Richards quoting from a letter he sent his aunt in 1961: "This morning on Dartford Station a guy I knew at primary school came up to me. He's got every record Chuck Berry ever made. He is called Mick Jagger."

It's like discovering Cleopatra's page-a-day diary, and the entry: "Tuesday, 4:30 PM: meeting with Mark Antony."

And so it goes on from here—recruiting all the Stones one by one, Bill Wyman sighingly tolerated because he has a better amp than anyone else. They work hard, but it comes ridiculously easy: the first song they ever write together—locked in the kitchen by their manager, until they come up with something—is "As Tears Go By," which both goes to Number One, and bags Jagger the beautiful Marianne Faithfull as a girlfriend. They buy houses. They buy drugs. Here's the Redlands bust, recounted by the man who owned the house: casually mentioning another guest—David Schidermann, the acid dealer. As the inventor of both the Strawberry Fields acid and the Purple Haze acid, Schidermann dosed the charts with two of the greatest psychedelic singles ever made.

Keith can tell us the Marianne Faithfull/Mars Bar story is a myth—but adds, casually, that he was the man who left a Mars Bar on the coffee table, as a snack, for when he was stoned.

Here's John Lennon—"Johnny. A silly sod, in many ways"—coming round with Yoko, and keeling over in the bathroom.

"I don't think John ever left my house, except horizontally," Richards sighs, having found Lennon—godhead for a generation—lying by the toilet, murmuring, "Don't move me—these tiles are beautiful."

On another night with Lennon, Richards tries to explain to him where the Beatles—the fucking Beatles!—have been going wrong, all these years: "You wear your guitar too high. It's not a violin. No wonder you don't swing. No wonder you can rock, but not roll."

Redlands burns to the ground, and Richards—high—escapes with only "a cutlass, and a box of goodies, hur hur. Fuck the passports."

Allen Ginsberg—the high priest of beatnik—is regarded as a bit of a twat: coming over to Keith's house, he "plays a concertina and makes 'Om-mmmmm' sounds," as Richards relates, still sounding beleagured by an unwelcome houseguest, thirty years later. Brian Jones is dismissed as little more than "a wifebeater."

In this rollercoaster blur, Altamont—where the Hell's Angels, high on LSD and speed, stab Meredith Hunter to death—is merely an incidental point. For generations of lazy documentary makers, it's been seen as the point that the sixties turned sour: the moment that Flower Power idealism dies; the undeniable beginning of the darkness.

To the man on stage at the time, however, playing "Under My Thumb" as Meredith dies, it's a story that merits little more than two paragraphs. The first Stones fan to die had been back in 1965—plunging from the balcony of an early gig. By 1969, Keith Richards had seen it all. He couldn't be surprised by anything.

But for all the drugs, car chases, jets, stadiums, Presidents, fistfights and deaths, the core of *Life* is a small, human, timeless story. The story of Keith

Richards' life revolves around two things: the friend he never quite understands, and the girl who got away: bandmate Mick Jagger, and former wife, and mother of three of his children, Anita Pallenberg.

Reading *Life*, I was shocked by how candid Richards is about his relationship with both Jagger and Pallenberg. Indeed, I gasped at two of the stories. My thought was, as I read them, "Keith Richards—you're going to be in trouble."

"In trouble?" Richards says, laughing. "Hur hur. Why?"

Well, let's take Mick Jagger. You reveal that your secret nickname for him is "Your Majesty," or "Brenda"—and that you openly had conversations with the other Stones, in front of Mick, referring to "that bitch Brenda." Your review of Mick's solo album, *Goddess in the Doorway*—which you refer to as *Dogshit on the Doorstep*—is "It's like *Mein Kampf*—everyone had it, but no one read it." You describe an annoying pet mynah bird as "like living with Mick." There's a chapter that starts, "It was the beginning of the eighties when Mick started to become unbearable." There are quotes like, "Mick plays harmonica from the heart—but he doesn't sing like that." "Mick Jagger is aspiring to be Mick Jagger." "I think Mick thinks I belong to him." "I used to love Mick, but I haven't been to his dressing room in twenty years. Sometimes I think, 'I miss my friend. I wonder, 'Where did he go?'"

Has Mick read the book?

Keith seems resolutely unfazed.

"Yeah!" he says, equanimously. "I think it opened his eyes a bit, actually."

"Were there any bits he asked you to leave out?" I ask.

Keith starts laughing again. "WURGH WURGH WURGH." It sounds like a crow stuck in a chimney.

"Yeah! Funnily enough, it was the weirdest thing he wanted taken out. I mean, look. You know, I love the man. I've known him since I was four years old, right. But the bit he wanted taken out was how he used a voice coach."

"Really?"

"Yeah! And everyone knew it anyway. It's been in a million interviews, but for some reason, he was like, 'You know—could we leave that out?' And I went 'No! I'm trying to say the truth here.'"

I pause for a minute. I clear my throat.

"So he didn't ask you to take out the bit about how small his cock is, then?" I ask, in a rather prim voice.

"Hey—I was only told that by others," Keith says, with a wolfish smile and a shrug.

This is the height of disingenuousness, because the "other" Richards is referring to is Marianne Faithfull—Jagger's girlfriend at the time—and a story that is one of the key "OH MY GOD!" moments of the book.

Rumors have long circled about just what was going on in 1969—the year the world's two most glamorous couples were Keith Richards and Anita Pallenberg, and Mick Jagger and Marianne Faithfull.

As Pallenberg and Jagger started work on *Performance,* in the roles of lovers, Richards was convinced that director Nicolas Roeg—whom he hates—is trying to get Mick and Anita together for real, so that he can have "hardcore pornography" in his film.

In one of the most evocatively written passages in the book, Richards describes how the jealousy and fear that he's losing Anita to Jagger, coupled with his escalating heroin abuse, results in him writing "Gimme Shelter" on a filthy, stormy day—staring out of the window of his house, waiting for the sound of Anita's car. It never arrives. She doesn't come home that night. He presumes she lies in his bandmate's bed.

Partly in retaliation, Richards then goes about bedding Marianne Faithfull. Despite the undeniable dark, fratricidal overtones of screwing Jagger's girlfriend, Richards' account of it in *Life* is recounted in Pirate Tavern mode, concluding with his joy at having "my head nestled between those two beautiful jugs."

When Faithfull and Richards hear Jagger returning home, Richards jumps out of the window, like Robin Askwith in *Confessions of a Window Cleaner,* leaving his socks, and his cuckolded bandmate's girlfriend, behind him. As a final stab, forty years later, Richards adds:

"[Marianne] had no fun with [Mick's] tiny todger. I know he's got an enormous pair of balls—but it doesn't quite fill the gap."

For a Stones fan, it's a real double-or-quits moment. On the one hand, as a description of what it's like to be inside a legendary song as it make landfall, Keith Richards' recollections of writing "Gimme Shelter" are without parallel. On the other hand, there is the massive risk that—after reading the chapter—every subsequent listening of the song will be haunted by the image of Mick Jagger's allegedly tiny todger, nestled on a pair of gigantic testicles.

It's one of those side effects of rock 'n' roll that no one ever warns you about.

"Well, I *did* say he had enormous balls," Richards says now, generously. "I'm sure he's had worse thrown at him by women. I mean, Jerry Hall pretty much decimated him anyway."

"It does seem like you're trying to . . . wind him up," I say.

"We've had our beefs but hey, who doesn't. *You* try and keep something together for fifty years," Richards says, palpably not caring.

There is similar, breathtaking candor in his recounting of his relationship with Anita Pallenberg. In a physically abusive relationship with fellow Stone Brian Jones, Pallenberg has the hots for Richards, and Richards has the hots for Pallenberg. When Jones gets hospitalized with asthma, Richards and Pallenberg end up together in a car, being driven from Barcelona to Valencia. Without a word ever being exchanged, Pallenberg kicks off their relationship by silently unzipping Richards' jeans and giving him a blowjob.

"I remember the smell of the orange trees in Valencia," Richards writes, still sounding post-coital, forty years later. "When you get laid by Anita Pallenberg for the first time, you remember things."

"Oh—the great blowjob in the car?" Keith says today, when I bring it up—again, quite primly.

"What was your chauffeur was doing all this time?" I ask, incredulously.

"He's got to keep his eyes on the road," Keith shrugs. "I should imagine he was going, 'about time,' to be honest. It had been in the air for ages."

Although it was Richards who eventually called time on the marriage, when Pallenberg's subsequent heroin addiction got out of hand, Pallenberg still comes across as "unfinished business" in *Life*—with Richards repeatedly addressing Pallenberg directly from the pages, calling on her to think of what would have happened if they'd managed to stay together, in rocking chairs "watching the grandkids." Although Richards is now married to, and has two children with, Patti Hansen, Pallenberg recurs through out the book like perfume; melody; a ghost. While Richards rails at Jagger, he sighs over Pallenberg. The girl that gave herself away.

Perhaps you keep coming back to Anita and Mick, I suggest to Richards, because as an artist, there's nothing to say about the people you love and understand. It's the ones who mystify you that you need to write songs and books about. That's how you try and figure them out.

"Yeah," Richards nods. "You've got nothing to say when it's all understood."

It's the best inference to make—because any other suggests Richards is still a little in love with the woman whose clothes he's wearing on the cover of *Their Satanic Majesties Request*.

At sixty-seven, having come into life-transforming wealth and fame in one of the most controversial bands of the counter-cultural era, one could easily assume that Keith Richards became a pirate *because* of rock 'n' roll—around the time the Stones went out on the road, and never really came back: "A pirate nation, moving under our own flag, with lawyers, clowns and attendants."

But the other revelation of *Life* is that this was how Richards was raised: Richards has always been a pirate. He describes post-war Dartford as somewhere where "everyone's a thief." Dartford—where the highwaymen would hold up the stage to London, explosions from the fireworks factory "would take out the windows for miles around," and patients from the lunatic asylum would regularly abscond.

"In the morning, you'd find a loony on the heath, in his little nightshirt," Richards recalls, fondly.

Richards' family were not respectable, or God-fearing. They numbered musicians, actors and prostitutes. His mother would "cross the road" to avoid the priest, and divorced his father to marry a younger lover.

Richards' mother, Doris, was a classic, working-class matriarch—her last words to Keith, as he played to her on her deathbed, were "You're out of tune"—and as an only child of a poor, bohemian couple, the only things Richards was brought up to respect were the local library and music. When he got his first guitar, he slept with it in his bed.

Twenty years later, guests to Redlands recall Richards' guitar collection being on every sofa and chair, and being left with nowhere to sit but the floor.

So when you come and talk to Keith Richards, this is who you feel you are meeting: not a millionaire Rolling Stone, with houses in Suffolk, Connecticut and Turks & Caicos—but the guy from Dartford who would always have been out of kilter with normal society, however his life had turned out. You get the very strong feeling that this is what Keith Richards would be like even if we were down the pub, instead of Claridge's, and Keith had got here on the bus—not least because his bandana is, on closer inspection, quite grubby, and he's wearing a pair of beat-up track pants, and the kind of incongruously bright turquoise sneakers you often see on meths-drinking tramps.

Ask him about his daughter—twenty-four-year-old Alexandra—doing a nude shoot for *Playboy,* and he seems truly baffled by notion he could have been disapproving.

"You know—my girls are like me," he says. "They try to avoid work as much as possible, hehehe. A bit of modelling is a bit of freedom. Hey, baby—with a frame like that, flaunt it."

The story of how he came to work with Johnny Depp on *Pirates of the Caribbean* is a case in point.

"It took me two years before I realized who he was," Keith says, lighting another fag. "He was just one of my son Marlon's mates, hanging around the house playing guitar. I never ask Marlon's mates who they are, because you know, 'I'm a dope dealer,' hahaha. Then one day he was at dinner"—Richards mimes Johnny Depp holding a knife and fork—"and I'm like, 'Whoa! Scissorhands!' Hahaha. Then I find out he's an actor, and like one of the biggest Keith Richards fans in the world—and how do I deal with that? 'Get over it, Johnny.' HURGH HURGH."

Depp and Richards are currently shooting *Pirates of the Caribbean 4,* where Richards plays, for the second time, Captain Jack Sparrow's father— "It takes two hours to put the wig and make-up on. Back into the hairy prison. 'Ooooh, sorry about my sword, babe,' hahaha."

Filming a barroom scene, Richards has roped in "a couple of mates. Well it's a bar-room, innit?"

In between the last film and this, Depp has been shooting a documentary on Richards: "Kinda behind the scenes stuff. Johnny does interviews. Dunno when it's going to be finished." He shrugs again. The idea of being followed around by a documentary crew, and one of the most famous actors in the world, seems resolutely normal.

Possibly because of his upbringing—"I'm just a retarded gangster, really. Maybe that's what I should have called the book. *Retarded Gangster"—* Richards seems genuinely at ease with his fame. He lives now, as he always has since a child, in a world outside most others'—he doesn't watch TV (*"Lovejoy,"* he says, finally, having struggled to think for some minutes about his favorite show), exists on old-fashioned comfort food (the book includes his recipe for bangers and mash: "Put the fuckers in the pan and let them rock"), has never voted ("I suppose democracy is the best there is to offer. But for a lot of people, it's like telling the slaves they're free. 'Hey man—where's the next meal coming from?'"), and as for when he last traveled by public transport, he wrinkles his forehead and asks, mistily, "Have they still got trams?"

This leaves him at ease in the company of other infamous people ("My favorite head of state? Václev Havel. Very impressed with the man. He had a telescope in his office, trained on his old prison cell. He used to refer to it as 'my old house.' I liked Clinton. He's a lousy sax player. A little indiscreet, but as a guy—I'd take him on any time. He's great." As for Tony Blair: "I wrote him a letter [about the Iraq war], telling him he had to stick to his guns. I got a letter back, saying 'Thanks for the support.'") He views the recent imprisonment of George Michael with equimanity, and not a little amusement.

"Fame has killed more very talented guys than drugs," he says, sighing.

"Jimi Hendrix didn't die of an overdose—he died of fame. Brian [Jones], too. I lost a lot of friends to fame. There's that bit in the book, where I talk about how I cope with fame, and say 'Mick chose flattery, and I chose junk.' Because I kept my feet on the ground—even when they were in the gutter. You know what? I bet George Michael is loving it. I say, 'Stay in jail, George.' There's probably some dope, and some gays. He probably won't want to leave—it's the best place for him. He's playing around with fame. I can't remember a song of his. I don't want to knock the guy, but I'm an immortal legend, according to some," he shrugs.

The implication is that, however wasted Richards got, he wouldn't have crashed into a branch of Snappy Snaps on something as lightweight as a joint.

Keith Richards is a man without regret. When I ask him if—given the chance to do it all over again—he'd start taking heroin, he doesn't pause. "Oh yes. Yes. There was a lot of experience in there—you meet a lot of weird people, different takes on life that you're not going to find if you don't go there. I loved a good high. And if you stay up, you get the songs that everyone else misses, because they're asleep. There's songs zooming around everywhere. There's songs zooming through here right now, in the air."

He looks up, as if he can see them, hovering over the grand piano.

"You've just got to put your hand out, and catch them."

During our whole chat, the only time he seems roused to genuine annoyance is when I ask him what I think might be the most amazing question of my entire journalistic career. Thanks to a meeting at a party last year, I am able to say to Keith Richards—one our greatest living rock stars—"Keith. I met Noddy Holder last year, and he's convinced you wear a wig." (For American readers: Noddy Holder is the permanently beaming, costermonger-lunged lead singer of British glam-rock legend Slade. Imagine Robert Plant, but dressed like a glittery clown.)

"Not yet!" he says, looking genuinely indignant. "Hey man, what's his problem with wigs?"

"He thinks both you *and* Mick wear them," I say, with mock disapproval.

"Get out of here!" Richards roars. He pulls down his bandana and shows me his hair—gray, a little wispy, but looking undeniably real. "Hey Noddy, you know, there more important things in life than hair. Mick definitely doesn't wear a wig. I KNOW! I've PULLED IT! What's Noddy's problem?"

"I think Noddy's just very proud he's still got a gigantic afro," I offer.

"Well, that's about all he's got," Keith says, sniffily. "Well done, Nod."

Our hour is up. Keith is off to get ready for another day of shooting on *Pirates*—possibly the most high-profile busman's holiday in show business.

"Any plans for the future?" I ask, as he picks up his cigarettes—still eschewing the British ones on the table.

"Well, you know, we'll be on the road again in the future," Keith says, pocketing his lighter. "Yeah. On the road. I think it's going to happen. I've had a chat with . . . Her Majesty. Brenda."

And Richards leaves the room, laughing. He's at it again. Winding up Mick; doing what he wants; being Keith Richards, for the sixty-seventh year in a row.

"I had to invent the job, you know," he said, earlier. "There wasn't a sign in the shop window, saying, 'Wanted: Keith Richards.'"

And he's done a bloody job of it.

I don't think I can hold out any longer: I think it might be Sherlock *time.* Sherlock *blew my mind like I wanted it blown—hard, fast, properly, and while I was too busy laughing to notice that it was also, quietly, and at the same time, breaking my heart.*

I loved the way it entered—kicking the door open shouting "BANG! And I'm in!" in such a confident manner that, twenty minutes into the first episode, people on Twitter were saying, "This really might be one of the greatest TV shows of all time." After twenty minutes! That is one hell of a mesmeric aura for a show to be throwing off.

When people said, smugly, "Oh, it's just because you fancy Benedict Cumberbatch as Sherlock," it was as if they were saying to a plant, "Oh, you only photosynthesize because of the sun." Well, YES. DUH. That's what the sun/Cumberbatch does to me/a plant. Why are you arguing against the miracle of Nature? You might as well punch a tree. Just buy the box set.

Anyway. Here's my review of the first episode, written with a spinning head and a bursting heart, and a bid going on eBay for a deerstalker hat.

Sherlock Review 1:
Like a Jaguar in a Cello

OH DEAR. That was bad timing.

In the week where Culture Secretary Jeremy Hunt questioned if the BBC license fee gives "value for money," the advent of *Sherlock* donked his theory quite badly. It's a bit embarrassing to be standing on a soap-box, slagging a corporation off as essentially wasteful and moribund, right at the point where they're landing a bright, brilliant dragon of a show on the rooftops, for 39p per household. And with the rest of the BBC's output that day—theoretically—thrown in for free.

The casting was perfect. Benedict Cumberbatch—the first actor in history to play Sherlock Holmes who has a name more ridiculous than "Sherlock Holmes"—was both perfect and astonishing: an actor pulling on an iconic character and finding he had infinite energy to drive the thing. He is so good that—ten minutes in—I just started laughing out loud with what a delight it was to watch him.

He looks amazing—as odd as you'd expect The Cleverest Man in the World to look. Eyes white, skin like china clay, and a voice like someone smoking a cigar inside a grand piano, this Holmes has, as Cumberbatch described it in interviews, "an achievable super-power." He might not have actual X-ray vision, but his superlative illative chops mean that London is like a Duplo train-set to him: an easily-analyzable system, populated by small, simple plastic people.

At one point, a suspect speeds away from him in a taxi. Holmes can call up the A-Z, and the taxi's only possible route, in his mind: "Right turn, traffic lights, pedestrian crossing, road works, traffic lights."

By climbing over the right rooftop, ducking down the right alleyway, and running very, very fast while looking hot, Holmes can beat the taxi to its destination: as easily as if he were the size of the Telecom Tower, or Big Ben, stepping over the city laid out on the rug at 221b Baker Street.

Of course, this view of humanity's masses makes him a high-functioning Asperger's/borderline sociopath. Questioning why someone would still be upset about their baby dying fourteen years ago—"That was ages ago!" he shouts with the frustration of a child. "Why would she still be upset?"—Holmes notes that the room has gone quiet.

"Not good?" he hisses to Watson.

"*Bit* not good, yeah," Watson replies.

So this is why Holmes needs Watson—their advent into each other's lives managed with three perfect flicks of the script. Yes, Watson is impressed by Holmes: "That's amazing!" he gasps, as Holmes deduces he has an alcoholic sibling, merely from scratch marks on his mobile.

"People don't usually say that," Holmes blinks, pleased. "They usually say, 'Piss off.'"

But this Watson isn't the usual, buff, conservative sidekick. In a role rivalling his turn as Tim in *The Office,* Martin Freeman's Watson is altogether more complex and satisfying. Yes, he's here as dragon-trainer—to whack Holmes with a stick when he starts monstering around, and climbing up on the furniture. But he's also as quietly addicted to "the game" as Holmes— it's Watson with the nervous tremors because he misses active service, in Afghanistan, Watson with the gun.

Sherlock is so packed with joy and treats, to list them means bordering on gabbling: Una Stubbs as secret dope-fiend landlady Mrs Hudson ("It was just a herbal remedy—for my hip!"), Mycroft Holmes's mysterious, posh, texting, superlatively composed assistant, "Anthea." The little nods to the possibility that Holmes might be gay. The insanely generous casting of Rupert Graves as DI Lestrade. The line "I love a serial killer—there's always something to look forward to!" And the perfect placing of what is, presumably, the series arc: "Holmes is a great man. And I hope, one day, a good one, too."

"Value for money" isn't even the start of it. Every detail of this *Sherlock* thrills. Given that it was written by Steven Moffat in the same year he knocked off the astonishing, elegant and high-powered re-booting of *Doctor Who,* at £142.50, Moffat's scripts alone are value for money.

If the funding is ever called into question, I'll pay it myself. In cash. Delivered to his front door step. With a beaming, hopefully non-stalkerish, "Thank you."

Then, two weeks later, it was all over: there were only three episodes in the first season. And I'd lost the bid on the deerstalker to someone in Leicester. I was gutted.

Sherlock Review 2:
The Frumious Cumberbatch

"BUT WHY ARE THERE only three episodes?" Britain asked, scrabbling around in the listings, in case there was a *Sherlock* left they'd overlooked, at the bottom. "Only three? Why would you make only three *Sherlocks*? Telly comes in SIX. SIX is the number of telly. Or TWELVE. Or, in America, TWENTY-SIX—because it is a bigger country. But you never have three of telly. Three of telly is NOT HOLY. WHY have they done this? IS THIS A GIGANTIC PUZZLE WE MUST DEDUCE—LIKE SHERLOCK HIMSELF?"

But yes. On Sunday, *Sherlock* came to an end after a fleet, flashing run. Like some kind of Usain Bolt of TV, perhaps it finished so early, simply because it was faster than everyone else. Either way, it had left scorch marks on the track: in three weeks, it flipped everything around. Sunday nights became the best night of the week. Martin Freeman went from being "Martin Freeman—you know. Tim from *The Office*" to "Martin Freeman—you know. Watson from *Sherlock*." Stephen Moffat had—extraordinarily—constructed a serious rival to his own *Doctor Who* as the most-loved and geekily-revered show in Britain. And Benedict Cumberbatch had, of course, gone from well-respected, BAFTA-nominated actor to pin-up, by-word, totty, avatar and fame: the frumious Cumberbatch.

"The Great Game" opened with Holmes—slumped in a chair, legs as long as the TV was wide—bored, shooting at the wall without even looking. Popping holes in that lovely 1970's wallpaper at 221b Baker Street; lead-like with torpor.

"What you need is a *nice murder,*" Una Stubbs's Mrs Hudson clucked, sympathetically, in the hallway. "Cheer you up."

So when Moriarty came out to play, Holmes's glee at the oncoming chaos was inglorious, but heartfelt. He received phonecalls from weeping innocents, parceled up with TNT. Moriarty told them what to say: they give Holmes a single, cryptic clue about an unsolved crime, and tell him he has twelve, ten, eight hours to solve it, or they will die.

With increasing dazzle, Holmes busts each case. On the foreshore by Southwark Bridge, with London frosty and grey behind him, Holmes looks at the washed-up corpse in front of him, and in less than a minute concludes that because this man is dead, a newly-discovered Vermeer—going on exhibition tomorrow—must be a fake. His torrent of illation is extraordinary—his mind has anti-gravity boots; he bounces from realization to realization until he's as high as the sun.

Ten minutes later, and he's in the gallery, staring at the Vermeer. He knows it's fake but doesn't know how to prove it. Then Moriarty's latest, TNT-garlanded victim calls him. The voice is tiny.

"It's a child!" Lestrade, Watson and the audience horror. "A child!" The child starts counting backwards from ten—Holmes has ten seconds to prove the Vermeer is a fake. The tension is insane—I was biting my wrists with distress—but when the answer bursts on Holmes, he almost doesn't shout out the answer in time: the pleasure he's had from smashing the case has him high as a kite. He is wired.

But the whole season has been building up to Holmes meeting Moriarty and, finally, in a deserted swimming pool, here he is: Jim Moriarty. Young, fast, Irish.

Sherlock seems oddly—*relieved* at finally meeting Moriarty. Yeah, he's completely evil—but he's also the only person in the world who doesn't, ultimately, bore Holmes. He's made the last week thrilling. Moriarty makes Holmes come alive—even when he's trying to kill him. And Moriarty knows this.

"Is that a Browning in your pocket—or are you just pleased to see me?" he asks.

"Both," Holmes says, during a scene that had an undeniable undercurrent of hotness.

But things suddenly turn. Moriarty knows that Holmes is bad for business. And—oh yeah—Dr. Watson's still standing in the corner, covered in TNT. Moriarty's threatening to explode him. I'd forgotten about that, during the hotness.

"The flirting's over, my dear," Moriarty says, warning Holmes off.

Holmes is in accord. "People have died."

And suddenly, the awfulness of Moriarty comes roaring out. "THAT'S. What people DO," he screams—eyes dilating so huge and black, I wondered if it might have been done with CGI. "I will BURN the HEART out of you," he continues, warning Holmes off his patch, boilingly insane. It was like when Christopher Lloyd shows his evil Toon eyes in *Who Framed Roger Rabbit?*—truly startling. Andrew Scott has some serious chops.

And there, five minutes later, we left them, on a cliff-hanger. Moriarty's snipers shining their laser sights on Holmes's and Watson's hearts; Holmes pointing his gun at a pile of TNT, telling Moriarty he's happy to blow them all sky high; *The Great Game* ended in checkmate. Not quite as amazing as the first episode—which was the televisual equivalent of someone kicking a door off its hinges, screaming, "I've COME to BLOW your MINDS!"—but a different league from Episode Two; and still the best thing on all week by several, palpable, indexable leagues.

Sherlock ends its run as a reekingly charismatic show, flashing its cerise silk suit lining in a thousand underplayed touches: Holmes watching *The Jeremy Kyle Show*—"Of course he's not the father! Look at the turn-up on his jeans!" The neat one-two of, "Meretricious!" "And a happy New Year!" A myriad of amazing moments from Cumberbatch, who will surely— surely—with his voice like a jaguar in a cello, and his face like sloth made of pearl—get a BAFTA for such a passionate, whole-hearted, star-bright re-booting of an icon.

No one can be in any doubt that the BBC will re-commission *Sherlock*, and that—so long as Steven Moffat and Mark Gatiss are in charge of the scripts, as they were for the first and last episode—it will continue to totally delight anyone who watches it.

But next time, in sixes, or twelves, or twenty-fours, please. Not threes. Threes are over far, far too quickly. Now Sunday is just . . . normal again.

I still haven't got round to doing what I propose in this next piece. I really must. I am still haunted by the boy in the playground. I wonder what he did next? I hope he continued to escalate his look commensurately with each passing year, and now walks around Solihull dressed like fucking Batman.

Hello. You Look Wonderful.

WHEN I WAS FOURTEEN, and bored, I used to walk the five miles into town, sit on the patch of grass outside St. Peter's church, and look at people. Obviously, at that age, it was mainly boys I was looking at. And obviously, given that I was sitting in the drizzle, staring at them, and wearing—it's a long story—a red, tartan bathrobe instead of a coat, they would cross the street, and go into Argos, to avoid me. But still, I would look. I would look and look and look. They literally could not stop me.

Anyone who'd seen Desmond Morris's *The Human Zoo* would suggest I was studying humans like animals, but I know that I was not. It was far more formless, and thoughtless, than that. I was definitely just staring—like a mono-browed lollygagger, creating a patch of unease by the village well.

I think that, at the time, I thought that if I looked at people—particularly boys—long enough, I would somehow work "it" out. That I had no idea what "it" was, of course, is one of the hallmarks of adolescence. If I'd been forced to put money on what "it" might be, it sadly would not have been, "Whether my life would be immeasurably improved if I stopped wearing a bathrobe, tried to be normal, and bought a coat, instead." I was, as you can see, quite hopeless.

We *all* look at people, of course. We cannot help it. Mankind has hot air balloons, and crampons, and mine shafts, and submersibles. Mankind has been on the Moon. Anywhere we look, people get in the way—hanging off ladders, falling from windows, putting their face a little too close to yours to ask you if you're alright. Everywhere we look, we are looking at people. They are like Nature's little screensavers.

But one of the things I most love about this country is that we do not, *will* not, stare at each other. The British will not spend all day gawping at each other in the drizzle, however odd we may look. The entire cast of *Priscilla, Queen of the Desert* could roll into Starbucks, with candy-colored cockatiels flying out of their hair, and—after a brief glance upwards—everyone would studiously go back to reading their papers, as if the door had merely been blown open by the wind. In a cramped, crowded nation, we know the essence of politeness is ignoring pretty much everyone around us.

And yet—and yet, this saddens me, also. For while it means we do not cause anguish in the hearts of the sweaty, the harried or the deformed, it means that, with the Olympic Committee of our gaze, we also fail to hand out gold medals to those who actually *should* be looked at.

Yes. I'm talking about people who look hot. People who look really, really hot. Not necessarily classically staggering, like a Moss, or a Best. But those who've put together a smoking outfit, done something foxy with their hair, artfully clashed their shoes with their bangles, or just gone whole hog, and back-combed their fringe until it looks like a hat. Straight boys in pink nu-rave hoodies. OAPs in scarlet ballet pumps. Waitresses with 1940s up-dos. Ghanaian girls in pig-tails and jodhpurs, trotting round Topshop like it's a gymkhana. These are the people who *want* to be looked at. They are abiding by Quentin Crisp's maxim—to live their lives as if they were in a movie. But their tragedy is that, by living in Britain, it's a movie that will be furtively glanced at, for a mere second, and then pointedly ignored.

For those who believe, as I do, that the next stage in human evolution will be neither a giant leap in intelligence, nor partial DNA-merge with robots, but all of us looking consistently better-dressed, it is a crime against Nature itself.

Instance: I was in Solihull last week, in a park. It was starting to look—as all parks must, in the middle of a wet September—a bit like a plate of boiled cabbage, with some swings stuck in it. Sitting on the edge of the skate-park was a boy of about fifteen, who had clearly recently seen *The Dark Knight* in the last few months, and was now desirous to be the Joker. On this day, he was doing so by dressing all in black—skater trousers, knee-length pea coat, beanie hat. When he took the coat off, it revealed a cropped black waistcoat over a white shirt—a shirt that bordered, thrillingly, on blouse.

While the other kids skated—in nondescript trousers, and greige tops—he leaned against the monkey-bars, smoking a fag, and photographed them with an impressively old-fashioned Nikon. Now, I'm not entirely deluded. I know that the photos were probably awful, the cigarettes had a one-in-three chance of giving him cancer, and he was in all probability, a bit of a dick. But I loved him. I loved him for treating his outfit like an atmosphere-controlled space suit, which shielded him from the world he was actually in. I loved that his clothes were a signal to vaguely like-minded people—the opening line of a conversation, which you could hear from the other side of the park.

But as I looked at him, I felt a melancholy steal upon me. I feared that, without the support of a watching world—a couple of thumbs-up here, a "nice one" there; maybe some winks from a bus-driver—he would eventually find that the leaden lure of sweatpants and a Nike hoodie too great to resist, and just give up on being beautiful. There is a paradox in being cool, as I have learned over the years from interviewing pop stars, actors and sundry cultural beacons. They have all noted that one of the little sorrows of being cool is that similarly cool people are too cool to ever come over and tell you you're cool—because that's just not cool. And so, gradually, the entire point of being cool is being eroded.

What the cool people need, then, is some gawping, moon-faced, resolutely non-cool person to come and tell them that they're cool instead.

To this end, I am about to order 1,000 old-fashioned calling-cards—string-colored, Verdana typeface, single-sided. They will read, "I just want you to know, I really appreciate your look." And I'm going to walk around London, handing them out as, and where, truly necessary.

Part **Two**

Homosexuals, Transsexuals, Ladies, and the Internet

In which we demand employment quotas for women while using a lengthy analogy about a pelican, nerd out with the gayest sci-fi series ever—Doctor Who—and point out that the internet was invented by humans, and not dystopian robots, or Satan. But first: back to me and Pete in bed again.

You might think there's too many of these conversations. On that basis, you would immediately be able to strike up a cordial and mutually agreeable conversation with Pete.

First Time Ever I Saw Your Face

IT'S 11:38 PM. The children have finally gone to sleep. The foxes have not yet begun their nightly panoply of dumpster diving, bag-shredding and mad fox love. It's the Golden Hour. It is peaceful. It is time for sleep.

"Pete?"

"No."

"Pete?"

"No."

"Pete?"

"I am asleep. No."

"Pete—what's the first thing you think of when you think of me?"

"What?"

"When someone says my name, or you think of me—what's the picture that comes into your head?"

"Please remember that I just said 'I'm asleep.' Please."

"For instance," I say, turning over into my "Interesting Chat" position. I have intrigued me with this question. This is a good question. "For instance, when I think of *you*, straight away—quick as a flash—I see you standing at the kitchen table, wearing a cardigan, and looking down at a pile of new records that you've just bought. You've put one on, and you're kind of bopping to it a bit, and you're eating a slice of bread and butter, while you wait for the tea to cook. You might be humming a bit. That's my go-to image for you. That's your essence. That's what I think of, when I think of you. In the kitchen, with your records, all happy."

There is a big pause. Pete appears to need a prompt.

"That's what I think of, when I think of you," I repeat. "So what about me? What do you see in your head when someone says my name? 'Cate.' What's in your head? 'Cate.' 'Cate.' What do you see? 'Cate.' 'Cate.' 'Cate.' 'Cate.' What you getting? 'Cate.'"

There's another pause.

"'Cate'," I say, helpfully. Third pause.

"Your face?" Pete replies, eventually.

"My face?"

I am hugely disappointed.

"My face?" I repeat. "I see a whole scene with you in it—I can even see what record you're holding: it's the best of Atlantic Psychedelic Funk. It's a gatefold—and you've just got . . . *my face?*"

I am determined to make Pete see that he actually sees more than that. There's no *way* all he sees is my face. We've been together seventeen years. I have blazed a cornucopia of images into his head. I've given him a visual love pantechnicon. The material is endless. Instance: he's seen me dressed as a "sexy Santa," falling off a castored pouffe. He's got loads in there.

"Okay," I say, patiently. "Look *down* from my face. What am I wearing?" I think this is all key questioning. I want to know what, in Pete's mind, is my "classic era"—my imperial phase. Does he remember me most vividly from the early years of our relationship, when I was a young, slightly troubled teenager with a winning line in bong construction—but also the dewy appeal of innocence, and youth? Or does his subconscious prefer me now—a far more rational mother-of-two whose knees are going, and who says 'Oooof!' every time she sits down; but who will also never again wake him up crying because the central heating has come on in the night, and she thinks her legs have melted, and got stuck to the radiator?

There is another pause.

"You're wearing your blue and white striped pajamas," he says finally, confidently.

This time, I pause.

"Blue and white striped pajamas?" I am wounded. "I've never had blue and white striped pajamas."

"You did!" Pete sounds a little panicked. "Once! Blue and white striped pajamas."

"Pete," I say, quite coldly, "I am a woman. I know every item of clothing I have ever owned. And I can tell you now—I have never had a pair of blue and white striped pajamas. Are you sure you're not getting me confused with the boy from *The Snowman?*"

"It's far too late at night for me to deal with you accusing me of imaginary pedophilia with a cartoon," Pete says, despairingly. "Again. And anyway—you *did* have blue and white striped pajamas."

"I once had blue and white *Paisley* pajamas," I say, grudgingly.

"There you go!" he says, triumphantly. "That's near enough!"

"No!" I say, outraged. "That's not a *memory*. That's not a *real memory*. You've made those pajamas up. You've just got this . . . fantasy version of me in your head, instead."

"Fantasy version of you! I've hardly gone into my brain, cut out a picture of your face and stuck it onto a picture of . . . Carol Chell from *Playschool*," Pete says, agitatedly.

"Carol Chell from *Playschool?*" I ask.

"She's a very pretty and lovely lady," Pete says, in a firm and non-negotiable manner.

"Carol Chell. Well," I say, staring up at the ceiling. "Well. Carol Chell. We've learned a lot tonight, haven't we? We really have learned a lot."

I let a vexed air fill the room. Let's see if you remember *this*, I think.

The Gay Moon Landings

LAST WEEK I WAS compiling a quick-cut YouTube montage of humanity's greatest moments—what can I say? The kids are seven and nine now; weekend activities have moved on from cupcakes and coloring—and came across an awkward fact: there is no Gay Moon Landing.

There are single, iconic images for every other blockbuster moment in humanity's progress: the Civil Rights Movement has Martin Luther King, giving his speech. The suffragette movement has Emily Wilding Davison, trampled by the King's Horse. The triumphs of medical science: the mouse with the ear on its back. And the Space Race has, of course, the Moon Landing—Neil Armstrong making the most expensive footprint in history.

But there is no single, iconic news image for gay rights. There's no five-second clip you can put in that marks a moment where things started getting better for the LGBT guys. The Stonewall Riots in '69 are an obvious turning point, of course—but footage of it needs captions to explain what's going on. Otherwise, it just looks like a lot of late-sixties men of above-average grooming experiencing a very unwelcome fire evacuation from a disco, while a load of policemen hit them. Anyone who went clubbing in the rougher parts of the Midlands, or Essex, at the time will have seen scenes almost identical. It's not particularly gay.

Perturbed by this lack of relevant news footage, I went on Twitter and asked what people would regard as a putative "Gay Moon Landing." There were dozens and dozens of replies: David Bowie and Mick Ronson's homoerotic sparring on *Top of the Pops*, John Hurt as Quentin Crisp in *The Naked Civil Servant*—dumb with lipstick, blind with mascara and brave as a lion.

Seminal teenage fumbling/nascent emancipation in *My Beautiful Laundrette* and *Oranges Are Not the Only Fruit*. Cindy Crawford—straight—acting all geisha, and slathering a beaming k.d. lang in shaving foam on the cover of *Rolling Stone*.

All of these instances crashed into people's front rooms and started things: conversations; realizations about sexuality; imagining, for the first time, a possible future. In that way—millions of lights, sparking up in millions of minds—they *were* news events; albeit ones that never actually made it onto the news.

Because what was notable was that nearly every single instance of a Gay Moon Landing suggested was from pop, TV, magazines or film. The history of gay rights, and gay progress, has included keynote speeches, legislation, protest and rioting—but the majority of its big, watershed moments have taken place in the art world. It was good to be gay on *Top of the Pops* years before it was good to be gay in Parliament, or gay in church, or gay on the rugby pitch. And it's not just gay progress that happens in this way: *24* had a black president before America did. Jane Eyre was a feminist before Germaine Greer was born. *A Trip to the Moon* put humans on the Moon in 1902.

This is why recent debates about the importance of the arts contain, at core, an unhappy error of judgment. In both the arts cuts—29 percent of the Arts Council's funding has now gone—and the presumption that the new, "slimmed down" National Curriculum will "squeeze out" art, drama and music, there lies a subconscious belief that the arts are some kind of . . . social luxury: the national equivalent of buying some overpriced throw pillows and big candle from John Lewis. Policing and defense, of course, remain very much "essentials"—the fridge and duvets in our country's putative semi-detached house.

But art—painting, poetry, film, TV, music, books, magazines—is a world that runs constant and parallel to ours, where we imagine different futures—millions of them—and try them out for size. Fantasy characters can kiss, and we, as a nation, can all work out how we feel about it, without having to involve real shy teenage lesbians in awful sweaters, to the benefit of everyone's notion of civility.

Two of the Gay Moon Landings Twitter suggested were *Queer as Folk*, from 1999, and Captain Jack kissing the Doctor in *Doctor Who* in 2008—both, coincidentally, written by Russell T. Davies. *Queer as Folk* was cited as a Gay Moon Landing because, when it aired, it was the first-ever gay drama, and caused absolute, gleeful outrage. Conversely, the *Doctor Who* gay kiss was a Gay Moon Landing because it caused absolutely no outrage at all. The two were separated by just nine years. I would definitely call that another big step for mankind.

But then, perhaps I'm barking up the wrong tree here. Maybe I don't need to look for a Gay Moon Landing, after all. As someone on Twitter pointed out, "The Moon Landing itself is pretty gay. A close-knit group of guys land in a silver rocket, make a really dramatic speech, and then spend half an hour jumping up and down? Please."

*Let's put the "Gay Moon Landings" piece next to my piece on transsexuals—
making a little LGBT ghetto within the book. These pages will have markedly
better delis and bars than the delis and bars in the rest of the book, and feature a mini-cab company run by a drag queen whose Grease-tribute act goes
under the name "Sandra Wee." You can find me on these pages most Friday
nights—wearing only one shoe and singing "Womanizer" by Britney Spears
with a male nurse wearing a sombrero, and waving poppers.*

We Only Had Two Transsexuals
in Wolverhampton

IN WOLVERHAMPTON IN 1991, we had two male-to-female transsexuals,
who would unfailingly be in the chip shop at the end of Victoria Street at
2 AM, sobering up on curry sauce and chips after a night out clubbing.

As I went past them on the 512 bus, I would feel a kinship with them—a
kinship that I would try to project through the glass.

"I feel as if I were born in the wrong body, too!" I would think, loudly,
at them. "You were trapped, unhappily, in the bodies of men. I too am
unhappily trapped—in the body of a fat virgin with a bad haircut. I wish *I*
could have an operation to sort things out, like you guys—I mean ladies."

I was reminded of what a moron I was this September, when a ten-year-
old boy returned to school after the summer holidays as a girl. As the media
coverage made clear, some parents at the school claimed to be "outraged."

"We should have been consulted," one said—presumably imagining a
scenario where parents regularly throw open the raising of their children
to a school-wide committee of other parents; possibly via a Facebook page
called "Penis or Vagina: YOU Choose Which One You Think Suits My
Weeping Child Best."

Then, last week, the Department of Education announced that it was considering that schoolchildren be taught about transgender equality—which was greeted, again, with a predictable series of complaints.

Margaret Morrissey, founder of campaigning group Parents Outloud, said: "We are overloading our children with issues they shouldn't have to consider."

This is an interesting stance to take on an issue—mainly because of its unappealing and extreme impoliteness. We have to remember that the descriptor "our children" includes both transgender kids (0.1 percent of the population), and kids who live in a world with transgender kids (the other 99.09 percent)—thus comprising 100 percent of all the world's children.

With those kinds of stats, it seems to be a good idea to enable children in learning about it nice and early on—before they start getting the kind of weird ideas adults have. We constantly underestimate children in these situations. I recall, when I was a teenager, the suggestion of "lessons" in homosexuality being decried for similar reasons of "complexity." A generation later, and I watch kids in the playground, arguing over who should play the bisexual Captain Jack Harkness from *Doctor Who*—who fancied both Rose *and* the Doctor. Not only do they seem to have got their heads around it quite easily—but they're incorporating it into games involving time-travel, wormholes and paradox, too.

And, anyway, as a general rule of thumb, I don't think we need worry much about overloading kids with interesting philosophical subjects that help them develop both understanding, and tolerance of, other human beings. That's like worrying that the Beatles might have made *Sgt. Pepper* "too good." That's what's supposed to happen. Carry on! Everything's fine!

One of humanity's less loveable tropes is an ability to get hurt, self-righteous and huffy about someone else's problem. It's amazing that "normal" people would turn on some transgender kid and go, "But what about meeeeee? What about myyyyyyy kids?" It's a bit like those dads in the maternity wards who complain about being exhausted.

And as a strident feminist, I'm always saddened by other feminists who rail against male-to-female transgenders—claiming you can only be born a woman, and not "become" one.

Holy moly, ladies—what exactly do you think is going wrong here? Having your male genitals remodeled as female, then committing to a lifetime of hormone therapy, sounds like a bit more of a commitment to being a woman than just accidentally being born one. And, besides, it's an incredibly inhospitable stance to take. Personally, anyone who wants to join the Lady Party is welcome as far as I'm concerned. The more the merrier! Anyone who's been rejected by The Man is a friend of mine!

Anyway. Since I was an ill-shorn sixteen-year-old on the bus, I've found out that the word isn't "normal"—it's "cis." In Latin, the opposite of "trans" is "cis"—and so most of humanity is "cisgender." This opens language up to a subsequent possibility: finally finding the "otherness" in transgender fascinating, and useful. We'll hurl satellites out into space, in order to find new and enthralling wonders—but we could simply turn to someone next to us, and ask a question about their life, instead. We endlessly debate what it is to be a man, or what it is to be a woman—when there are people who walk the Earth who've been both. If transgender people didn't exist, we'd probably be trying to spend billions of pounds trying to invent them. Instead, we won't even tell kids they exist.

Is it time for my Lady Gaga interview? Let's do my Lady Gaga interview—given that this is the gay ghetto of the book, and Gaga is the most gay-friendly pop-star ever.

Interviewing Gaga was one of the more extraordinary moments of my life—not just the night out with her itself, which is all in the feature, but the reaction to it afterwards, as well. I posted it on Twitter on the day of publication with the message, "I'm not being funny, but you really won't ever read a better interview with Lady Gaga than mine." This is mainly because I was drunk when I tweeted it—but also because it's got the lupus exclusive, and a sex club, and her having a wee, and an empowering talk about feminism, and us getting hammered, and me exclusively finding out she didn't have a penis, and me ruining a couture cloak. Everything you want, really.

In the three days following my tweet and the link to the piece, it got re-tweeted over 20,000 times. It went around the world. I lost count of the people who read it and told me they liked it—mainly because I have both very poor both long- and short-term memory. My favorite person who told me they liked it was some orange, handsome dude I met at the Glamour Awards in 2010. We were in the smoking area having a puff and, when I told him my name, he went, "Oh, you! You went to the sex club with Gaga!" and we had a lovely chat. Throughout our conversation, I was aware of an odd atmosphere around us. A semi-circle of women had gathered, and were watching us with expressions of what can only be described as "hunger."

When we finally finished our fags and bid each other adieu, the moment Mr. Orangeio walked away, a woman, who looked on the verge of fainting, went "What's he LIKE? I CAN'T BELIEVE YOU WERE TALKING TO HIM!"

Turned out he was some bloke from Sex and the City who all the birds fancy. I didn't have a clue. I hate that show like bum-plague. I thought he was the PR for Vaseline Intensive Care, which was sponsoring the awards. No wonder he looked confused when I asked him if he took his work home with him, and used it to keep his elbows moist.

Mind you, that was the same party where I talked to an old dear in a tiara for ten minutes, thinking she was the editor of Glamour'*s mum—and it turned out to be Home Secretary Theresa May. I'm not so good with the faces.*

Come Party With Gaga

THERE'S NOTHING QUITE LIKE watching a plane take off without you to really focus your mind on how much you want to be on it. As flight BA987 knifes off the runway, and begins its journey to Berlin, I'm watching it through a window in the Departures Lounge—still holding the ticket for seat 12A in my hand.

Due to a frankly unlikely series of events, I got to Heathrow three minutes after the flight was closed. Although no missed flight ever comes as a joy, this one is a particular mellow-harsher because, in five hours, I'm supposed to be interviewing arguably the most famous woman in the world—Lady Gaga—in an exclusive that has taken months of phonecalls, jockeying and wrangling to set up.

It's not so much that I am now almost certainly going to be fired. Since I found out how much the model Sophie Anderton earned as a high-class call-girl, my commitment to continuing as a writer at *The Times* has been touch and go anyway, to be honest.

It's more that I am genuinely devastated to have blown it so spectacularly. Since I saw Gaga play *Poker Face* at Glastonbury Festival last year, I have been a properly, hawkishly devoted admirer.

Halfway through a forty-five-minute-set that had five costume changes, Gaga came on stage in a dress made entirely of see-through plastic bubbles, accompanied by her matching, see-through plastic bubble piano. You have to respect a woman who can match her outfit to her instrument. Although the single "Poker Face" is a punching, spasmodic, Euro house stormer, Gaga took to her piano and started to play it as cat-house blues—all inverted chords and rolling fifths, with falling, heartbroken semitones on the left hand; wailing out like Bessie Smith sitting on the doorstep at 4 AM.

It was already incredible *before* she did the second half of the song standing on her piano stool, on one leg—like a tiny, transvestite ballerina.

Twenty minutes later, she ended her set literally bending over backwards to please—fireworks shooting from the nipples of her pointy bra, screaming, "I fancy you, Glastonbury—do you fancy me?" The audience went wholly, totally, dementedly nuts for her.

It caused me to have this—unprecedented—thought: "She's making Madonna look a bit slack and unimaginative here. After all, when Madonna was twenty-three, she was still working a Dunkin' Donuts in New York. She weren't playing no rolling fifths."

Since then, I have followed her career like boys follow sports teams. As a cultural icon, she does an incredible service for women: after all, it will be hard to oppress a generation who've been brought up on pop-stars with fire coming out of their tits.

She's clearly smart and clearly hilarious—she pitched up at the Royal Variety Performance on a sixteen-foot-high piano, modelled on Dali's spider-legged elephants—but has never ruined the fun by going, "Actually, I'm smart and hilarious" like, say, Bono would.

And, most importantly of all, she clearly couldn't give a f*** what anyone says about her. When she appeared on *The X Factor,* it was the week after Simon Cowell had said that he was "Looking for the new Lady Gaga." She performed *Bad Romance* in an eighteen-foot-long bathtub with six dancers—then played a piano solo on a keyboard hidden in a pretend sink, while sitting on a pretend toilet. Clearly, Simon Cowell would never sign up anything like that in million, billion years. It was very much in his face.

So yes. I am a Gaga supporter. I'm Team Gaga. She's my girl. My pop Arsenal; my dance Red Sox; my fashion England.

AT HEATHROW, AS I go through the rigmarole of booking the next available flight—which will get me to Berlin two hours after my appointed slot—I know what awaits me at the other end. Angry Americans. Very angry Americans from her management team.

Because in the year since Glastonbury, Gaga has taken on a semi-mythic air, like Prince, or Madonna. Since she has sold fifteen million albums and forty million singles, and has become a tabloid staple, she now rarely does interviews. The last one she did in the UK—with *Q Magazine*—ended with her leaving halfway through, in tears. Pap-pictures of her looking spindly—covered in scratches and bruises—have carried with them the inference of those most female of traits under stress: eating disorders, self-harm. There have been collapses: last minute cancellation of concerts in Indiana, West Lafeyette and Connecticut after irregular heartbeats and exhaustion; near-collapse onstage in Auckland.

When you've just been named one of *Time* magazine's "100 Most Influential People in the World," this is, traditionally, where you are expected to start going a bit . . . Jackson.

It's incredible I was ever granted access at all—and now I've, unbelievably, stood her up.

I will be genuinely, tearfully grateful if I get even a ten-minute Q&A from a piqued megastar pulling a gigantic huff, and answering all my questions with monosyllabic, "yes/no" binary tetchiness.

This is the worst day of my life that hasn't involved an episiotomy.

"Hi!"

Gaga's dressing room, backstage at the 02 World Arena in Berlin. With the walls and ceiling draped in black, it resembles a pop-gothic seraglio. But while scented candles burn churchishly, a gorgeous vintage record player on the floor—surrounded by piles of vinyl—and works of art hung on the wall give it a cheerful air. There is a table, laid with beautiful china. There are flowers, growing in the dark. And at the head of the tea table, amongst the flowers: Gaga.

Two things strike you about her immediately. Firstly, that she *really* isn't dressed casually. In a breast-length, silver-gray wig, she has a black lace veil wound around her face, and sits, framed, in an immense, custom-made, one-off Alexander McQueen cloak. The effect is having been ushered into the presence of a very powerful fairytale queen: possibly one who has recently killed Aslan, on the Stone Table.

The second thing you notice is that she is being lovely. Absolutely lovely. Both literally and figuratively, what's under the veil and the cloak is a diminutive, well brought up, New York Catholic girl from a wealthy middle-class family, with twinkly brown eyes, and a minxy sense of humor.

"So glad you finally made it!" she says, giving a huge, warm hug. "What a terrible day you're having! Thank you so much for coming!"

Holding her for a moment, she feels—through the taffeta atmosphere of billowing McQueen—borderline Kylie Minogue-tiny, but warm, and robust. Like a slender, teenage cheerleader. This is some surprise, given the aforementioned presumption that she's cracking up.

So when Gaga says, with warm good manners, "This tea is for you," gesturing to a bone china cup hand-painted with violets, I can't help myself from replying, uncouthly: "I know you're tiny and must get knackered—but why do you keep collapsing?"

"My schedule is such that I don't get very much time to eat," Gaga says, holding her teacup daintily. I don't think the teacup is her infamous "pet tea cup" that she took everywhere with her earlier in the year—including nightclubs. Perhaps it's too famous to be merely drunk from now. Maybe it has its own dressing room.

"But I certainly don't have an eating problem," she continues. "A little MDMA once in a while never killed anybody, but I really don't do drugs. I don't touch cocaine anymore. I don't smoke. Well, maybe a single cigarette—with whisky—while I'm working, because it just frees my mind a little bit. But I care about my voice. The thrill of my voice being healthy on stage is really special. I take care of myself."

Later on in the interview, Gaga takes off the McQueen cloak—perhaps pointedly, for the nosey journalist—and reveals that, underneath, she's only wearing fishnets, knickers and a bra. As someone who is practically seeing her naked, from two feet away, her body seems non-scarred, healthy: sturdy.

She is wiry, but not remotely bony. It's a dancer's body—not a victim's.

I hand Gaga a page torn from that day's paper, which I read on the plane. It's a story about her performance at the Met Ball in New York—one of the big events of the global celebrity calendar. In the report, it is claimed that Gaga "angered" organizers by "refusing" to walk the red carpet, and then suffered an attack of stage fright so severe she locked herself in her dressing room, and had to be "persuaded out" by "her close friend Oprah Winfrey." It's merely the latest of the "Gaga cracking up" stories in the press.

"Is this true?" I ask her.

She reads through the story—frowning slightly at first, eyes wide open by the end.

"I wasn't *nervous!*" she says, witheringly. "To be honest with you? I don't give a fuck about red carpets, and I never do them. I don't like them. First of all—how could any of these outfits possibly look good with an ugly red carpet under them?"

For a moment, I recall some of Gaga's more incredible rig-outs: the silver lobster fascinator. The red PVC Elizabethan farthingale. The tunic made of Kermit heads. The red lace outfit that covered her entire face, peaking in a two-foot-high crown. She has a point.

"It's just visually horrid," Gaga continues, in a merrily outraged way. Her manner is of your mate in the pub, slagging off the neon smock she's been forced to wear working at Boots. "Hollywood is not what it used to be. I don't want to be perceived as . . . one of the other bitches in a gown. I wasn't *nervous*," says the woman who appeared in her "Telephone" video dressed in nothing more than "POLICE: INCIDENT" tape, strategically placed across her nipples and crotch. "Don't be SILLY!"

But still these rumors persist—of collapses, and neuroses. "You are, after all, a twenty-three-year-old woman coping with enormous fame, and media pressure, on your own. You are currently the one, crucial, irreplaceable element of a 161-date world tour. How do you keep depressive, or panicked, thoughts at bay?"

"Prescription medicine," she says, cheerfully. "I can't control my thoughts at all. I'm tortured. But I like that," she laughs, cheerfully. "Lorca says it's good to be tortured. The thoughts are unstoppable—but so is the music. It comes to me constantly. That's why I got this tattoo," she says, proffering a white arm through the black cloak-folds.

It is a quote from the poet and art critic Rainer Maria Rilke: "In the deepest hour of the night, confess to yourself that you would die if you were forbidden to write. And look deep into your heart where it spreads its roots, the answer, and ask yourself: 'Must I write?'"

"I think tattoos have power. I did it as a way to kind of . . . inject myself with a steadfastness about music. People say I should take a break, but I'm like, 'Why should I take a break? What do you want me to do—go on vacation?'"

On stage, later that night—dripping in sweat, just after playing a version of "Bad Romance" where the chorus sounds even more tearfully euphoric and amazing than usual—Gaga shouts to the crowd, "I'd rather not die on a vacation, under a palm tree. I'd rather die on stage, with all my props, in front of my fans."

Given that one of her props is a six-foot-high hybrid of a cello, keyboard and drum machine, with a golden skull nailed to the side of it—something that makes the "keytar" look like a mere castanet—you can see her point.

But it has to be said, for a twenty-three-year-old, death is a recurrent theme in her performances. The thematic arc for the Fame Monster tour was "The Apocalypse." In the current "Monster Ball" tour, Gaga is eventually eaten by a gigantic angler fish—a creature she was terrified of as a child—only to be reborn as an angel. Her MTV Awards performance of "Paparazzi," back in September, had her being crushed by a falling chandelier—amazing—before bleeding to death while singing.

"What's the nearest you've ever come to death?" I ask her. "Do you have any recurring illnesses?"

She goes oddly still for a moment, and then says, "I have heart palpitations, and . . . things."

"Recently?"

"Yes, but it's okay. It's just from fatigue and . . . other things," she shrugs, before saying, very carefully, "I'm very connected to my aunt,

Joanne, who died of lupus. It's a very personal thing. I don't want . . . my fans to be worried about me."

Her eyes are very wide.

"Lupus. That's genetic, isn't it?" I ask.

"Yes."

"And have you been tested?"

Again, the eyes are very wide and steady. "Yes." Pause. "But I don't want anyone to be worried."

"When was the last time you called the emergency services?" I ask.

"The other day," Gaga says, still talking very carefully. "In Tokyo. I was having trouble breathing. I had a little oxygen, then I went on stage. I was okay. But like I say—I don't want anyone to worry."

It's a very odd moment. Gaga is staring at me calmly, but intently. Lupus is a connective tissue disease, where the immune system attacks the body. It can be fatal—although, as medicine advances, fatalities are becoming rarer. What it more commonly does is cause heart palpitations, shortness of breath, joint pain, and anemia, before spasmodically but recurrently driving a truck through your energy levels, so that you are often too fatigued to accomplish even the simplest of tasks.

Suddenly, all the "Gaga cracking up" stories revolve round 180 degrees, and turn into something completely different. After all, the woman before me seems about as far removed from someone on the verge of a fame-induced nervous breakdown as is possible to imagine. She's being warm, candid, smart, amusing and supremely confident in her talent. She's basically like some hot, giggly pop-nerd.

But if she were regularly running into physical difficulties because she has lupus—being delayed on stage, cancelling gigs, having to call the emergency services—you can see how a world press, desperate for stories about her, ignorant of any other possibility, would add these things up into a wholly different picture.

Gaga is certainly very affected by her aunt's death: the date of her death, in 1976, is interwoven into her Rilke tattoo on her arm. When I ask her if she ever "dresses down," she says the only thing remotely "dress down-y" she has is a pair of pink, cotton shorts—embroidered with flowers—that once belonged to her aunt.

"They're nearly forty years old," she says. "But I wear them when I want her to . . . protect me."

The story that I thought I would find when I met Gaga—dark, otherworldly, borderline autistic diva-genius failing under the pressure of fame—just dissolves, like newsprint in the rain.

All that's left is a mardy pop sex threat—the woman who put out three, Abba-level classic singles in one year, at the age of twenty-three, while wearing a lobster on her head. As Ali G. says at times like this, "Booyakasha."

"What's the best thing you've spent your money on so far?" I ask, in a far more cheerful mood.

"I bought my parents a car," Gaga replies. She has often spoken of how close she is to her parents—particularly her father, whom she appears to borderline worship. Presumably, she sees herself in him—a self-made man, he started as a rock 'n' roll bar musician, before making his fortune as an internet entrepreneur. By the time Gaga was thirteen, the family was rich enough to send her to the same school as heiress Paris Hilton.

Gaga is not faking her current outsiderness—even then, when she was still just Stefani Germanotta, she was the goth girl with dyed black hair, obsessed with Judy Garland, Led Zeppelin and David Bowie, and wearing her skirts really high.

"It's a Rolls Royce," she continues, sipping on her tea, daintily. She has lifted the veil now: she looks as casual as it is possible to in a wig and couture. "It's black. My dad's very Italian, so I wanted to get him a real Godfather car. I had it delivered on their anniversary."

When Gaga rang her father and told him to "Go outside!", he refused. "He thought I'd got him a dancing gorillagram," she giggled.

The car had a huge bow on it, and the message "A car to last like a love like yours." At first, Gaga's parents thought they had it just for the day, to drive round in. When she told them it was theirs to keep, her father shouted "You're crazy!" and burst into tears.

"You see, I don't really spend money, and I don't really like fame," Gaga says. "I spend my money on my shows—but I don't like buying *things*. I don't buy diamonds, because I don't know where they came from. I'll spend it on fashion." She hugs the McQueen cloak close.

"I miss Lee every time I get dressed," she says, sadly. "But you know what I spend most of my money on? Disappearing. I hate the paparazzi. Because the truth is—no matter what people tell you—you can control it. If you put as much money into your security as you put into your cars or your diamonds or your jewellery, you can just . . . disappear. People who say they can't get away are lying. They must just like the . . . big flashes."

The conversation turns to the music industry. Gaga has an endearingly schoolmarmish belief that most acts are "lazy."

"I hate big acts that just throw an album out against the wall, like 'BUY IT! FUCK YOU!' It's mean to fans. You should go out and tour it to your fans in India, Japan, the UK. I don't believe in how the music industry is today. I believe in how it was in 1982."

She explains she doesn't mind people downloading her music for free, "because you know how much you can earn off touring, right? Big artists can make anywhere from $40m for one cycle of two years touring. Giant artists make upwards of $100m. Make music—then tour. It's just the way it is today."

While on this huge, technically complex, sell-out world tour, Gaga has written and recorded the majority of her next album: "I don't understand bands who say they'll tour for one year—then record the next!" she exclaims at one point, going Thatcher again. "I make music every DAY!"

Although she "can't talk about it yet," she is clearly excited about the next album. She keeps trying to tell me things about it, then claps her hands over her mouth, going, "I can't!"

"But everyone's going to fucking know about it when it comes out," she says, excitedly. "You know when people say 'If you could say one sentence about who you are, what you life is?' It's that. *For the whole album.* Because I recently had this . . . miracle-like experience, where I feel much more connected to God."

You were raised a Catholic—so when you say "God," do you mean the Catholic God, or a more spiritual sense of "God?"

"More spiritual," Gaga says, looking like she's biting her tongue. "I don't want to say much, because I want it to stay hidden until it comes out—but I will say that religion is very confusing for everyone, and particularly me, because there's really no religion that doesn't hate or condemn a certain kind of people, and I totally believe in all love and forgiveness, and excluding no one."

"Would you play for the Pope, if he asked you?"

"Yeah," Gaga says. There's a pause. Perhaps she considers her current stage show, and the section where her male dancers grab their gigantic, fake white penises, and bounce them off their palms to *Boys Boys Boys*.

"Well. I'd do an acoustic show for the Pope," she amends.

ASTONISHINGLY, GIVEN HOW LATE I was, Gaga has given me a full hour of interview time. I later find out that she turned down doing a video acceptance speech for the World Music Awards in order to fit me in. I feel I've done amazingly well, considering how badly the day started. Then Gaga puts her cup down, and turns to me.

"You should come out with us tonight," she says, warmly. "Actually, I've never had a journalist come out with me, so you'd be the first. It's going to be fun. It's like an old sex club, in Berlin. Come party with Gaga!"

IT IS MIDNIGHT. GAGA came off stage half an hour ago. Dressed, once again, in knickers, bra, fishnets and her black taffeta McQueen, she has been standing in freezing, driving rain outside the 02 World, signing autographs for fans.

Her fans are infamously, incredibly devoted—as she is to them. She calls them her "Little Monsters." They draw pictures of her, get tattoos like hers, weep when she touches them. Her den-mother championing of "all the freaks"—fat girls, gay boys, lesbian girls, Goths, nerds. Everyone who gets picked on at school—allied to her global pop juggernaut, makes her relationship with her fans intense. When you watch her with them, you see that culturally, what she's doing is . . . providing a space for them. Giving them somewhere to meet.

Then, her security guy gives the signal, and we are all bundled into people-carriers with blacked-out windows, and whizzed across Berlin.

Paps in cars try to follow us, but it seems what Gaga said earlier was true: if you spend enough money on security, they can't follow you. She simply has two burly men stand in front of their cars, impeding them, until we have vanished.

"It's, like, a sex party," Gaga explains. "You know—like in *Eyes Wide Shut?* All I can say is, I am not responsible for what happens next. And wear a condom."

As we take the alleyway to the sex club, security men appear and close off the alleyway with giant, blacked-out gates.

The club—The Laboratory—is an industrial, maze-like building. To get to the dance floor, you have to pass a series of tiny, cell-like booths, decked out with a selection of beds, bathtubs, hoists and chains.

"For fucking," a German member of our entourage explains—both helpfully, and somewhat unnecessarily.

Despite the undoubted and extreme novelty of such a venue, Adrian—Gaga's British press officer—and I give away our nationalities instantly when we comment, excitedly, "Oh my God! You can SMOKE in here!" It seems a far more thrilling prospect than . . . some bumming.

It's a small entourage—Gaga, me, Adrian, her make-up artist, her security guy, and maybe two others. We walk onto the small dance floor, in a club filled with drag queens, lesbians dressed as sailors, boys in tight t-shirts, girls in black leather. The music is pounding. There is a gigantic harness hanging over the bar.

"For fucking," the same German says again, helpfully.

Gaga is heading up our group. Even, like, Keane would slope off to a VIP booth at this point, and wait for people to bring them drinks.

Instead—cloak billowing, and very much looking like one of the Skeksis in *The Dark Crystal*—Gaga marches up to the bar, leans on it in a practiced bar-fly manner. With a bellowed, "What does everyone want to drink?" she gets the round in.

It reminds me of what was possibly the best moment of this year in Gaga world: the tabloids running a shot of Gaga—dressed only in fishnets, a bra and leather cap—sitting in a pub in Blackpool, with a pint of Stella and a plate of chips.

"I really love a dingy, pissy bar," Gaga says. "I'm really old-school that way."

We go into an alcove with a wipe-clean banquette—"For the fucking!" the German says, again—and set up camp. Gaga takes off her McQueen cloak, and chucks into a corner. She's now just in bra, fishnet and knickers, with sequins around her eyes.

"Do you know what that girl at the bar said to me?" she says, sipping her Scotch, and taking a single drag off a fag before handing it back. "She said, 'You're a feminist. People think it means "man-hating," but it doesn't.' Isn't that funny?"

Earlier in the day, conversation had turned to whether Gaga would describe herself as feminist or not. As the very best conversations about feminism often will, it had segued from robust declarations of emancipation and sisterhood ("I am a feminist because I believe in women's rights, and protecting who we are, down to the core.") to musing on who she fancied ("In the video to 'Telephone,' the girl I kiss, Heather, lives as a man. And as someone who does like women, something about a more masculine woman makes me feel more . . . feminine. When we kissed, I got that fuzzy butterfly feeling.")

We had concluded that it was odd most women "shy away" from declaring themselves feminists, because "It really doesn't mean 'man-hating.'"

"And now she's just said the same thing to me! AND she's hot!" Gaga beams. She points to the girl—who looks like an androgynous, cupid-mouthed, Jean-Paul Gaultier cabin boy. "Gorgeous," Gaga sighs.

This is Gaga off-duty. Although the booth becomes by way of a shrine to her—between now and 4 AM, fully two-thirds of the club come over to pay obeisance to her: drag queens and tom-girls and superfreaks, all acknowledging the current definitive pop cultural salon keeper—Gaga alternates being wholly gracious and welcoming to them, and getting absolutely off her cake. With the thrill of like recognizing like, I realize she's a total lightweight—giggly after two Scotches, dancing in the booth after three, and wholly on the prowl after four.

"Are you straight?" she asks some hot, American boy we've been talking to at one point, in the manner of someone who needs to make plans for the rest of the evening based on the reply. When he says, regretfully, "No," her attention seems to, amusingly, wander.

But that's just for sex. Gaga's devotion to, and promotion of, every aspect of gay culture is legendary. Bisexual herself, while her musical education might once have been classical, her cultural education was homosexual, and comes to a head in the video to her forthcoming single, "Alejandro."

Sprawled across the banquette, in a mood of eager excitement, Gaga shows me stills from the video shoot on her BlackBerry. She's dressed up as Joan of Arc, with a ferocious Purdey haircut. To be honest I can't see much more than that, because she's a bit pissed, and her thumbs keep getting in the way.

The video is about the "purity of my friendships with my gay friends," Gaga explained, earlier. "And how I've been unable to find that with a straight man in my life. It's a celebration and an admiration of gay love—it confesses my envy of the courage and bravery gays require to be together. In the video I'm pining for the love of my gay friends—but they just don't want me."

We look at the photo on her BlackBerry again.

"I'm not sure about my hair," Gaga says, suddenly, staring at the Black-Berry.

3 AM. I AM pretty wasted. I am kneeling on the banquette, with Gaga lying by my knees. I have just come up with the theory that, if you have one of your heroes lying tipsily next to you, you should tell them all the pretentious pop culture theories you have come up with about them. So I slurringly tell her that the difference between her and, say, Madonna, is that you don't penetrate Gaga. Her songs and videos are—while sexual—about dysfunction and neuroses and alienation and self-discovery. They're not, in any sense, a come-on. Despite having worn very little clothing for most of her career, Gaga is not a cock-tease.

"Yeah! It's not what straight men masturbate over when they're at home watching pornography," she confirms. "It's not for them. It's for . . . us." And she gestures around the club.

Earlier in the day, she had said—somewhat unexpectedly—"I still feel very much like an outsider. And I have zero concept of how I'm assessed in the world." As one of the most-discussed women in the world, this is a surprise. Does she really not read her press? Perhaps this is how she's stayed so . . . normal. Ordering drinks, chatting to everyone. She's the least pretentious multi-million-selling artist I've ever met.

A minute later, Gaga springs up, and beckons for me to follow her. Weaving her way down a series of corridors, we eventually end in—the VIP toilet.

"You're wearing a jumpsuit," Gaga says, with feminine solidarity. "You can't get out of one of those in the normal toilets."

As I start to arduously unzip, Gaga sits on the toilet with a cheerful, "I'm just going to pee through my fishnets!" and offloads some of those whiskies.

For the first year of her career, massive internet rumors claimed that Gaga was, in fact a man—a rumor so strong that Oprah had to question her about it when Gaga appeared on her show.

Perhaps uniquely amongst all the journalists in the world, I can now factually confirm that Lady Gaga does not have a penis. That rumor can, conclusively, die.

4 AM. Time for bed. We pull up outside the Ritz Carlton, in a people carrier with blacked-out windows. Gaga opens the door, and totters out, looking—despite the McQueen cloak—like any tipsy twenty-three-year-old girl on a night out in Newcastle, on a Saturday night. Her gray wig looks dishevelled. Her face-sequins are wonky. Her eyes are pointing in slightly different directions—although, to be fair, I can only focus on her myself if I close one eye, and rest my head against the window. Tonight, she played to 40,000 fans. Tomorrow, it's Sting's Rainforest Ben-

efit, where she takes her place among the pantheon: Debbie Harry, Bruce Springsteen, Elton John.

She leans against the car for a moment, issues a small hiccup, and then turns, dramatically.

"I. Am. KNACKERED!" she roars. She then walks, slightly unsteadily, up the steps of the Ritz Carlton hotel. A total, total dude.

Gaga is, of course, the perfect bridging subject between "ranting about gays" and "ranting about feminism." And so we move on, to the vexed subject of wondering where all the clothes went on MTV.

MTV Hoes

"I WISH," MY FRIEND Jenny tweeted last week, "there was an MTV Normal. For people who love pop—but don't want to watch a load of girls dressed as hoes."

I knew exactly what she meant. Twenty-first–century pop music presents one of the biggest vexes for the modern feminist—and by "feminist" I mean "all women," really; unless you have recently and decisively campaigned to have your voting rights removed.

When I was a teenager, all my pop heroes were Britpop and grunge— unisex jeans and sneakers for all. I was raised with the expectation that, if I wanted to, I could sell twenty million albums with my upper arms covered at all times.

My daughters, on the other hand, are being raised in the Era of the Pop Ho. This is a time when the lower slopes of Britney Spears's leotard-clad pubis mons are more recognizable than—although oddly redolent of— David Cameron's face, and pop videos for female artists have become so predictable, I can run you through what will happen in 90 percent of them, right here:

1. "Just checkin' my legs are still there." Self-groping which begins with a lascivious sweep across the collarbone, develops into decisive breast-rubbing, and then ends with some pretty full-on caressing of your own buttocks, belly and thighs. The ubiquity of this dance

move is baffling: however much healthy, positive self-love a woman has, she's still not going to be this mesmerized and excited by having an arse by the age of twenty-three. She knows it's there. She doesn't have to keep checking. By and large, women generally can keep their hands off themselves for the three minutes it takes to make a pop video. I know up to nine women, and none of them have ever had to excuse themselves from the table, saying, "Sorry—just going to feel myself up in the coat closet. Back in a moment."

2. Having sex with an invisible ghost. Sooner or later, every modern popstress is going to have to vibrate in a squatting position, in order to pleasure the Ghost of Christmas Horny. That's what we ladies do in 2011. We hump spooks.

3. "Making your booty touch the ground." Women of pop—if you want to get to Number One, you will, at some point, have to make your "booty" (bottom) touch the ground. It is as regulation a move in twenty-first–century pop as having incredibly dry-looking hair was in the 1980s. Of course, making your booty touch the ground isn't that difficult—almost any woman can do it, given a full minute or so to get down and up again, and allowed to repeatedly say "Ouf!" and "Argk!" while clutching at the mantlepiece. In the scheme of things, it's no biggie. But what may sadden the viewer, after a couple of hours, is noting how "booty grounding" is solely the province of women. You never see the boys doing it—despite them having legs that are anatomically identical to women's, and rocking the consid-erable advantage of not being in six-inch heels. I have never seen Bob Dylan make his booty touch the floor. It is not something that was asked of Oasis.

4. "Having some manner of liquid/viscous substance land on your face, then licking it off lasciviously." In no other field of human ex-perience does someone busily engaged in their work—in this case, miming to their latest single—have something land on their face, and react with anything other than a cry of "WHAT? WHAT IS GOING ON? I am gonna start effin' and jeffin' if we cannot keep

107

the rain-machine/mud/custard off my face, Andrew. Just—stop hurling stuff at me! I'm trying to look thoughtful! I sold fifteen million singles last year!"

Do not get me wrong. It's not as if I *dislike* women acting all fruity in videos—I was raised on Madonna. Beyoncé and Gaga are my girls. Put the Divinyls' *I Touch Myself* on, and I will terrify you on the dance floor. Literally terrify you. You will want to leave.

It's just the . . . *ubiquity* of female pop stars dressing up as hoes that's disturbing. It's as weird and unnerving as if all male pop stars had decided, ten years ago, to dress up as farmers. All the time. In every single video. Imagine! Sitting down to watch your 5,000th video incorporating a hay-baler, and a man in a straw-covered gilet giving medicine to a coughing ewe. You'd think all men had gone insane. But that's what it's like with the women, and the ho-ing.

Anyway, I've finally found the best moral through route for watching MTV with my daughters, without making them feel that if they want to sell twenty million albums, they must dress like hoes. And it is pity. Every time we see Rihanna on her hands and knees with her coccyx hanging out of her knickers, my girls will shake their heads, sadly, and say, "It is a great song—but we feel sorry for Rihanna. If she was really one of the biggest pop stars in the world, she'd be allowed to wear a nice cardigan once in a while. Poor Rihanna. Poor, cardigan-less Rihanna."

Rihanna has too few clothes. Someone in a burqa, meanwhile, could be argued to have too many. Sometimes, it's hard to be a woman. Your wardrobe might as well have "socio-sexual-political minefield" written on it.

I lifted a paragraph of this column—on burqas—from How to Be a Woman, *but have included it in full here, because the idea of a "woman-made religion" continues to deeply intrigue me, to the point of maybe making one myself. After all, how much did L. Ron Hubbard coin off inventing Scientology? And that's a* bollocks *religion. People being controlled by tiny aliens inside? You've just lifted that off* The Twilight Zone, *Ron. It's pathetic.*

Burqas: Are the Men Doing It?

OVER THE LAST FEW WEEKS, I've whiled away hours imagining how different the world would would be if the major religions—Christianity, Islam, Judaism, Sikhism, Hindusim—had been invented by women. As someone who had atheism burned into them when they were fifteen and noticed a) all the terrible, unanswered suffering in the world and b) the first growths of a desperately unwanted woman-mustache, apparently given to me by a cruel God, my subsequent interest in theology became one of sociological curiosity: looking at religions' rules, and working out why people thousands of years ago would have invented those particular guidelines in the first place.

Lots of them are obvious and laudable morality—not killing, not lying, not stealing, doing your very best not to have sex with next door's wife; or else common sense housekeeping tips for hot countries—pork and shellfish would have been perilous in a pre–Sub-Zero era in the Middle East, for instance. They're all fine.

Then there are the more questionable rules. For anyone who's watched

Jerry Springer or read *Us Weekly*, "respecting your parents" doesn't make sense if your father is basically Frank from *Shameless*, or your mother some neurotic socialite who abandoned you to a host of disinterested nannies.

And, finally, there are the rules—scattered across all religions—that would only have been made up in an era where women were second-class citizens, i.e., any point before the release of *Working Girl* in 1986. The value on female virginity; female sexuality being "dangerous"; divorce being considered shameful: understandable rules from a pre-contraceptive society where women's main purpose was to keep family bloodlines undisputed, and prevent small, muddy villages exploding in a series of *General Hospital*–like plot-lines.

And, so, to the burqa—currently the world's most controversial outfit. Last week, the French government brought in a law making the burqa illegal in public places—prompting complex, but often inconclusive, emotional reactions, from pub gardens to broadsheets.

On the one hand, there feels something deeply amiss about seeing a woman walking down a street, in twenty-first century Paris, shrouded from head to toe as if she were some ghostly, flickering projection from 1,000 years ago. Some official urge to address this seems understandable.

On the other hand, the pictures that went around the world on the day the laws came into statute—French policemen grabbing a woman, on her own, and dragging her away; the inference, if not the actuality, being that they would then strip the *burqa* from her face, even as she protested—were also deeply disturbing. Xenophobic governments telling immigrant women what to wear—making laws about their wardrobes—*also* feels medieval. With another cultural shift, what other laws could be brought in to legislate against the clothes on women's backs: Fur? Mini-skirts? Pants? You could find passionate advocates against all of them. But in the case of the French government against burqas, who is *really* telling who what to wear here?

Well, I have a rule for working out if the root problem of something is, in fact, sexism. And it is this: asking "Are the boys doing it? Are the boys having to worry about this stuff? Are the boys the center of a gigantic global debate on this subject?"

And this is basis on which I finally decided I was against both the French legislation *and* women wearing burqas. France was the last European country to give women the vote, the French senate is 76.5 percent male, and it's never passed a law on what French men can wear. Not even deck shoes; or alarming all-in-one ski suits in bright pink nylon. So there's clearly some sexism going on there.

Secondly, meanwhile, the logic of the burqa is a paradox. Yes, the idea is that it protects your modesty, and ensures that people regard you as a human being—rather than just a sexual object. Fair enough.

But who is your modesty being protected *from?* Men. And who—so long as you play by the rules, and wear the correct clothes—is going to protect you *from* the men? Men. And who is it that is regarding you as just a sexual object, instead of another human being, in the first place? Men.

And—most importantly—which half of the population has never been required to walk around, covered from head to toe, in order feel like a normal human being? Men.

Well, then. Burqas seem like quite a man-based problem, really. I would definitely put this under the heading, "100 percent stuff that the men need to sort out." I don't know why women are suddenly having to put things on their heads to make it better.

Men invented burqas—men are banning burqas. And they are the only people who *would* have invented them. Because I can't believe a female-invented religion—with a female god, female prophets, and laws based on protecting women's interests—would *ever* have invented an item of religious clothing that required so much ironing.

Other times, however, fashion is a bit easier to deal with. You just have to look its insanity firmly in the eye, and say, "No. No, fashion—stop being silly. Shoo. I am too busy for this nonsense, as well you know."

This Cape Makes Me Look Like Wizbit

I LOVE THIS TIME of year, when the autumn/winter trends are minutely detailed in the media, and womankind can observe the fashions which are bearing down upon it at 100mph.

As someone who is both technically and actually a woman, I would never wish to absent myself from these vital dispatches. So, as is tradition, I spent this summer holiday as I have the last five—casting an eye over the forthcoming fashion weather, and making my wardrobe calculations accordingly. I learned that the forecast for 2011 is both varied and absorbing.

Capes, for instance, will continue to be a hot look—despite their unnerving ability to make the wearer look like Wizbit and/or someone who's had their arms chopped off in a jousting tournament, and is inexplicably coy about admitting it in front of their peers. (Wizbit was a triangular children's TV character who had very few distinguishing character traits other than being triangular in shape. He is not one of British TV's most legendary inventions.)

"No—no, there's nothing wrong. Just gonna wear this cape for a while. No reason. Could you just . . . put that sandwich in my mouth, please? It's for . . . a dare."

Should you not favor the cape, and/or prefer to have the use of your arms, there is apparently another option for you: the "Mannish Coat," instead.

"It should look like it's borrowed from the man in your life," *Vogue* explained, over shots of tweedy, boyish, single-breasted numbers.

This, of course, would be fine advice if the man in your life were Benedict Cumberbatch in *Sherlock*, who rarely has less than a grand's worth of hot and alluring tailoring hanging on the peg by the front door. Were I to wear a coat borrowed from the man in my life, however, I'd be pitching up at smart dinners in a bright yellow Radiohead Pac-a-Mac, decorated with one of Thom Yorke's trademark cartoons of a sad, abused panda.

When it comes to actual clothes, the summary for F/W11 is apparently "sophisticated" and "modest." In a post-Middleton era, it's "all about" pussy-bow blouses, tight midi-skirts, and court shoes. I cannot say I receive this news with great joy. At thirty-six, I'm a seasoned Fashion Veteran now—and in all my years of Style Combat, I have come to have a particular reason to view tight midi-skirts with Feud Eyes.

Don't get me wrong—your *Mad Men*–style skirt looks great when you're lolling around in it, smoking a fag. Attempt to get down a flight of stairs in one, however, and the extreme restriction around the knees becomes apparent, causing all manner of problems in posture and gait. However many icy martinis you're holding at the time (and FYI more than two is difficult, although certainly possible, particularly if you're not shy about utilizing the crook of your elbow), it's hard to maintain an air of sophisticated allure when you're having to kick your calves out sideways, in the style of a windup plastic bath frog. And court shoes look Thatcher. Always have done, always will do. And they tend to fall off when you're running, like you're some union-crushing Cinderella.

So—having spent my holiday debriefing myself on the F/W11 mood board I returned this week to London, and did what all women do every year, head full of the "must haves," "directional pieces," and "looks" we'll be "channelling" until spring: went to Topshop, and bought whatever made me look thinnest.

Obviously that's not the *entirety* of my F/W11 wardrobe makeover—I also popped into Mango and Zara, as well, and bought whatever made me look thinnest there, too. And I certainly wouldn't rule out, at some later point, buying something from H&M if it in any way makes me look a bit like Elizabeth Taylor drinking gin while sitting on Richard Burton's lap. But, frankly, that's it. When all the fashion editors were on Twitter in August fretting about which coat they were going to go for this autumn, I just looked in my coat closet, noticed that my duffel coat was still there, and said, "Yes. I know which coat *I* am going for this autumn. The one that I already have."

Because the truth about the gigantic hoopla of each new season's developments is this: there is no must-have, platinum-plated, worn-by-Anna-Wintour item in the *world* any woman would wear if it does anything other than make her look thin and a bit "likely."

On top of this, *Vogue* can list as many "must have" "directional pieces" as they like—if it's not in a shop we're wandering past we're going to kind of . . . forget to buy it. Yes. That's right. Simply not get around to it. We might sometimes *like* the idea of getting the £600 green snakeskin belt by Dior but—like whale-watching in Peru—it's not very local, and would, financially, require canceling Christmas in its entirety.

This is why the phrase "I wear a mixture of high-street and vintage"—the "quirky" wardrobe descriptor claimed by Alexa Chung, Kate Moss, et al—amuses me so much. That just means "a mixture of cheap stuff and old stuff." That's what we're *all* wearing, dear. That's what we'll all be wearing in F/W11.

Some discrimination isn't bad, ladies. Like positive discrimination. That's the good discrimination.

We Need Quotas, Ladies. Or We Will Be Lonely Pelicans.

IN A REPORT AS interesting to read as it must have been wearying to compile, *The Guardian* recently ran statistics on the male dominance of British public life.

Over a month, they painstakingly recorded that 78 percent of newspaper articles, 72 percent of *Question Time* contributors and 84 percent of the presenters and guests on Radio 4 were men. Ninety-three years after women got the vote, they still aren't saying very much. Well, obviously they *are* saying a *lot:* they're in the kitchen getting the tea ready, and shouting at Toby Young spraffing on on *Today*—his ability to be a total tit about any and all events so reliable, you could use it to power an atomic clock. But. Still. Women aren't getting paid to say things *publicly.* That—like coal mining, and arranging illegal dog fights—is still the domain of men.

If you do ever see women commenting on current affairs, it's usually as a vox-pop of "just" "a mum" outside a shopping center on the *Six O'Clock News,* being asked what she thinks of the government's plan to open up a Hellmouth, just by the ring-road, and let all the demons of the lower realms pour forth.

"I don't know much about these things," she will say, doubtfully, jiggling the buggy to keep the baby quiet. "But it worked out quite badly that time when they raised all the dead, and let them traverse the streets at night, eating cats to fuel their evil quests. *And* they've closed the library. I sometimes worry they might have gone too far. Not that I'm political. Sorry."

So. Given that these are pretty embarrassing statistics for a first world country in 2011, what are we going to do about it? Many, of course, would say that "we" shouldn't "do" anything—that attaining a position in public life is just something best left to Nature. Women should think of themselves as salmon, say—and just keep trying to leap up that waterfall, over and over again, until they finally get to the top and lay their eggs (appear on *Newsnight* talking about Syria).

Personally, however, I think that idea is—to use the technical term— bollocks. Society isn't Nature—it's made by people. Hopefully, polite and civilized people. And if society isn't working for 52 percent of the people, then it would be mannerly to change it so that it does. That's why I'm totally in favor of employment quotas and positive discrimation.

"But Cate," those who object will say, who know what my nickname is. The good nickname. Not "Snakey Mome Rath." "But Cate—if you insist 50 percent of your workforce is women, and force employers to hire them, that means you're gonna get women who are wildly ill-qualified desk-meat, smashing at the keyboards with their faces, and making a total hash of it. Women racketing around the office who don't know the difference between 'up' and 'down,' keep pressing buttons on the air conditioner saying, 'This printer isn't working,' and posting confidential client information on Twitter. That can't be right!"

Well, it's not "right." It is, however, totally normal. After all, in an office that's 70 percent men, at least 20 percent of *them* are going to be wildly ill-qualified desk-meat, smashing at the keyboard with their faces, and making a total hash of it. Of course they are. That's just statistics. People who are anti-positive-discrimination are ignoring the fact that we've been giving jobs to MILLIONS of stupid, unqualified people for millenia: men.

Please don't misunderstand—I am not prejudiced against the stupid men. Or the stupid women, for that matter. As we all know, any office— from Budgens in Crouch End to the White House—only needs three clever people to run it. Everyone else there is essentially just a background extra, to keep the important, capable people from feeling lonely. And that's another reason why we need quotas. When women are in a minority in any situation, they feel as understandably odd and stressed as two pelicans in a camel enclosure. And the camels can't help but look at the pelican beaks oddly, and go off and do "camel things" in the corner, while the pelicans feel awkward and alone, and go on a weird diet, out of self-loathing.

In this situation, you just need to wang half a dozen stupider pelicans into the enclosure, to keep the best pelicans company, and even out the numbers—so that both "being a pelican" and "being a camel" is totally normal in London Zoo's New Pelican & Camel Experience.

Men who complain about positive discrimination look like—to use the technical phrase—girls. Let's face it—the next Bill Gates or Barack Obama isn't going to be held back because AAAAAAABBA Office Supplies in Dartford has been forced to hire three female accounts managers. Come ON! Do you really think you have something to complain about? Do you really think you're at a disadvantage? Stop whining! Rosa Parks managed to kick-start the Civil Rights movement in America, on a bus, WHILE CARRYING SOME GROCERIES. You need some perspective on just how hindered you really are.

Here I can go into a lovely segue—from the politeness of female employment quotas, to the politeness of chivalry—all as smoothly as a local radio presenter going from the sport into travel and weather. And that's plenty smooth.

As "Downton Fever" (some people watching Downton*) swept the nation in 2012, an interview with Michelle Dockery, who plays Lady Mary, and— as revealed later in this book—crunks to "No Diggity," provoked controversy when she lamented the end of chivalry in an interview in the* Radio Times.

"Those old manners—such as men standing when women arrive at the dinner table, or opening doors for you—are lovely, and it's lovely when you see a man doing that today," she said. "But young men wouldn't think about that for a second [now], because that's not the culture anymore."

This prompted much squabbling over the desirability of a chivalric revival, with many women and men arguing against it, as they believed all chivalry was essentially men patronizing women, and implying they were weak and helpless.

I strongly disagreed—primarily on the basis that I like sitting down.

I Would Like Some Chivalry, Please, Dude

THERE HAS RECENTLY BEEN some debate on the place chivalry has in the modern era—prompted by the massive success of *Downton Abbey,* which shows a forgotten world of gentlemen rising as a lady enters the room, using quadrille gloves when engaged in quadrilling, and making only the faintest legal protest over women gaining the vote in 1918.

Having observed its full glory on television, modern opinion seems to be split on the desirability of now staging a full chivalric revival. The main argument against it is that it presupposes weakness in women. The common complaint is that if a man, say, stands up to give his seat to a woman on the Tube, he is basically saying, "Lady, I think you are having a massive period, and might faint if you remain standing. That would then delay this Tube for all of us normal, non-menstruating people. So, on behalf of everyone with a tight schedule, have my chair and sit tf down, lest we all suffer from your physical misfortune."

And I can see why that might be slightly annoying—if you were, perhaps, a hale and hearty wench, who prides herself on her upper body strength, and can climb up a rope rather than hanging at the bottom of it, uselessly, like a 5'5" lady-bauble.

However. Speaking as someone who, four days a month, really *might* faint on the Tube if someone doesn't give up their seat, I am eternally grateful for any gentleman who stands as I limp into his car. Sometimes, I have been suffering so badly on public transport I have inadvertently let out a low, animal-moan of "Maaaaa"—then had to style it out by pretending to be a slightly unhinged person, singing along to *Mama Mia* on my iPod. I have had swooning moments so intense I had to rest my head on a Slovakian's rucksack, while mouthing the words "Don't faint, Cat-Mo; don't faint" into a gigantic outside pocket.

And that's before we even mention pregnancy. The first three months of gestation—when there are no visible indicators to the onlooker—are a panoply of astonishing and dehabilitating physical side effects. I had one incident where my feet became so mysteriously hot, I eventually had to go into a changing room in New Look, and sluice them down with a bottle of Purdey's. All kinds of head spinning insanity can be going on inside a woman's body. Some days, it's like we're covering up a circus that's on fire, using only an A-line skirt and a blouse. Underneath, there are clowns jumping out of windows, and crying seals everywhere.

In these circumstances, then, any man aware of what women might be enduring, and offering some manner of solidarity, is a kind, gentle, bright brother to me. He is doing something both polite, and hot. He is a man who has quietly concluded that—given how frequently women are dealing with some manner of Big Top Crisis—it's generally best for men to give us *all* both the benefit of the doubt, and their seats. I suspect this was the origin of chivalry in the first place—a simple, kind logic.

The only alternative to universal, automatic chivalry, of course—giving up seats for all women—is to make chivalry more specific. In this system, women who were physical indisposed would have to indicate their situation with some manner of "period badge," or "special pregnancy hat"—so that men may only offer courtesy to those who are genuinely in need of it. As you can see, that would be only slightly worse than having to walk around in public with your teenage diary entries pinned to your chest. Most women would die of mortification on their first commute to work. It would be a massacre.

Of course, there are bad men—men who abuse the concept of chivalry. Their unspoken deal is, "Yes, I am going to open this door for you, Amelia—but I will leer at you as you walk past me, then maintain a vague air of 'ownership' over you all night: as if I am a great silverback who has now inducted you into his harem of lady gorillas. You will now bare my gorilla babies, in my mind."

But here, ladies, we must keep some manner of perspective. Given how much random perving the average woman will have to put up with in the course of a week—I was once perved when I was nine months pregnant, wearing a duffel coat and carrying a Vileda Supermop back from a local hardware store. I really was not the Girl from Ipanema—at least we have got something out of this particular perv-instance: in this case, being spared the indiginity of having to open a door with our teeth, because our arms are ladened with bags and coat.

At least, in this instance, we're a door opening up on the deal. For that reason alone, I'm pro-chivalry.

On top of this baffling rejection of men being nice—LADIES! In turning down acts of chivalry, we are behaving in an unchivalrous manner! The irony would kill me were I not already reeling from the impossibility of a situation where OPENING A DOOR is seen as an aggressive act. Come on, fellow breastkateers—we can be more noble that this. Why not pat these well-meaning fellows on the back, and simply say "Thank you"? That's a) manners and b) what you would want in return.

I write a lot about the internet. There are two reasons for this. The first is because it is, quite clearly, the greatest invention of the twentieth century: the equivalent of the wheel, or fire, but for the mind.

With mass communication no longer limited to newspapers or TV companies—to which access was previously and jealously guarded by professional writers and broadcasters—the nearest thing to a meritocracy of opinion and experience has now come about, thanks to Tumblr, Facebook, YouTube and Twitter. Some teenage kid in Buttfuck, Idaho, can come up with a joke, campaign or picture of a funny raccoon, and, if it catches people's imagination, it can be (ironically) making old-fashioned newspaper headlines by sundown. Ideas and thoughts and experiences can spread like pollen in the air, blood in water. For good or bad, of course: the unsayable becomes the unstoppable just as easily as some beautiful attempt for a better world. There are people whose lives have literally been ruined by a bad picture on Facebook, or an email being sent to the wrong address—then being passed on across the world.

But the sheer, awesome, exhilarating power of the internet is absolutely captivating: it is the biggest game on Earth. The twenty-first century equivalent of the birth of rock 'n' roll. For those who don't work in it—who are merely customers, rather than Mark Zuckerberg—having access to it is like standing on a rocky ledge, halfway down Victoria Falls, in the middle of an all-enveloping monsoon. The roar and the spray—the constant motion and hydrating mist— are intoxicating. Thousands of new things tumbling past you every second— swept into the river above in the flood—that you can just reach out and grab. Maps and shops and faces and friends from 1987 and that clip from that show that time, and snowflakes, and explosions, and Crosby, Stills and Nash singing "Helplessly Hoping" in three part harmony, as many times as you want.

The idea of moving away from it—back inland, back off-line—seems wholly desolate and mean. Dry. Silent. How would you know . . . anything, without the internet? How could you make things happen? What would be left of you? Just some jumped-up hapless monkey in a dress, trying to buy a train ticket to Nottingham by being put on hold by another jumped-up yet hapless monkey in a dress.

No, no—every time I am off-line, I am half-off. I can't get anything done. I love the internet. It is where I live.

And the second reason I love it is because pissing around on Twitter is an excellent *substitute for smoking. I think I'm on 120 Twitter a day. I am* chaining *that shit.*

In the following piece, I explore—with another smoooooooth segue from the last column—the lack of chivalry on the internet.

Don't Feed the Troll

THE THING I LIKE most about the internet is that it's just humans, interacting with other humans—but in a sufficiently novel manner for new guidelines to be needed. Because there's no one in charge—no, despite the claims of thousands of teenage boys, "King of the Internet"—online is a world where billions of people are trying to get through another day of posting amusing pictures of cats, typing in capital letters and lying slightly about how amazing they are—all while not getting in each other's way, or offending each other.

By and large, it works so well as to stir the heart. Observed from above, the internet must look like the Magic Roundabout gyratory system in Swindon: trillions of opinion-cars from all over the world, ploughing into what seems like certain fatality—only for everyone to, at the last moment, avoid each other, and seamlessly continue their journey to Bristol/some pornography. No international wars have *ever* been declared on the internet. It is a remarkably amiable place.

But there are exceptions. "Trolls": anonymous posters whose kink is making deliberately inflammatory comments—then getting visibly high off others' subsequent outrage. Imagine an adolescent boy breaking wind at the breakfast table—then smirking as everyone shouts, "Jesus, that smell has irradiated my Weetos. Why? WHY would you DO that Julian, WHY?"

Typical troll behavior would be, say, going on a Beyoncé fansite, observing the conversation for a few minutes, and then saying, "Yeah—but she's got a fat arse, hasn't she?" As more inexperienced fans castigate the troll for sexism, possible racism and stupidity, older hands utter one of the internet's most used catchphrases: "Don't feed the troll." In other words: if some anonymous armchair cowboy pitches up and deliberately provokes a fight, don't satisfy his need for attention. Ignore him. Don't feed the troll.

Until recently, I, too, would intone, "Don't feed the troll." Firstly, it's a waste of time that could be spent engaging in a pleasant early summer stroll, searching out the first buds of pussy willow. And, secondly, there's always the undeniable feeling that, as you castigate a troll, he's rubbing his *Red Dwarf* mouse pad against his crotch and sighing, "Angry liberal women typing at me. Oh yah. That's how I like it."

But then I started to notice that, as a phenomenon, trolling isn't just confined to pseudonymous IT workers hanging around Justin Bieber fansites, making fourteen-year-old girls furious. When, a few weeks ago, on *Top Gear,* Jeremy Clarkson made his "amusing" remark about Katie Price having a "pink whore's box"—"I meant PINK HORSE BOX!" he corrected, knowingly it occurred to me that Clarkson's entire career is essentially an exercise in trolling: gleefully vexatious comments on Mexicans, homosexuals and women, thrown out with the "Ho ho! Our 'PC' friends won't like THIS!" expression that is the carat mark of the true troll.

Clarkson isn't the only professional troll on the block: consider his friend, the *Sunday Times* columnist A. A. Gill, with his liberal sprinkling of references to "dykes," "ferret-faced Albanians" and the "ugly Welsh." Both Clarkson and Gill know that these kinds of comments provoke massive reactions—in their cases, to the point where ambassadors from other countries get involved. Essentially, they're trolling the entire concepts of diplomacy and civilization for a reaction. This is something to which some hopelessly small-town troll, flaming for kicks on the breastfeeding boards of Mumsnet, can only sighingly aspire.

If there is one thing that defines the troll worldview, it's a sour, disatissfied sense that the world is disappointing. Trolls never troll enthusiasm.

The default troll attitude is one of inexplicably vituperative disapproval for something millions find joy in. The first time I thought that sentence, I went, "Oh my God—you know what this means? The *Daily Mail* is the fucking LODESTONE of trolldom! It's the Magna Carta of Trolldom! It's the Dead Sea Trolls!"

Because if you look at the *Mail*'s website, your presumption that *Daily Mail* readers actually like bitchy headlines about female celebrities putting on weight ("Fuller-Faced Cheryl Cole"), is blown out of the water. All the comments are actually from reasonable people baffled by the *Mail*'s tactic ("Can't celebrities put on an ounce without it being news?" Ivy, Barking)— making you realize that the *Mail* is, in practice, trolling its entire readership. Amazing.

So this is why I can't agree with the internet's first rule: "Don't feed the trolls." It's *fine* when it's just some spenk on a message board, with only five users. Ignoring provocative nonsense is only right and sensible. But when millionaire celebrity broadcasters, and entire publications, start trolling, ignoring them isn't really an option anymore. They are gradually making trolling normative. We have to start feeding the trolls: feeding them with achingly polite emails and comments, reminding them of how billions of people prefer to communicate with each other, every day, in the most unregulated arena of all: courteously.

Throughout this book, a few recurring themes will make themselves apparent: a fear of the sixteenth century; continuing enjoyment over the Moon Landings; the bangingness of Sherlock; *an irresponsible love of alcohol and loud pop music; and a deep, beyond primal adoration of the BBC series* Doctor Who.

In this feature, the BBC let me go around the Doctor Who *studios, where I found the Face of Boe in a warehouse and sat on him. For two years, a picture of me doing so was the screensaver on my laptop. There is no doubt in my mind that, when I'm dying, and my life flashes before my eyes, that particular picture will get a longer slot than many other pivotal life moments, with a caption saying "WINNING!" flashing over it.*

On the Set of *Doctor Who*

CARDIFF TRAIN STATION, 10 AM. The cab driver is unsure as to where, exactly, we are going. He pulls to a halt at the end of the rank, and hails the cab opposite.

"I've got passengers for *Doctor Who*," he says, with an expansive gesture at us in the back. "Where do I turn off?"

"For *Doctor Who*?" the other cab driver says. "For *Doctor Who*?"

There's a huge pause, where a more overexcited cab passenger might begin to speculate as to whether *Doctor Who* is actually shot on Earth at all. Maybe it's only accessible via a closely guarded magnetic anomaly, in a disused bronze mine, guarded by the Sontarans!

"You go right at the BP petrol station, mate."

DOCTOR WHO AND DOCTOR WHO'S spin-offs—*Torchwood, The Sarah Jane Adventures, Doctor Who Confidential* and *Totally Doctor Who*—occupy

Cardiff, in much the same manner an army barracks occupies a small town. With a crew of 200, 180 special FX technicians, 200 prosthetics technicians, 2,000 extras and 200 guest stars, the population of the city is divided into civilians and non-civilians; *Who* and non-*Who*. The pivotal question in Cardaffian nightlife is "You on *Who*, then?"

"Some of them act a bit cliquey, like they've seen attack ships on fire off the shoulder of Orion," a friend who lives in Cardiff said. "When, in actual fact, they've just spent all day waving a foam rubber leg around."

But much like the army, this clannishness is understandable—*Doctor Who* is both a huge, and a hugely secretive, operation. Having made the decision to try and keep the plots a surprise—extremely rare in television, where tabloid pre-publicity is key in getting ratings-spikes—phenomenal amounts of thought and energy are put into keeping details from the public. On the way to Cardiff, the show's press officer, Lesley, has a wary weather eye out for possible leaks.

"We can't discuss the show on the train," she says, firmly, as soon as we sit down. "People have done it before, and had passengers who've overheard ring the tabloids. Everyone knows what you're talking about as soon as you say 'The Doctor,' you see."

So an hour later, when I am standing in a dark, otherwise deserted warehouse, with the TARDIS looming over me like the monolith in *2001*, I feel genuine frissons of both privilege, and slight fear. Privilege, because I am in a place where thousands of fans of the show would love to be. After all, a mere twenty feet away, there's a top secret spaceship being referred to as "the James Bond set," which will tittivate the spod-glands of any western adult between the ages of seventeen and fifty.

And fear, because the TARDIS—despite sitting on top of a pallet— looks unexpectedly legendary. It has the aura of something that has bounced off comets, arced over nebulae and oscillated through the furthest reaches of spacetime. Even though, when I knock on its door, it's clearly made of wood.

The *Doctor Who* warehouse is a surreal place. Despite our last sighting over the Cybermen being during Season Two, when an impassively muscular army of millions tried to take over the Earth, there are, in fact, only ten Cybermen in existence. Well, four now, due to breakages. I can see three of their legs poking out of a large cardboard box, at right angles. The Daleks, meanwhile, are—contrary to all lores of celebrity—actually *bigger* than they seem on TV.

Being quite common, my first instinct it to steal something cool. I cannot be alone in this impulse. These warehouses are, presumably, an open invitation for cast and crew to take "mementos." Everyone wants a Cyberman codpiece on their mantlepiece, surely?

"To be honest, no," says our tour guide, Edward Russell, Brand Executive of *Doctor Who*. "It's like a family. It just wouldn't be worth their while to steal anything, because, if they got caught, they'd never work again. Everyone on this show is very protective."

He makes it sound as if, in the event of any possible transgression of trust, a hit squad of Daleks can be seen trundling into a local pub, and emerging again, minutes later, with smoking plungers.

Of course, an operation this big and, indeed, a universe this vast would all be pretty pointless were we to venture into it without a charismatic galactic chaperone. As we all know by now, the resurrection of *Doctor Who* is down to one man—the joyous, expansive and prodigiously talented Russell T. Davies, the man who traded all his success with *Queer As Folk*, *Bob & Rose* and *Casanova* in order to do what the BBC had thought impossible for sixteen years—regenerate the abandoned *Who* into the BBC's flagship. It is he, above all others, who is responsible for the best program in Britain in the twenty-first century being, against all the laws of probability, a children's show, made on a miniscule budget, in Wales, by gays.

But it is, perhaps, in Davies's choice of the Doctor that he made his most crucial decision. For while, in the first season, Christopher Ecclestone's leather-jacketed, slightly demented hard-nut Doctor was the right person to make a full break from the show's heritage of frock coats, frilly cuffs and hammery, it is in David Tennant, the tenth and current Doctor, that the show has found its most appealing emissary. While Ecclestone approached the role prosaically, as a difficult job to be done well, Tennant has taken on the role with, well, to be frank, love. A fan of the show since childhood, he has been voted "The Best Doctor Ever" in acknowledgment that it is his performance, above all others, that has best embodied the show's values: anarchy, vigor, moral rigor, silliness, and a reverential awe at how big, scary, complex, beautiful and full of bipedal aliens made of foam rubber the universe is.

Meeting with him—in the tea rooms of the Landmark Hotel in Marylebone—it's clear to see why Davies cast him in the role. He has quick wit, excess energy, and self-deprecates at every available opportunity ("Look at my mobile! It's really boring! It's about as intergalactic as a brick!") He is, also, let's be frank, the first hot Doctor. He is the primary Timephwoard. He has been voted "Hottest Man in the Universe" by *The Pink Paper*, while *New Woman Magazine* placed him at Number 13 in its poll of 10,000 women's crushes—just below Brad Pitt.

Tennant, however, disputes his assignation as the First Hot Doctor.

"Tom Baker!" he says, with a Bakerish roar. "Come on! He was a huge hit with the ladies."

He was more of a specialist taste, I offer, primly. Something WHSmith would keep behind the counter, and you'd have to ask for.

"I'm sure Peter Davidson was in polls at the time," he continues, gallantly. Perhaps aware that he is seconds away from attempting to mount a defense of the sexual allure of Sylvester McCoy, Tennant changes the conversation with a confidence that just, to be honest, proves how hot he is.

"This is a terrible anecdote, so I must tell it," he says, settling into a chair with a coffee. "Last year, Bille [Piper] and I kept getting invited to guest at award ceremonies but we could never go—we were either filming in Cardiff, or because we would be presenting Best Wig or something, and what's the point of that? But when the Brit Awards rolled around, we let it be known, through our 'people,' that we'd love to present a Brit for Best Drunkard, or something. But—pleasingly for the laws of hubris—they said 'No, we'll be fine, thank you.' They turned down the Doctor and Rose! Famous across the universe!"

Tennant does a self-deprecating boggle.

Talking to him is an experience of mild surreality. On the one hand—it's the Doctor! You're talking to the Doctor! On the other hand, he's as obsessive and passionate about the show as any fan. This is a man who can talk about the Gravitic Anomalyser without any protective layer of irony.

Dismissing the possibility that, paradoxically, becoming the Doctor could ultimately ruin the show for a him—"I know what you mean, because all the surprises are gone, but I'd have gone mad if I'd turned it down and watched someone else do it"—Tennant, instead, spends the next hour discussing the show with all the enthusiasm and mild geekery of a fan, albeit a very privileged one. Discussing certain titillating morsels that Russell T. Davies has thrown into previous episodes and then not returned to—such as the intriguing news that the Doctor has, at some point, been a father—Tennant yelps, and then says, "I know! I'll be reading these things, going 'When are you coming back to that?' Often he does. But sometimes," he says, leaning forward, "he just drops them in for wickedness. There's something he's done in the next season, and I said, 'What's that all about?' and he replied, 'Oh, I've just put it in because it's funny.' The internet forums will go into meltdown."

He beams. "But you know—he knows what he wants as a fan. You want to be discussing it all the next week. You want to float your different theories on what will happen next. That's part of the pleasure."

Together with Russell T. Davies, he comes across like a steam enthusiast who's taken over an old rail line. Every detail of the show thrills him—even the clothes. Indeed, perhaps the most surprising moment comes when he explains how the image of his Doctor was, fairly unguessably, based on the savior of our fat school children, Jamie Oliver.

"I'd always wanted a long coat, because you've kind of got to. You've got to *swish*. Then when Billie was on *Parkie*, she was on the same week as Jamie Oliver, who was looking rather cool in a funky suit with sneakers were the one thing I did go to the wall on." Tennant bashes his hand down on the table, and then laughs.

"Although," he adds, "I have to say, I do regret it when I'm doing a night shoot in a quarry of stinking mud, and they're putting plastic bags on my feet."

The big news for the forthcoming season, of course, is that Billie Piper, who played the Doctor's assistant, Rose, has left. As well as being phenomenally popular in the role—she was credited with bringing a young, female audience to a show that had previously lacked one—she and Tennant formed a famously matey duo. They always emanated the vibe of having spent their down time in Cardiff Nandos, eating huge amounts of fried chicken with their hands and laughing with their mouths open. When discussing her departure, Tennant becomes quite tender.

"The last scene we shot was for [the episode called] 'The Satan Pit.' Our very last line was someone saying, 'Who are you two?', and we reply 'The stuff of legend,' and then zap off in the TARDIS. We just could not get a take where we weren't crying. If you look very carefully, you can still see us starting to go 'Wah!'"

Tennant, however, is stalwart in his enthusiasm for the new assistant, Freema Agyeman.

"It's a totally different energy—she comes from a totally different starting place. She's very upfront about fancying [the Doctor], and so he has to be very upfront about not being into it. It's a completely new dynamic. She's a completely new girl."

It's *Who*—2.1, perhaps, I suggest.

"Yes!" Tennant beams. "*Who* 2.1!"

BREAKING FOR LUNCH, THE whole crew travels down the hill to the "base station"—a line of location buses and Portakabins. When David Tennant turns up, dandy and wire-thin in his new, electric-blue suit and precipitous quiff, the effect is roughly equivalent to the advent of the Fonz in Al's Diner. He is clearly lord of this domain—he manages to simultaneously hail, chat to and tease three crewmembers at once.

By contrast, John Simm's entrance onto the set is intense and lowkey. As the pivotally evil Mr. Saxon, Simm is in a black suit, wearing an ominous-looking ring, and eschewing the buffet in favor of a quiet lunch in his trailer.

"I can't tell you anything," he says, sighing. "I don't think I'm even officially here, am I?" he shrugs.

LATER ON, IN A waterfront bar back in Cardiff, Simm starts an admirably brisk line of whisky ordering, and explains exactly why he left a three-week-old baby to spend a month in Wales, on the side of a windy hill.

"It's *Doctor Who*, innit?" he says, with admirable succinctness. "You've got to do it. And Christ, the energy they all put into it. Julie Gardner [producer] and Russell T. Davies were getting on midnight trains up to Manchester, to the set of *Life on Mars*, to ask me to do it."

The deciding vote, though, was cast by Simm's five-year-old son, Ryan. "He's *Doctor Who* mad. He's got the lunchbox, the dolls, the screwdriver. As a dad of a small boy, you kind of have a moral duty to be a baddie on *Doctor Who* if you can, don't you?"

Simm is keen to illustrate just what he and Tennant have gone through to thrill this new generation of *Who* fans—just how far their dedication extends.

"We were shooting one scene, just me and David, on top of this deserted mountain top. We're giving it our all when, from fuck knows where, you can hear the faint sounds of an ice cream van. David carries on, so I thought well, I'm not going to stop if you're not going to stop. So we carried on right to the end—despite the fact that this must be the only ice cream van in existence that does the theme tune to *The Benny Hill Show*. The least inter-galactic sound imaginable!"

He shakes his head.

"We were, looking back, very professional that day."

FOR SEASON THREE, THE BBC have taken the publicity for *Doctor Who* out of their own, often ramshackle, house, and placed it in the hands of Taylor Herring—PR to Robbie Williams, *Big Brother* and Al Gore.

The new PR team, seemingly more aware of just how much interest there is in the show, have accordingly ramped up the screenings of the first two episodes. While screenings normally consist of a small room, forty scruffy journalists and a table of coffee and buns, the *Who* screenings are treated like a movie premiere. Outside the Mayfair Hotel, fans scream as a phalanx of paparazzi snap at the guests. While the celebrities do, by and large, look like someone took a van down to the BBC canteen and shouted, "Anyone want to come and watch *Doctor 'oo?*"—Ian Beale, Michelle Collins, Reggie Yates—there is also Jonathan Ross, Catherine Tate and Dawn French.

Freema Agyeman is wearing a pair of £4,000 earrings, and both David Tennant and Russell T. Davies are resplendent in sharp suits, and working the line of TV crews like pros.

At the beginning of the screening there is, momentarily, no sound. The TARDIS, iconic as ever, spins through electric-blue spacetime to complete silence. Then the audience, as one, begins to sing the theme-tune themselves: "Oooo WEEE oooooo/OOOO ooo." There is even an impressive counter-accompaniment of "De duddle le dum/De duddle le dum." It's a moment of happy, communal rejoicing.

Russell T. Davies floats around, looking as joyous and serene as someone recently voted "The Third Most Powerful Man in British Show Business" should, upon pulling off another considerable success.

"The show is simply one of the best ideas ever, really, isn't it?" he says, dragging on a ciggie and beaming. "So simple, yet so complex. How can you not love a sexy anarchist, roaming through time and space?"

When asked if—given that *Doctor Who* has now, to all intents and purposes, over-taken *EastEnders* as the BBC's flagship show—a larger budget would be more useful, he says a series of vaguely blustery and on-message things before roaring, dramatically, "Yes! Yes! Yes, I want more money, goddamnit!"

And it's hardly surprising that he does, considering that *Who* is still not being shot in HD—surely a foolish short-term economy, given the show's inevitably longevity in repeats and DVD sales.

But in all, "I am a happy man," Davies sighs, exhaling, and staring across the room at the Doctor, his assistant, and a circle of a dozen grown adults, all squealing with excitement about being about to touch the TARDIS. "A very happy man."

And he should, perhaps, feel a quiet satisfaction. After all, in a world where very little is a surprise, and everything is viewed with cynicism, *Doctor Who* is a genuine rarity. It represents one of the very few areas where adults become as unashamedly enthusiastic as children. It's where children first experience the thrills and fears of adults, and where we never know the exact ending in advance. With its ballsy women, bisexual captains, working-class loquaciousness, scientific passion and unremittingly pacifist dictum, it offers a release from the dispiritingly limited vision of most storytelling.

It is, despite being about a 900-year-old man with two hearts and a spacetime taxi made of wood, still one of our very best projections of how to be human.

Last piece for this section—on the curious phraseology of the anti-choice move-ment in America. "A gift."

This Is Not a Gift

THERE'S SOMETHING DISTURBING ABOUT the idea of someone press-ing something unwanted—wholly unwanted—in your hands, saying, "It's a gift! It's a gift!"

And you demure, politely at first—saying, "How lovely, but no. I do not want this gun/modern sculpture too large for my house/a sack of oys-ters—to which I am allergic—thank you. It is lovely that you thought of me: but no."

But the insistence increases.

"It's a GIFT," they insist, forcing it into your palm. "A PRESENT. YOU MUST HAVE THIS GIFT."

And now your hands are bleeding, and you're truly alarmed, and you try to back away. But you find that the law is changed, overnight, and you are legally obliged to take this gift—even as you stand there with your hands torn, saying, "But surely a gift is something wanted? Something *suit-able*? A stranger's hand putting something into my pocket is the same as a stranger's hand taking something *out* of my pocket. Really, there should be no hand there at all."

And the gun goes off, and the sculpture is wedged in the doorway, im-movably, and the oysters leak, slowly, onto the floor. Things that would have been wanted elsewhere cause chaos here. They do not fit, and they cause grief. And the stranger walks away from you. Having pressed his gift upon you, his work is done. And you do not understand why he ever came to your door.

Republican candidate Rick Santorum's comment that, if his fourteen-year-old daughter were raped, and became pregnant, he would not want her to have an abortion—but think of the baby as a "gift" from God—has been one of the defining quotes of the year.

As contraception and abortion become, yet again, controversial—the UK facing the second proposal, in as many years, for pro-life organizations to counsel women wanting an abortion; in the US, Rush Limbaugh and Rick Santorum speaking out against contraception, even for married couples—the idea of babies as a "gift" becomes a pivotal one.

"Gift" is a key concept. If all babies are a "gift," then a pregnant woman seeking abortion becomes unforgivably "ungrateful." Similarly, contraception is bad, because it is the rejection of yet more "gifts."

Let us think of all the inferences of "gifts." If I give you a gift, it is usually a surprise. It is probably something you would not have gotten for yourself. And after I have given it to you, I would not see it again. I leave you with the gift. Gift-giving leaves the person who receives the gift essentially powerless—not a problem if it's an incongruously brightly colored wristwatch; a great deal more so if it's a human being for whom you bear responsibility for the rest of your life.

Babies being "given" to women as gifts makes the women sound powerless. Just something that a present was put onto, like a bookcase, or a shelf—rather than a reasoning adult, who decided they were ready to be a mother, instead.

Calling a baby "a gift" also sounds—let us be honest—like the phrasing of someone who has not spent much time bringing up children. It seems unfair to use visceral language to describe the reality of parenthood—but as anti-choice, anti-contraception campaigners are quite happy to use visceral language themselves ("slut," "prostitute," "whore," "murder"), I have to presume they would be all right with it.

From the shop floor of pregnancy, childbirth and motherhood, here's what that gift can entail: tearing, bleeding, weeping, exhaustion, hallucination, despair, rage, anemia, stitches, incontinence, unemployment, depression, infection, loneliness. Death. Women still die in childbirth. Not as many as used to—but notably more die than while receiving any other "gifts," such as scented candles, or long weekends. Additionally, "gift" sounds hopelessly inadequate to describe your children, whom you would die for in a heartbeat, inhale like oxygen, and swoon over like lovers. I have never done this over a foot spa or vase.

The worry of the anti-abortion and anti-contraception campaigners is that women rejecting these "gifts" are rejecting the gifts of Nature, or God. It is in obeisance to them that we should not turn to contraception, or abortion. But Nature, of course, turns to contraception and abortion all the time: the diseases that make you barren; the sperm-counts that fall to zero. Blocked tubes and blown wombs and the thousand sorrows of the infertile. The one-in-three first pregnancies that end in miscarriage—miscarriage that is just like abortion, we must remember—a potential life ended—except miscarriages are unwanted, and often dangerous; while abortions are safe, and wanted.

Nature also, clearly, believes in non-procreative sex: for twenty-seven days a month, sex is non-procreative. Sex after menopause is non-procreative. Statistically, most sex is non-procreative. Clearly, sex *isn't* just for procreation: it's also for the creation of happiness, or excitement, or contentment.

Those things that really are gifts; and are always wanted. Those things that do not scare me, when pressed upon me.

Part **Three**

Parenting, Politics, and the Posh

In which we boggle over Downton Abbey, *mount a defense of parental binge drinking, discuss the heaviness of poverty, and call for Lola from* Charlie and Lola *to be rubbed out forever. But before that, a domestic interlude.*

While my job involves a lot of brief, yet incongruously intimate, encounters with all kinds of people, my ability to just "get on" with anyone—put them at their ease, make time with me a pleasant experience—is never more pertinently exposed than in the late night conversations I have with my husband. In many ways, I feel these chats encapsulate marriage in a nutshell: one person bursting with ideas they feel they can only share with one, special, most-beloved; the other just wanting to go the fuck to sleep.

All the Ways I've Ruined Your Life

IT'S 12:04 AM. I'm on the woozy half-slide of sleep; the cotton-wool duvet of more weightless thought. There's something about my teeth growing bigger. I'm falling, leg first, into a dream.

"Cate." It's my husband, sitting up next to me.

"Wh?"

"Cate." He, apparently, is not falling asleep.

"Wh?"

"I've just found your Mooncup under my pillow."

For those who have never come across one, a Mooncup is a . . . lady thing, which you use at . . . lady-time, to do . . . lady-business. For some reason, I always seem to be losing them—then finding them in unexpected places. The second most embarrassing thing that has ever happened to me is having my best friend's one-year-old son walk into the kitchen, my Mooncup wedged in his mouth, like a pacifier. I still can't talk about the most embarrassing thing that ever happened to me. Needless to say, I was not expecting to see that twenty-one-year-old accountant on my landing at that particular moment.

"Why is your Mooncup under my pillow?" Pete asks. Oh dear.

"I wondered where it was!" I say. Maybe my cheeriness at having found it again will infect Pete, and he will be happy for me.

"I'm not happy for you about this," he says. "If that's what you're thinking."

"I am sorry," I say. "It is just the way of my Mooncup. It is like all scissors and cheese graters—I never, ever know where they are. They seem to flit between parallel worlds. It's mad!"

"I don't think your Mooncup has made it to underneath my pillow via string theory," Pete says, still looking quite awake. "Because it's one of many, many of your things that have ended up in the wrong place, and I don't think even an infinite universe has that many wormholes."

"What do you mean?" I say.

Clearly I am not going to sleep any time soon. Pete is obviously a little het up about this. I have to say, I find this desire to chat during sleepy time somewhat thoughtless. I would never do this.

"Well, yesterday I found a slice of half-eaten bread and Marmite on top of my Pentangle boxed set," Pete says, sounding genuinely quite annoyed. "I was going to have a go at the kids—until I recognized the gigantic, foot-wide mouth print of the person who'd been eating it."

"Me?" I say.

"Well, it was either you or a wandering T-Rex," he says. "You appear to have the mouth span of something that can dislocate its lower jaw and eat a piano, whole."

"Well, that's not so bad, is it?" I say. "Toast on a CD? After all, they do look like coasters. They're easy to wipe clean. In a survival situation, they'd be an obvious substitute for melamine picnic plates. I think that's quite reasonable."

"You just shouldn't leave your lunch on my records!" Pete says, sounding a little bit emotional. A bit like a woman, I have to say. "I wouldn't—" he casts around for a comparable event "—put a pork pie in your handbag."

"I wouldn't mind if you did," I say, reasonably. I am very reasonable.

"I know you wouldn't!" he says. "I've seen you put falafel in the glove compartment! You have very low standards of hygiene! After sixteen years, I accept that in you! I just don't accept it in you on my stuff!"

"Is it so bad?" I ask. I'm rather hurt. I have improved my standards since we've been together. When I moved into his flat, in 1996, I brought two black garbage bags of dishes with me. Dirty dishes. That was by way of my trousseau. In one bag, there was an ashtray. Full. But I wouldn't do that now. I have changed.

"You leave your dirty tights in the kitchen. I found one of your flip-flops in my computer bag. Yesterday, I took my Oyster card out of my coat and it had one of your blister pads stuck to it—I had to stand at Holborn peeling it off. You threw my Le Creuset oven glove out of the window."

"I've already done a column on that," I say. "To my mind, it's been dealt with."

"I came down after one drinking session and found you'd stubbed your fag out on Nancy's special *Little Mermaid* plate," Pete continues. "You try to squeeze the blackheads on my nose when I'm driving; you come in and start conversations with me when I'm on the toilet; you've ruined all the BBC Four reruns of 1976's *Top of the Pops* by repeatedly saying, 'I hope when the punks finally turn up, they've got GUNS and KILL J. J. Barrie.'"

"Is this," I say, hopefully, "one of those arguments where you list all of the ways I've ruined your life—but, by the end of it, you feel oddly saucy, and the argument segues into some sex? Like in *Moonlighting*?"

"And you compare everything to *Moonlighting*, even though you know I've *never* seen it," Pete says.

The pleasures in having children are uncountable. The touch of a sticky, star-fish hand on your face. The walk to school where you merrily slag off half their classmates together. The mammalian joy in watching an ill child find comfort, and fall asleep, in your arms.

On top of this, if you're a lighthearted newspaper columnist charged with taking a wry, sideways glance at life until life knows the fuck it's been wryly glanced at sideways, they're always good for rinsing out a quick 850 words on a tight deadline. If anyone calls it child exploitation, you can point out that the Lego Death Star costs £274.99—and so therefore who, really, ultimately, is screwing whom over here?

I Refuse to Make You Goody Bags. Leave Before I Summon a Policeman.

I AM NOT A curmudgeon when it comes to my children's birthdays. Not at all. I *make* them a card, I *make* them a cake. Let's cut to the chase—I made *them*. I am a birthday originator. If it weren't for me, they'd just be cardless, cakeless, aimless sperm.

But while there is no end to the amount of delight I am prepared to shoehorn into my daughters' big days, I do draw the line at one thing: goody bags. I find goody bags unconscionable. I will not hand them out. I think they are the symbol of a decadent and corrupt regime. There is no logical reason why they ever have come into existence, or why we—as reasoning, sane people—should continue to support them.

In the sixteen, peaceful years my husband and I have had together, there are only two subjects on which we come to blows. The first is over his repeated, intolerable desire to own an oven mitt—MAN UP AND USE A FOLDED TOWEL. YOU DON'T NEED SOME MANNER OF

PAMPER MITTEN TO GET A TRAY OF OVEN CHIPS OUT, YOU
THUNDEROUS NANCY.

And the second is goody bags. Twice a year, it is the same argument.

Him: "Party tomorrow. Better get the goody bags ready."

Me, reasonably: "Pete, as those children leave, they will already HAVE a
goody bag. The bag is their own heads—and the gifts inside are the memo-
ries of a great day, spent violating a balloon animal man."

Him, not listening at all: "I don't want to put the same things in it this
year as I did last year. Last year I did mini Rubik's cubes. It's got to be
something different."

This desire for "unending bag surprise" has led my husband down some
unexpected goody-bag alleyways. Last year, he made every single kid at
Lizzie's ninth birthday a compilation CD of songs he thought they'd like.
We never got any feedback on the ninety minutes of the "more accessible"
works of Stackridge, Kraftwerk and psychedelic folk-jazz titans Pentangle—
possibly because kids these days have everything on MP3, instead. They
must have been intrigued by the odd rainbow coaster in their bag. Perhaps
they thought it was a pirate Blue-ray of *Avatar*.

Pete's problem is that he is essentially a good man, trying to make sense
of a bad system—but he should never have been pushed into the invidious
position of trying to get seven-year-old children into psyche-folk in the first
place. Why on *earth* would a child attending a party receive, essentially, a
gratuity? It's like we're tipping them on the way out the door.

Let me make this clear: I am not *thanking* them for coming. I've
just laid on three hours of food, amusement, and tolerance in the face of
Alfie taking over the handicapped bathroom at Pizza Express, and using
it as his own private office-cum-hangout, much in the manner of the
Fonz conducting his "business" from his favorite booth at Al's Diner. I
have also had to deal with Emily, who has explained her attitude to pizza
thus: "I don't have the pizzas with tomato sauce, or cheese, on. Not
those."

The message I have, to twenty-four departing children, is not, "Here
is your treasure bag. I am grateful for this special time with you." It is,

"You've had your fun—now sling your hook, sunshine, before I summon a police constable."

I don't believe in children's goody bags in the same way I don't believe in "The Gifting Room" at awards ceremonies. People rocking up at the Oscars don't need to be taken into a room full of high-end consumer durables and/or "pamperment experiences."

By the time you're walking down a red carpet, a kilo heavier from all the diamonds, all your life is basically one big gift. You know—Mariah Carey's had a great day. She's gotten out of the house, worn a nice frock, had a conversation with John Travolta she probably didn't understand, and now she's going home again. She doesn't need a Diamonique-covered Magimix and some spa vouchers to sweeten the deal.

And yet this pointless giving of gifts continues, unstopped. Parents are brought to the edge of despair by it. You see them, the day before a party, wandering around shops with that "goody-bag look" in their eye.

"I just need a collection of stuff that comes to no more than £2 per child," their posture is saying. "It honestly could be anything. I will put an apple, a box of tacks and a copy of the *Express* in there if I have to. I just need a quantity of stuff to weigh a child's hand down as it goes out of the door."

The honest, untrammelled reaction of a child, meanwhile, reminds you of the pointlessness of the whole thing.

"Oh," they say, looking inside the bag. "This eraser is all covered in frosting."

And then they throw the whole lot in the garbage can.

More parenting fury—this time, over the monolithic merchandising cash cow that is Charlie and Lola. *At the time I wrote this, it didn't seem appropriate to mention in* The Times *that I've "got my eye" on husky-voiced, awkward Marv—Charlie's best friend—and would totally Mrs. Robinson him when he reaches the age of majority; some four years hence from his age in the books. Somehow, though, it seems okay to say it here. The italics oddly make it okay.*

I Hate *Charlie and Lola*

IN THE EARLY DAYS of parenthood you aren't, of course, so picky. In those first, panicking years, anything that entertains and diverts your children for ten minutes—allowing you such fripperies as falling asleep face down on the landing, or the time to slough crusts of spit-up from your unflattering parenthood pantaloons—is gratefully embraced. You would put on a DVD of any old toot for five minutes' respite from a 3 PM toddler, who is freaking out, *Gremlins* style, about contact with sunlight. It's hard to explain to a non-parent how very low your standards—and, indeed, morals—become. Once, on one of the very worst days—when no TV show seemed to please them—I remember thinking, "Hitler apparently had a mesmeric oratory style. Audiences would listen, silent and rapt. I wonder if I could order something from Play.com."

But they get older, it gets easier, and you can, finally, afford the luxury of quality control. You can begin to cast a critical eye over just what it is your children are staring at, saucer-eyed, and evaluate it in the same way you used to evaluate your own collection of music, DVDs and books.

And when I started to do this with my children's very favorite program—one of the most famous and successful of the last ten years—I had a creeping realization: I hate Lola from *Charlie and Lola*.

There. I've said it.

For those who've never watched the program, the setup is this: Charlie and Lola are two middle-class, bohemian children who live in a world of eclectic Scandinavian textiles and irregularly-drawn eyes. Where their parents are, no one knows—judging by their house, mum is probably appearing on *Newsnight Review* wearing spendy shoes and analyzing *Peep Show*, while dad drops some rare Twinkletronica and Humbient grooves at an online nu-rave club, via Skype.

In their absence, bright, chatty, intolerable four-year-old Lola is being raised by her older, put upon, tousle-haired brother, Charlie. Charlie has a lot endure. "I am a fussy eater!" Lola declares, cheerfully—necessitating Charlie to spend a whole show renaming carrots "orange twiglets from Jupiter," until his sister finally gets her tea down her. He has to rename mashed potatoes "cloud-fluff from the pointiest peak of Mount Fuji," because Lola is a child who won't eat mashed potatoes. A child who won't eat MASHED POTATOES! Honestly, I have more tolerance for the Ku Klux Klan.

"I honestly, totally and completely can look after your dog!" Lola promises Charlie's friend, Marv—immediately losing the dog, and probably getting Marv beaten that night.

"I am too absolutely small for school," Lola says—crocodilian eyes calculating exactly how long she can play Charlie for a rube, wringing bribes and concessions out of him, before she finally knuckles down and goes through the school gates LIKE SHE KNOWS SHE HAS TO.

Charlie's age is never specified, but he looks around eleven—on the cusp of puberty. That he has to spend his days humoring a girl who opens all his birthday cards, breaks his rocket, and thinks she's Mariah Carey at her most mad ("All the world should have rainbows and ice creams!") must, surely, be a ballache of titanic proportions. His parents have created a lisping, eating-disordered monster—and then left him to deal with it while they take their Pashleys to La Fromagerie, to choose between their two favorite ash-rolled goat's cheeses for supper. Guys! Just get some Kraft slices and bail this kid out! Bail *us* out.

For the real basis of my hatred of Lola comes from her terrifying power as a role model to my daughters. She has raised intolerable expectations of what a twenty-first century child's bedtime might reasonably consist of—demanding tigers drinking pink milk, lions to put the toothpaste on her toothbrush, and three whales in her bath before she'll even deign to put on her pajamas. This is, obviously, roughly equivalent to pressing a button labelled "Drive all parents mad NOW." It's certainly not how I was raised. My bedtime ritual consisted of my mother pointing upstairs, and shouting, "GO THERE." That was very much a ritual I intended to pass on to my own children, until this . . . termagant came along.

What will become of Charlie and Lola in adulthood? Although it's theoretically too early to call it, Charlie's clearly going to be a total hotty by the time he hits sixteen. Given his appearance and upbringing, he'll end up forming an awkward, middle-class, Radiohead-type band, tour for a couple of years, then get a gig composing the incidental music for *Skins*. His early experience with a capricious younger sister will make him prime husband material, and his high-achieving wife will happily indulge his twice-yearly snowboarding sessions, and on/off weed habit.

Lola, on the other hand, will be one of the high-profile auditionees on *The X Factor* who tanks out spectacularly at Bootcamp, wailing "PLEEEASE, Simon—I absolutely completely and totally know I can do this!"

Yes. In thirteen years, Lola will be Zooey Deschanel's evil twin.

Still, I'm aware that being a father is just as hard as being a mother. Especially when your kids start talking.

The Horror of
Daddy's Special Lemonade

I WAS SITTING AT the kitchen table last week, flicking through the newspapers, and observing just how many confusing and/or alarming things I could absorb before breakfast. Here was the news that David Cameron is apparently taking "anti-posh" lessons—surely an ill-advised move in the middle of an election campaign, given that, were it successful, the Conservative Party would be left with little more than a pair of trousers, and a name-tag reading "Dave."

On the next page, another mention of how the Mayans believed the world would end in 2012—a theory which is now beginning to rattle me quite badly. What, I panic, in the name of *Moses*, is going to go down at the London Olympics? How badly wrong can an opening ceremony featuring Paul McCartney, David Beckham and Stomp go? The only thing that could possibly make the End of Days worse is knowing that its epicenter was in Stratford, and that all the disruption of building the East London Line had been a complete waste of time, after all.

But then I turned the page and saw a picture of convicted pedophile Sidney Cooke, and felt suddenly and enormously reassured.

Now he really *does* look like a pedophile, I thought to myself happily. No doubt about that. He's a *classic* beast. He looks like he's from some putative Deviant Central Casting Agency. If I saw him in a playground, I thought, there would be no doubt or uncertainty. I would be evacuating the swings immediately. So long as there are pedophiles who look as obviously up to no good as Cooke, there is less confusion and worry in the world. He has that certain, unmistakable, alarming "something" that sets the nerves jangling. Thank God for Cooke.

I turned the page in the newspaper, finally feeling more relaxed about the world.

But of course, that certain, alarming "something" is not just restricted to things that actually warrant alarm. Sometimes, we are alarmed by things that shouldn't really be alarming at all.

I was given cause to reflect on this the next day, when we had some friends over. Lizzie greeted them in the hallway.

"I've been helping Daddy make his Special Lemonade!" she said, brightly. My husband does, indeed, make very good lemonade. As lemonades go, it really is quite special. But as I caught the momentary quizzical looks of my friends, I realized that the phrase "Daddy's Special Lemonade" has a certain . . . dubious quality to it.

"I love Daddy's Special Lemonade!" Lizzie continued, cheerfully, as we all went into the kitchen. The situation started to feel bad.

"It's got limes in it," I said, briskly. My husband, however, had already noticed the glances.

"Oh, I wish I'd never called it that." He sighed, pouring lemonade out into glasses. "Daddy's Special Lemonade was a bad idea. It's like that tickle thing, all over again."

The "tickle thing" was an unfortunate incident a couple of years ago, when we had to leave a playground after a very young Lizzie shouted, "Daddy! Tickle me in my special place!"

As it happens, her "special place" was a particularly ticklish spot under her chin—but the looks on the other parents in the playground suggested they did not believe this to be the case. We actually never went back to that playground again—which was a shame, as there was particularly good mobile reception there, and I used to read all my emails while she was on the slide.

It is a sad fact that, over the last few years, both "special" and "Daddy" have taken on a slight tinge of . . . unsavoriness. Menace. Perhaps it's the racks of misery memoirs that have them in the title—*Please Daddy, No*; *What Daddy Did*; *Daddy's Special Girl*—but two ostensibly benign words are becoming loaded with unhappy inference. To the point that, when I see a greeting card with "To a Special Daddy" on the front, I can barely repress a shudder. A Special Daddy? A Special Daddy must be the very worst. That's some seriously gnarly ominousness. What manner of monster is Hallmark catering to?

As things stand, at this point in the twenty-first century, we're on the verge of losing our innocence toward words "daddy" and "special." I feel like homophobic bigots must have felt in the 1970s, as they watched the word "gay" slip from their vocabulary.

Lexical tectonic plates are shifting. Special Branch, the Special Olympics, the Specials, Special K—all will have to be renamed, as the word shifts from "something unique and significant" to "a terrible traumatic secret, such as would be a major plotline development in *General Hospital*." As a consequence, the words "specialization" and "specialist" will sound little better than an outright admission of having studied evil at the PhD level.

As for Daddy's Special Lemonade—we've told Lizzie to refer to it as Lime Surprise from now on. As a matter of some urgency.

"Mummy's Special Lemonade," on the other hand, is a much different beast. It's a gin and tonic with a massive wedge of lemon.

In Defense of Binge Drinking

ACCORDING TO A BBC *Newsround* report last week, 70 percent of children have seen their parents drunk—and, of these, 46 percent don't think their parents should ever drink in front of them.

Before we go any further, let's just tackle the obvious yet necessary points: if we're talking about parents who go completely woo-hoo/Bill Sykes on the sauce; or who are only getting through half the school drop-off before sitting down in the middle of the road, puncturing a Gaz canister with their keys and sucking out the contents with a "special" straw, then guys, you need help. I am not interested in "partying" with you. If you come round my house with a bottle of peach Schnapps, I will hide in the coat closet, while phoning in a perfect description of you to Social Services. You are not my good-time bredren. Consider yourself eschewed and betrayed by me.

Everyone else, however, is welcome to join with me in faintly piqued incredulity at the children of today. WHAT MORE do they WANT from us? Don't they KNOW how this system WORKS? Mummies and daddies have to drink lots of wine down in one go on Friday night—because the schedule doesn't *allow* it the rest of the week. It's called TIME MANAGEMENT. If I don't drink a whole bottle of wine on Party Night, I probably wouldn't get time to drink at *all*—and that, obviously, would be ridiculous. Parents drinking is the reason you came into the world, and if we didn't keep doing it, then by God, it would be the reason you went back out of it.

This is one of those many occasions where adult reason must overrule the ill-thought-out utterances of the young and stupid. You don't want us to drink in front of you? Where, pray, are we *supposed* to drink? Obviously we'd *like* to go to the pub—we'd *like* to go to Harry's Bar in Venice, in 1951—but we can't, because we're *looking after you*. And, I might add, looking after you in the best possible way: has mummy ever been more entertaining than when she stood on the patio table, opening and closing the big parasol, and singing "You Know I'm No Good" by Amy Winehouse? Or when she had a little "wine nap" at the bottom of the garden, and Uncle Eddie and Uncle Jimmy wrote "BALLS" on her forehead in magic marker, and you got to color in her nose and ears blue? If CLOWNS were doing this in a CIRCUS you'd think it was hilarious. And, let's face it, it's the only time mummy can be half-way bothered to play Super Mario Kart with you.

But by the skewiff logic of the younglings, my father had a better attitude to drinking—in that we never actually *saw* him drink. Instead, we'd be left outside the Red Lion in a Datsun, engine running so that Radio One could entertain us. As we howled along to "Take On Me" by A-ha, Dad would occasionally reel out of the saloon bar door, push a packet of potato chips through the crack in the window—saying, "Remember you're a Womble" (for a detailed explanation of what a Womble is, please see my first book, *How to Be a Woman*, page 179)—before going back into the pub again.

Three hours later, he'd suddenly come bombing out holding something incongrous like a fish tank, hissing, "It's all gone a bit *serious* in there," and pulling away from the curb at 60mph. Then he'd pass out on the hall floor, and we'd rinse his pockets for spare change.

Was he ultimately the better parent? The fact that I once watched him throw two liters of petrol onto a bonfire—"Because *The Two Ronnies* is on in ten minutes"— thus setting fire to our garden fence, means that I can answer this, frankly, "No."

But we are, at least, of accord on the issue of parental drunkenness. Look, man. I don't do fox hunting, diamond collecting, spa weekends, or that much nitrous oxide anymore. My leisure time has to operate within the boundaries of being conducted a) within forty feet of my children; b) between the hours of 6 PM and 1 AM, Fridays only; and c) costing no more than £30. Therefore, I like to get a very, very cheap bottle of supermarket whisky—the kind that, when you drink it, turns you into a pirate: closing one eye and shouting "ARGH!"—sit down with a couple of chatty people, and get a bit toasted.

If you're of joyous mind, that kind of drinking is like a long weekend—as exhilarating an experience as spending three days sightseeing in Rome, or walking Scafell Pike. You'll have imperially wiggy conversations, solve the world's problems three times over, spontaneously remember all the lyrics to "I Don't Know How To Love Him" from *Jesus Christ Superstar*, and wake up in the morning feeling oddly cleansed, and cheerful.

And if the kids don't like it? Darlings, you talk this much nonsense, and fall down the stairs that dramatically, *every day of the week*. You haven't got a leg to stand on.

Want some more about my childhood? Here's the bit where I was in a camper in Aberystwyth, listening to Nightowl *by Gerry Rafferty and semi-convinced that, when I grew up, I'd marry Joey Boswell from* Bread. *I always enjoy writing about my childhood. It requires absolutely no research and always seems pleasingly improbable—like something I dreamed of when I fell asleep in a wardrobe, looking for Narnia.*

Aberystwyth:
The Only Place I Stop Wanting

WE FIRST WENT TO Aberystwyth when I was thirteen, at the height of my parents' hippydom. We had no TV, we lived on huge pans of lentil soup, and I ran barefoot across fields so long, the skin on my soles was like cork tiles.

We were spending our summers in a camper with no toilet in a field outside Pontrhydifendigaid, near Tregaron: eight kids, two parents, and three huge dogs. In my memory, when you walked towards the camper, the faces and legs of all the humans and animals were pressed up against the glass of the window, like a terrine. That camper was very full. When my parents had sex, the van would rock like a fairground ride, and all the kids would sit in the front room, quietly singing "California Girls" by the Beach Boys—to block out the sounds—until it was over. Our harmonies were terrible. We were not the Wilsons.

We had a Volkswagen campervan—the greatest vehicles ever created; a cheery cupboard on wheels—and when my parents had finished noisily co-joining, they would take us on post-coital journeys all across West Wales: up to Port Madoc, down to St. David's—right round the yawning pig-jaw of Cardigan Bay. Wide white estuaries, book-stack fishing villages, and bleak, wet-slate hamlets where it always lashed rain against the single, solitary phone-box.

I don't know why it took us four months to finally go to the nearest, biggest town—Aberystwyth—but when it did, some inner room in my heart twanged; some lever was pulled. It wasn't like falling in love—I was thirteen, and had never been in love. I just felt—not unhappy anymore. The quiet litany of pubescent frets that I counted, daily, like rosary beads—I was fat, I was lonely, I knew too much about my parents' sex life, I didn't have any shoes, and I wanted, more than anything, to be the best friend of the Duchess of York—all stilled the first time our van drove down Darkgate Street, and turned left onto the seafront.

There was something so perfect about Aber that it halted my lifelong internal monologue. I needed silence, to fully take the place in. It had a Gothic university like a castle, castle ruins like a smashed cake, a cliff-top Victorian theme park that appeared to have been commissioned by a drunk H. G. Wells (a funicular railway! A camera obscura! A golf course using GIANT golf-balls!) and then—slicing the town in half like a fabulous blindness—the cold, hard, glitter glue of the sea. Apparently, dolphins chased by the rock pools, at dawn.

Face pressed against the window, wetting it with breath, I wanted to concentrate on this town. And then eat it, whole, like a potato chip sandwich, but even better. For the first time ever, my heart stopped wanting.

"This place is shitting brilliant!" I chirped, from the back of the van.

"Don't swear in front of the fucking kids," my dad replied.

TWENTY-THREE YEARS LATER, and I'm back with my husband, and my kids, to the only place still that makes me happy and quiet. I came here with Pete when we were first in love, then again with each baby; and now we come every year, at the end of August: migratory creatures that can be followed on a map. We take the same apartment on the seafront, go to the same restaurants, do the same things, have the same days. I think even the conversations are the same: "No beach has better pebbles!" "No castle has better views!" "No freak shops have a better array of skull-shaped bongs, dude!"

The first day is Arrival—falling from the car on a journey that is always an hour longer than you remember, dehydrated and shrunken-legged. Aber's magic is that—ninety miles from the nearest motorway—it is near to, and on the way to, nothing, except the dolphins in the Bay. You only come to Aber if you're going to stay in Aber—a night, at least; a week, usually; the rest of your life, if you're one of the hippies who first pitched up here in the 1960s, or one of the 8,000 students a year who come here for their degrees, then just . . . don't leave.

We throw everything into the apartment, then walk along the seafront— the sea! The sea! Sailor blue! Or else, with bad weather, as hard, thrilling and unstoppable as a sword—to The Olive Branch, on the corner Pier Street. It's a comfortable, higgledy, pine-and-spiderplants joint and, if we're lucky, the window table will be free. We'll eat good Greek food—my husband is Greek, so he's picky about these things—while staring across the Bay to the distant shadows of Anglesey and Snowdonia. Because it's the first day of vacation, I will have had at least two glasses of wine by the time we finish, and go down to the beach for the first time: Pete and I leaning against each other as the kids fall into the waves for the first, and then the second time; wringing out their shorts, and spreading them on the beach to dry.

It's a fine, pebble-and-shale beach—crunchy, not clacking—and the currents bring a junk shop variety to the stones on the tide line. Quartz, slate, igneous Ordovician, meta-limestone from the Lleyn, cider-bottle glass smoothed to emerald—we fill our pockets with the most interesting ones; the ones shaped like letters, or animals or, once, a Volkswagen caravanette, just like the one we used to have.

You can crab, happily, for hours, off the boardwalk, legs hanging into the sea. In summer, the boardwalk is filled with coachloads of Orthodox Jews—hats and curls buffeted by the sea breeze. It seems right that they'd come here—Barmouth is too normal, Tenby too twee. Aber feels as practical and time-suspended as they are. It's far too windy for urban spores of anti-Semitism to take a hold here.

The sea turns silky, and electric-green, as the sun goes down—tide rising by the minute, and sucking at your knees until you leave the bay and walk home. Safe, from the apartment window, the bay explodes into sunset—fire, fire, pink nuclear fury, and then the utter insanity of Welsh starlight, mirrored in the trawler lights, heading for Ireland.

The next day is a proper beach day, and we head sixteen miles up the coast, to Ynyslas. There's a picnic in the trunk from Ultracomida, on Pier Street—a jewel-like Spanish restaurant/deli with breads, cheeses, olive oils and pastries—and the drive takes you high enough to see the lionback Cambrian mountains, chasing you all the way to the end of Dyfed. Ynylas is National Nature Reserve consisting of nothing but sky, sand pools and dunes: over a morning, you follow the tide out, over endless, new, creature-filled sandpools, until you reach a newly-revealed sandbar, miles out to sea.

The afternoon is then spent in slow, contemplative retreat back to the mainland as the tide comes back in—racing across the sand, throwing up instantly-doomed sand-castles, and writing our names—"MUMMY" "DADDY" "LIZZIE" "NANCY"—in meter-high letters on the beach, in the way that, two decades ago, my siblings wrote their names—"CAIT" "CAZ" "EDDIE" "WEENA" "PRINNIE" "GEZMO" "JIMMY" "JOFISH"—in the same, not-same sand.

The third day will rain   Cluedo—and the fourth rain, probably, too: the Ceredigion Museum, on Terrace Road, is Aberystwyth's old theatre, now filled with curious agricultural tools, archeological finds, stuffed animals, maritime oddities and a dinky café, all in a Womble-ish jumble. Then Wasabi—Aberystwyth's sushi restaurant, on Eastgate—before home, and the concluding round of Cluedo.

Day five is probably my favorite: full immersion in Aber. A half-hour walk takes you to the top of Constitution Hill, and Luna Park—the benevolently ghosty Victorian amusements on top of Aber's outcast cliff. A candled, rickety shrine to the Virgin Mary, halfway up the path, is the point where you stop to eat crisps. At the top, it's tea and Welsh cakes. Then the Funicular Railway down lands you in the center of town again, and lunch at the Treehouse—another of Aber's jumbled, pitch-pine joints, this time selling soul-cheering local wholefood and chili hot chocolate.

You can spend hours here, on a rainy day, as the windows mist up, the smell of fenugreek and jasmine tea and goat cheese making the room pleasingly dreamy as you do the crossword, or stare out of the window at the million grays of wet, Welsh slate rooftops. And then, when the weather breaks, the Castle: a green hill overlooking the sea, with the rib bones of a fourteenth-century castle poking through. The view is the very best, the one I bone-ache for in London: Cardigan Bay from end to end; the full length of Wales visible in one, long sweep. The first time I saw it—thirteen, standing here in a wet, crocheted poncho, holding my squalling two-year-old brother—I felt insane, wild jealousy towards Prince Charles.

"I can't believe he's the Prince of all this!" I shouted, into the wind. "I would KILL for this!"

And then I remembered that, of course, in a roundabout way, he had.

But there's a quiet, stubborn, time-biding, self-contained Welshness to Aberystwyth that makes the idea of being "ruled" over laughable. This place simply disbelieves it belongs to anyone but itself. In the playground, in the dip next to the Castle—sheltered, and lavish with white clouds of hydrangea—the slate gravestones from a demolished church have been laid, like purple flagstones, around the perimeter. So many are in Welsh—the stories of farmers and captains and politicians and priests who would have no idea of England's existence as they lived, and died, here: traveling no further than the mountains behind us, and the sea in front.

As the wind blows across again, and the grass sings lysergic, rain-drowned green, and the bay looks like a billion smashed fish scales, stretching all the way forever, who could ever imagine England, east of here: flat, dusty, half-colored, quiet and so, so distant?

In the car, home, I cry, like every time since 1988.

As me and all my siblings were taught at home, the local library was the extra room of our home: it was our schoolhouse and our playground. Oh, it was a million more things besides—not least an easily-accessible toilet if you were caught short on Warstones Drive—and so when the Coalition started closing libraries—shooting out their lights and leaving the buildings to rot—I wrote this piece, which got the biggest response of any piece I've ever written for The Times. *It ended up being included in a very worthwhile anthology about libraries,* The Library Book, *whose proceeds went to a pro-library charity.*

Libraries: Cathedrals of Our Souls

HOME EDUCATED AND, BY SEVENTEEN, writing for a living, the only alma mater I have ever had is Warstones Library, Pinfold Grove, Wolverhampton.

A low, red-brick box on grass that verged on wasteland, I would be there twice a day—rocking up with all the ardor of a clubber turning up to a rave. I read every book in there—not *really*, of course, but as good as: when I'd read all the funny books, I moved on to the sexy ones, then the dreamy ones, the mad ones; the ones that described distant mountains, idiots, plagues, experiments. I sat at the big table and read all the papers: in public housing in Wolverhampton, the broadsheets are as incongruous and illuminating as an Eames lamp.

The shelves were supposed to be loaded with books—but they were, of course, really doors: each book-lid opened as exciting as Alice putting her gold key in the lock. I spent days running in and out of other worlds like a time bandit, or a spy. I was as excited as I've ever been in my life, in that library: scoring new books the minute they came in; ordering books I'd heard of—then waiting, fevered, for them to arrive, like they were the word

Christmas. I had to wait nearly a year for *Les Fleurs du Mal* by Baudelaire to come: even so, I was still too young to think it anything but a bit wanky, and abandoned it twenty pages in for Jilly Cooper. But *Fleurs du Mal,* man! In a building overlooked by a Kwiksave where the fags and alcohol were kept in a locked, metal cage, lest they be stolen! Simply knowing I could have it in my hand was a comfort, in this place so very very far from anything extraordinary or exultant.

Everything I am is based on this ugly building on its lonely lawn—lit up during winter darkness; open in the slashing rain—which allowed a girl so poor she didn't even own a purse to come in twice a day and experience actual magic: traveling through time, making contact with the dead—Dorothy Parker, Stella Gibbons, Charlotte Brontë, Spike Milligan.

A library in the middle of a community is a cross between an emergency exit, a life raft and a festival. They are cathedrals of the mind; hospitals of the soul; theme parks of the imagination. On a cold, rainy island, they are the only sheltered public spaces where you are not a consumer, but a citizen, instead. A human with a brain and a heart and a desire to be uplifted, rather than a customer with a credit card and an inchoate "need" for "stuff." A mall—the shops—are places where your money makes the wealthy wealthier. But a library is where the wealthy's taxes pay for you to become a little more extraordinary, instead. A satisfying reversal. A balancing of the power.

Last month, after protest, an injunction was granted to postpone library closures in Somerset. In September, both Somerset and Gloucestershire councils will be the subject of a full judicial review over their closure plans. As the cuts kick in, protesters and lawyers are fighting for individual libraries like villagers pushing stranded whales back into the sea. A library is such a potent symbol of a town's values: each one closed down might as well be six thousand stickers plastered over every available surface, reading "WE CHOSE TO BECOME MORE STUPID AND DULL."

While I have read a million words on the necessity for the cuts, I have not seen a single letter on what the exit plan is: what happens in four years' time, when the cuts will have succeeded, and the economy gets back to "normal" again. Do we then—prosperous once more—go round and re-open all these centers, clinics and libraries, which have sat, dark and unused, for nearly half a decade? It's hard to see how—it costs millions of pounds to re-open deserted buildings, and cash-strapped councils will have looked at billions of square feet of prime real estate with a coldly realistic eye. Unless the government *has* developed an exit strategy for the cuts, and insisted councils not sell closed properties, by the time we get back to "normal" again, our Victorian and post-war and 1960s red-brick boxy libraries will be coffee shops and pubs. No new libraries will be built to replace them. These libraries will be lost forever.

And, in their place, we will have thousands more public spaces where you are simply the money in your pocket, rather than the hunger in your heart. Kids—poor kids—will never know the fabulous, benign quirk of self-esteem of walking into "their" library and thinking, "I have read 60 percent of the books in here. I am awesome." Libraries that stayed open during the Blitz will be closed by budgets.

A trillion small doors closing.

Shall we do another righteous column? While I've got my serious face on? These are the ones I think of when people go, "Oh, I read your stuff! You're not bad! I think my dad likes you!" and I'm all like "Yeah, I'm changing your life with my Marxist/feminist dialectic! Check out my rad moves!"

Then it turns out, further into the conversation, they were just thinking of the funny one where I try to get Pete to call me "Puffin," instead.

Unlike Most of the Coalition, I Was Raised on Benefits

UNLIKE MOST OF THE people voting on the proposed £18b cuts to the benefits budget—as it shuttles between the Commons and the Lords—I was raised on benefits. Disability benefits—collected every Tuesday from the Post Office, in a shuffling queue of limpers, coughers, and people with their coat hoods pulled right up.

Perhaps if you drove past the queue, you would presume the ones hiding their faces were doing it because they were on the fiddle—"playing the books." In reality, they were the scared kids with mental problems on Incapacity Benefit, who you'd see trying three times, and ultimately failing, to get on a bus. Good luck with getting them on a Re-Start scheme, you would think. Good luck with trying to funnel that terror into a cardboard hat in McDonald's.

Public housing on benefits isn't what you think—if you must imagine it, rather than remember, or just look out of the window. Popular imagination has it that it's full of obese, track-suit–wearing peasants smoking Rothmans on the front doorstep, rehearsing for their spot on *Jerry Springer* while spending their fraudulent benefits on a plasma TV.

Benefits spent on plasma TVs is the totemic fury-provoker of the professionally angry social commentator—"They're spending YOUR taxes on A FORTY-TWO INCH SONY!!! You couldn't MAKE IT UP!"— ignoring the fact that if you live somewhere with broken-glass parks and looming teen-clusters on each street corner, and gave up on the idea of having a car or a vacation long, long ago, then staying at home, safe, together as a family, and watching fifteen hours of TV a day is a peerlessly cost-effective, gentle and harmless way of trying to buy happiness.

Besides, they almost certainly won't have spent "your" taxes on it. They'll have incurred a massive overdraft, like everyone else in the Western World. They'll have gotten your telly the way you got your telly. People on benefits are just people—on benefits. Some of them are dodgy, most of them are doing their best, and a few need more help than we could ever imagine. The mix is about the same as on your street. If you are having to imagine it—rather than remember it, or look out of the window.

What's it like, being on benefits? Being on Disability Benefits—"I've had a hard day's limping, to put that tea on the table!" my dad would say, as we sat down to eat something based around a lot of potatoes, and ketchup. Well, mainly, you're scared. You're scared that the benefits will be frozen, or cut, or done away with completely. I don't remember an age where I wasn't scared our benefits would be taken away. It was an anxiety that felt like a physical presence, in my chest—a small, black, eyeless insect that hung off my ribs. Every Tory budget that announced a freezing of benefits—new means-testing, new grading—made the insect drill its face into the bone. They froze benefits for four years in a row, as I recall: "freezing" being the news's way of telling you that you—already poor—will be at the checkout, apologizing as you take jam and squash out of your bag, put them back on the shelves, and ask them to add it up again. Every week you fear that this is the week the pennies won't stretch any further, and something will disappear: gas, food. Your home.

Eventually—and presumably to the endless gratification of Richard Littlejohn, a right-wing columnist whose love of assailing the disadvantaged in print runs through women, prostitutes, the poor, homosexuals, lesbians and immigrants, and will presumably, one day, continue on to mete out a thorough chiding to the ill, suicidal, and dead—they did take the telly away; halfway through *Twin Peaks*. All the kids cried and cried and cried. There wasn't really anything left to do. I invented a game where you lay on the bed staring at the telegraph lines outside the house for so long, without blinking, that you would start crying. The house was very cold. Dad spent whole days in bed—huge white plastic jar of painkillers on the floor beside him, looking like a ghostly barrel.

All through history, those who can't earn money have had to rely on mercy: fearful, changeable mercy that can dissolve overnight if circumstances change, or opinions alter. Parish handouts, workhouses, almshouses—*ad hoc*, make-shift solutions that make the helpless constantly re-audition in front of their benefactors, exhaustingly trying to reinvoke pity for a lifetime of bread and cheese.

That's why the invention of the Welfare State is one of the most glorious events in history: the moral equivalency of the Moon Landings. Something not fearful or changeable, like mercy, but certain and constant—a right. Correct and efficient: disability benefit fraud is just 0.5 per cent. A system that allows dignity and certainty to lives otherwise chaotic with poverty and illness.

Certainty, that is, until you cut the budget so savagely, some benefits disappear all together. Then, you bring back all the fear of the alms house, and the parish dole. Then, you cut this country back to Victorian times.

I remember it, from my childhood. I can feel the dreary terror from here.

One more.

I Know What It's Like to Be Poor.
They Took Away the TV, and We Cried.

WE'VE RECENTLY HEARD A lot about the gulf between the rich and the poor—the difference between those with money, and those without.

Well, I've been poor, and I've been rich. When I was poor, I knew I was poor because we lived on benefits, slept on mattresses on the floor, and would share a Mars Bar between ten for dessert.

Now I'm rich, I know I'm rich because I've got underfloor heating, and could afford to eat out at Pizza Express up to three times a week, if I so chose. I'm basically living the life of a billionaire. I am loaded.

So, having been a rich person and a poor person, what I notice is how similar they both are, really. There's not that much difference at all. Everyone cheerfully plays the system they find themselves in.

In Wolverhampton, when you needed dodgy inspection papers for the car, an uncle's mate would be given a tenner "for a pint," and an exhaust pipe would magically appear out of somewhere—to the ultimate financial detriment of the garage it had been lifted from, but hey-ho.

Now I'm in London, friends of friends recommend good accountants who will "sort out" your VAT problem for a pint-equivalent fee—to the ultimate economic detriment of the country, but hey-ho.

We're all just monkeys using sticks to get grubs out of logs, really. However. There is one, massive difference between being rich and being poor, and it is this: when you are poor, you feel heavy. Heavy like your limbs are filled with water. Perhaps it is rain water—there is a lot more rain in your life, when you are poor. Rain that can't be escaped in a cab. Rain that has to be stood in, until the bus comes. Rain that gets into cheap shoes and coats, and through old windows—often followed by cold, and then mildew. A little bit damp, a little bit dirty, a little bit cold—you are never at your best, or ready to shine. You always need something to pep you up: sugar, a cigarette, a new fast song on the radio.

But the heaviness is not really, of course, from the rain. The heaviness comes from the sclerosis of being broke. Because when you're poor, nothing ever changes. Every idea you have for moving things on is quashed through there never being any money. You dream of a house with sky-blue walls; wearing a coat with red buttons; going out on Saturday and walking by a river. Instead, you see the same crack in the same wall, push-start the same car down the same hill, and nothing ever changes, except for the worse: the things you originally had are now slowly wearing out—breaking under your fingertips, and left unreplaced.

This has the effect of making your limbs feel heavy; like you're perpetually slightly drowning. You're dragging ten years of non-progress behind you like a wheel-less cart. Perhaps there's something out there you would be superlatively good at—something that would give you so much joy, you feel like you are flying. But you'll never find out: the world is a shop and it is closed to your empty pockets, and you are standing still, heavy, in the dead center of your life. You look around, and start to suspect you might not exist. After all, you appear not to be able to make an impression on the world—you can't even change the color of your front door. Twenty-six years, now; forty-two, and you've never even been to your neighboring town—it's too far away. And so you sit. You sit still. Because your limbs are so heavy. They are full of rain.

If you've never been poor, I don't think you could imagine what it's like—simply because of the timescale. You could envision a day, maybe, or a year—but not a lifetime. Not generations of it, passed down like drizzle, or a blindness. Not how, if kids from a poor background achieve something, it's while dragging this weight behind them. How it takes ten times the effort to get anywhere from a bad postcode.

My children can't imagine it. They love to play at their Sylvanian Family rabbits being "poor": they love the ingenuity of a sofa turning into a bed for five rabbits; of having only one thing wear.

"It's all cosy," they say. "It's all—little."

I can see how if you were—say—a Coalition government consisting of public school kids and millionaires, you could convince yourself that the poor are snug in their motor homes. That all they need to bridge the "gulf" between them and the rich is for things to be less cosy. That making *their* life harder—withdrawing benefits and council housing—incentivizes them in a way making life harder for the wealthy—imposing higher tax-rates— would apparently *disincentivize* them.

But the last thing—the very last thing—anyone poor needs is for things to be harder. These limbs are full to bursting.

There's something to be said for the more misty aspects of human behavior. People operating on less coherent, yet still surging, instincts. People just . . . gathering.

The Occupy London movement set up camp outside St. Paul's Cathedral in September 2011, and stayed until they were finally moved on in March 2012. Many commentators derided their well-meaning incoherence. I loved it.

I Love a Protestor. You Don't Need Answers—Just Questions.

I LOVE A PROTESTOR. We all protest, of course—getting out of bed with "My back!", shouting at the television: "You ASS!", reading the headlines with furious exclamations of "We did WHAT?"

But that's just a sentence or two—a minute of remonstration, and then back to wiping down the counter, stacking papers and talking about the profound oddness of the people next door. We protest for the benefit of our own blood pressure, then forget again.

But a protestor—a proper protestor; someone out there, protesting—I find to be a beautiful thing. An objection made flesh, a whole body made over to do one thing—voice disapproval, simply by standing somewhere.

In a world where a minute's remote dabbing at your computer can transfer thousands of pounds, order a car to your door or petition against a death sentence, there's something so simple, elegant and forceful about putting your shoes on, walking out of the front door, and going somewhere where you body is a vote, instead.

There's a group of Chinese Falun Gong protestors who've taken it in turns to man a small table, covered in leaflets, outside the Chinese Embassy on Portland Place, since 2003. Every time I walk past them I think of how there are no elections in China at all: this is the only vote they have; standing in the rain, trying to protect the bright yellow tablecloth with a spoke-spined umbrella, for eight years. Just standing.

If I'd had two gins and felt a bit whirly, I'd claim occupation-protesting lay on the borderline between politics and art—that by placing yourself, say, outside a cathedral, you mean, and become, something wholly different to when you are placed in a supermarket, buying vegetables. You put yourself somewhere you shouldn't be. You are the odd thing out. A misplaced item in the bagging area. And this is how you want to change the world: just by being a misplaced particle. Difficult to tidy away.

And, so, to the protestors outside St. Paul's Cathedral, objecting to the global banking crisis. Their presence has caused so much commentary—and from so many different viewpoints—that it is clear they have stopped being merely a news item—a fact to be told—and have crossed over into being an infinitely malleable metaphor for whatever the commentator wishes to project on them, instead. Toby Young in *The Telegraph* saw them as "preening narcissists," only protesting because they "want to be on the news—that's all they care about." Richard Littlejohn, meanwhile, saw them as "a gormless rent-a-mob . . . layabouts from Mickey Mouse universities." I could spend hours suggesting why it might be that those particular people chose those particular epithets. Actually, I couldn't—it would take less than a minute and consist of shouting, "POT! POT! POT!" over and over again, until my Kettle Black Timer went off.

Anyway. Nearly all those who protested against the protestors commented on two things: how unwashed and scruffy they are, and how the protestors have merely "vague slogans," and have failed to say what their solution to the banking crisis would be.

To the first comment, one can only reply, "But dudes—they are in tents. It would be alarming and disconcerting if people sleeping on roll-mats in Central London emerged from their bivvies at breakfast, box-fresh, and sporting a crease down each leg of their slacks. Your insistence that the revolution be 'smart-casual' suggests a lack of any pictorial reference points to previous revolutions. They tend to be fairly 'festival chic.'"

With the second caveat, I would be a little more disappointed that it had ever been voiced in the first place. Is this now the entry qualification for voter-protest—that we must have all the answers, before we are allowed to speak? That when it comes to a global banking crisis so severe and complex that the combined powers of the European Union cannot come up with a solution—other than going "Text China! They're LOADED!"—voters can't comment on it unless we've got a massive folder full of equations with "SOLVED! The Banking Crisis" written on the front?

If we insist protestors must shut up unless they have answers, we are confusing them with columnists, academics, advisors, politicians. And, at root, protestors exist for a wholly different reason to these people. It misses the point of why people put on their shoes, leave their houses, and stand in the wrong place for a long, long time. Protestors don't have the answers. They would never pretend that they are. What they are is a question mark. St. Paul's currently stands over a square full of question marks—each tent a black punctuation mark in the middle of the City. A huge black question mark we now see every night on the news, and in the papers.

And the question being asked, over and over again, "What are you going to do about this?"

They don't need to be anything more than that. Asking questions is beautiful. Asking questions is enough.

I found it one of the more incongruous coincidences that the slow dismissal of the underclass came at the same time as ITV1's massive them-and-us, upstairs/ downstairs, master-and-servant blockbuster, Downton Abbey. I have a complex relationship with Downton. Well, not really. I think it's stupid—like a big dog in a dress, galloping around—and I delight in boggling at its every, demented, over-blown, eye-rolling move it makes.

I'd been writing about how enjoyably dumb Downton is for a year before I started to be quite good friends with Dan Stevens, who plays the show's Matthew Crawley—or "Handsome Cousin Matthew," as I always like to refer to him in print, because I know it makes him a bit awkward, even though he cannot deny he is handsome. Incredibly handsome. Honestly, sometimes it's like sitting in a bar with the sun.

Dan—and I know he won't mind me saying this, mainly because he's too busy to read this, and so will never know—is a skilled party maximizer. A dedicated and joyous boozer with some manner of supernatural, endlessly forgiving liver. I once saw him accidentally fire a champagne cork at a tramp in Soho—but he subsequently apologized so profusely and literally handsomely that, in the end, I think the tramp felt flattered to have been assaulted by someone so facially perfect. That was the night that ended with him and Michelle Dockery—who plays Lady Mary in Downton, also a bit of a dude—crunking to Blackstreet's "No Diggity" in a nightclub at 2 am. As I watched them, my mind made them wear corsets and World War One military garb. Given the amazing plotlines of Downton, it may well be something that actually happens in a subsequent season.

My favorite night out with Dan was when we attended an Olympic Ball together in West London, and vowed not to tie one on, as it was a school night. Everything went well until—on our way out of the venue, pretty sober—we passed a bar.

"We need cider. For the taxi," Dan said, decisively. And bought four bottles.

Obviously, by the time we'd chucked that down in the back of the cab, we were wasted before we were even halfway home, and ended up going back to my house, and drinking half pints of port while listening to records.

At 1 am I failed to find the record I was looking for—a bootleg of Elton John singing Nick Drake demos. Amazing—and went upstairs to wake my husband, who knows the location of all the records in our house.

"Pete," I said, cross-eyed on port. "Downton wants Elton Drake. Semergency."

He's still in my mobile as "Downton."

Downton Abbey Review 1:
Lady Mary's Haunted Vagina

DOWNTON ABBEY RETURNED—FINALLY, FINALLY—ON Sunday night. I'm sure you're aware of this. You would have to have been on a spiritual retreat down a deep well, with your eyes closed, to have missed it—in the matter of promotion, ITV1 has been acting like a gangster-made-good, parading its beautiful-yet-spoiled daughter around a Mob restaurant, boasting about how beautiful she is.

"Have you seen her? Look at her! Look at her! She's *gorgeous*," all the channel's full-page ads in the national press screamed. "Look at my little *Downton*. She's real classy. Nominated for Emmys and everything. She's my princess. Nuffink's too good for her. *Nuffink*. If you touch her you're dead, sunshine."

But then, who can really blame ITV1's pride? *Downton* is currently in the *Guinness Book of Records* as "the most critically-acclaimed television show of all time"—a fairly astonishing accolade when you bear in mind a) *Twin Peaks,* say, or *Life on Earth;* and b) *Downton's* much more urgent deserving of another record: that of Guinness's "silliest television show of all time."

Honestly, *Downton* is off its chanks. Sometimes it plays as if writer

Julian Fellowes sits at his writing bureau—overlooking his extensive lands, including *three rivers*—sucking on a helium balloon, and giggling as he starts bashing at his typewriter. This is, after all, the drama where an evil, chain-smoking maid caused her mistress to miscarry by deliberately leaving lilac-scented soap on the floor, which she slipped on. Yeah, that's right. She killed the unborn Earl of Downton with soap. This is a plot twist not even *Dynasty*, at its most gibbering, considered.

So here we are in Episode One, Season Two. It is 1914. All we can see is a nightmare-ish vision of mud and barbed wire. Shells whistle and explode as men fall to the ground, broken. In the trenches, men no more than boys weep, lighting cigarettes with bloodied, muddied hands. There's no two ways about it: this dinner party is going really badly.

Through the labyrinthine tunnels the cameras roam, until they find the man they seek: Matthew Crawley, played by Dan Stevens. In many ways, Crawley is the center of *Downton's* world: as the middle-class solicitor now unexpectedly due to inherit Downton itself—plus one-half of the Lady Mary/Matthew Crawley on/off love story—Crawley's character touches on every issue of class, destiny and desire.

More importantly than this, however, Crawley is unbelievably handsome. It is notable that, in this Stygian quagmire, he alone is immaculate. While everyone else looks like a bog troll, he is blonde, burnished and pristine. Perhaps the mud—being French—is asthetically highly-tuned enough to respect his beauty, and refuses to cling to his astonishingly well-cut trenchcoat and buttermilk skin, out of sheer love.

Either way up, Julian Fellowes knows the assembled nine million viewers haven't rocked up to ITV1 for *Wilfred Owen: The Movie*. There are nine million Cup-A-Soups going undrunk as the audience shouts, "This is a bit of a downer. Where's Maggie Smith looking snooty about someone using the wrong boot-buttoner?"

To this end, two minutes in, Matthew Crawley stares out into the middle distance of WAR.

"When I think of my life at Downton, it seems like a different world," he says, impossibly yearning, as the scene fades to black.

And so we're back to lovely old reassuring Downton itself, where all the things *we* yearn for occur: flighty maids making up beds with billowing linen; frisky footmen standing to attention as ladies alight from carriages; posh girls setting down their tortoiseshell-backed hair brushes and weeping over thwarted love affairs. Life is carrying on at Downton, despite the war—or "This DAMNED war," to give it its full name.

And its full name is being used often. People are referring to the war a lot. Despite the First World War being, surely, one of the Top Ten Events It's Unneccessary To Back-Ref, it seems any slight change to the domestic routine since Season One must be contextualized with a quick mention of the ongoing world-wide conflagration.

While this is amusing during a scene of overdue cushion-plumping in the drawing room—"There's a war on. You cannot keep standards as high."—it reached its apogee when Lady Sibyl bumped into Lady Cora in the hallway.

"This is early for you to be up, Mamma."

"War makes early risers of us all."

This begs the viewer to ask, "Really? Is the sound of shelling in the Dardenelles carrying all the way to Yorkshire?"

As well as being a hinderance to cushion plumpness, war, we discover, is also a massive bummer. Lady Sibyl receives a letter telling her a former beau, Tom, has caught it in Flanders.

"Sometimes, it feels as if all the men I've ever danced with are dead," she sighs. Darling, I've been to office Christmas parties too. I know exactly how you feel.

And it seems love is being thwarted left, right and center. Sexy DILF butler Bates looks like he's finally going to get it on with housemaid Anna, after spending all of Season One mooning after her like a calf on Wobbly Eggs. He even gets around to telling her his plans for their future life:

"I want to open a little hotel, in the countryside," he says, holding her hand outside the scullery.

The Bates Hotel? Really? That's honestly his plan? You can imagine Julian Fellowes taking a particularly huge hit off his helium tank as he wrote that line. As fans of the show will know, Fellowes seems to reserve all his most wiggy helium moments for Bates. Bates, let us not forget, was the one who wore a "secret leg-stretching contraption" in Season One—until he wearied of the pain, and hurled it into a lake.

Anyway, Bates's Season One Secret Leg Contraption Agony is as nothing compared to the torments Fellowes has for him in Season Two: seconds after announcing his Bates Love Hotel plan, Bates's evil, estranged wife turns up to banjax everything.

Understandably, one-legged, love-calf Bates is initially unwilling to receive her—keeping her waiting in the kitchen for half an hour.

"Sorry to keep you waiting, Vera," he says, finally arriving. "I've been . . . up in the lofts. Sorting out . . . some cupboards."

One look at Vera Bates's Super Evil face tells you that, with excuses like this, Bates is gonna be dog-food. She will screw him over, right into Season Three. All housemaid Anna can do is run off, and cry into her apron near a butter churn.

Upstairs, and love is equally complex. Home on leave, the luminously handsome Matthew Crawley attends a fundraising concert at Downton, allowing him to bump into Lady Mary for the first time since she dumped him, then he dumped her back (it's complicated. Just go with it).

Despite Matthew now being engaged to the sappy Lady Lavinia, and Lady Mary being pursued by Richard Carlisle ("You mean Sir Richard Carlisle? Who runs all those ghastly newspapers?" Lord Crawley expositions, handily. Often, *Downton* might well be renamed *Exposition Abbey*), we know Lady Mary and Matthew Crawley will end up together, eventually. Their love is real and true—for Matthew still loves her, despite her Terrible Secret: a brief fling with a Turkish diplomat, which ended with him dying in her bed.

Although I'm not certain of all the technicalities, I think this means Mary's private parts might now be haunted by the ghost of Mr. Kemal Pumak. I keep waiting for it to jealously go "WoooOOoooo" every time she looks at Matthew Crawley.

Alas—as Episode One finished, I was still waiting. There's no dice as yet—but with another seven episodes to go, and *Downton* reliably demented, I'm pretty confident that I'll hear Pumak's muffled "WooOOOooo" by the end.

I went through a spell of reviewing Downton *every single week—just because simply describing what was happening often made me senseless with laughter.*

Downton Abbey Review 2: SEX WILL BE HAD! SEX WILL BE HAD!

"DO THE PLOTS IN *Downton* move too quickly?" is the question many are asking at the moment. And with good reason. After all, as we realized last week, the entire First World War has only taken five episodes of *Downton*. At this rate, Maggie Smith could be making imperious comments about the etiquette of Neil Armstrong landing on the moon ("But has he been intro-*duced* to the Clangers? Does he know their *family*?") by Christmas.

But you know what? As long as you just strap yourself in—and maybe partake of a medicinal sherry beforehand—the rapid pacing is fine. It's a hoot! Just think of an episode of *Downton Abbey* as a "Haunted House" style ride—such as you would find at a fair, or on a pier. You burst in through the double doors to find the Earl of Grantham (Hugh Bonneville) kissing a widowed housemaid in the pantry, mount a gantry to view Ethel's illegitimate baby in the pantry—then take in a final straight that includes an elopement, a miracle cure and a revelation of unrequited love before the final credits. Put your hands in the air, and scream if you wanna go faster! It's only two quid, fun for aaaawl the family.

Of course, some fast plots are bigger than other fast plots. The megaplot that *Downton* currently revolves around is the state of Cousin Matthew's (Dan Stevens) trousers. It is all going off in Cousin Matthew's trousers, these days. That's where all the narrative is being stored.

Cousin Matthew, you may recall, is the preternaturally beautiful blonde heir to Downton Abbey, who bravely went off to the hell of war to serve his King and country—only popping back to Downton half-a-dozen times for key concerts, balls, scenes where it just generally felt good to have him around, and angsty forbidden-love stare-offs with Lady Mary (Michelle Dockery).

At one point, Cousin Matthew popped back from the war halfway through Lady Mary singing *If You Were the Only Boy in the World* at a concert—then joined her in a loving duet for the last verse, before immediately going back to the war again. It's the scene Vera Brittain never had the balls or insanity to write in *A Testament of Youth*—but, now, finally brought to life by Julian Fellowes in *Downton*. Hurrah! If the thinking remains as blue-sky as this, Season Three of *Downton*—set in the Depression—can have Bugsy Malone with a splurge-gun, or even—fuck it!—Scarlett O'Hara escaping a burning Atlanta in a horse and cart, with Miss Melly giving birth in the back. You might as well go for it, that's what I say! Scream if you wanna go faster!

Anyway. Matthew's trousers. In a war full of unspeakable atrocities, the Hun's most beastly move has been an attack on Cousin Matthew's— possibly literal, given his poshness—crown jewels. When he returned from the front in Episode Five, it was in a wheelchair—"an impotent cripple, smelling of sick," as he called himself, clearly on a bit of a Downton downer.

For a few, amazing moments, it seemed as if *Downton* might have gone the whole hog, and written in a character who'd had his nads blown off in the heat of battle—only the second-ever drama to attempt this, after the BBC's groundbreaking, testicle-exploding *Lilies* in 2007.

And, indeed, the first scene of last Sunday's episode seemed to confirm this: the Earl of Downton watching solemnly as a car departed down the driveway, his somber expression suggesting that the vehicle contained Matthew's balls on a tray, being taken off for a decent burial.

But—to infinite rejoicing—we found this was not the case. Not the case at all. Matthew was, in fact, *trousioso intacta,* as I'm sure the Latin would have it. The contents of his orangery were all present and correct—it was merely the "sexual reflex" that was missing. Or was it? Ten minutes later, sitting in his wheelchair, Matthew stared out into the middle distance.

"Bates," he said to his valet. "If I were to feel a . . . tingling, what would that mean? The doctors keep saying it's the memory of a tingling—but I keep feeling it."

"If something is changing, it will make itself known," Bates said, with all the wisdom of a man who'd had a broad country upbringing.

Although it sometimes felt like it, *Downton* was not all about Cousin Matthew's trousers, of course. My favorite subplot involved the villainous Mrs. O'Brien and Thomas entering the post-war black market economy—and trying to rip off the Downton estate by selling hooky foodstuffs to Cook.

While initially keen on sourcing such luxe ingredients—"I've not seen this since before the war!" Cook exclaimed, holding up candied peel as if it were an unquestioning attitude of deference toward the upper classes—Cook found, on tasting the resultant cake, that Thomas had been sold a pup.

"This is plaster dust!" Cook shouting, spitting cake all over the floor, then getting all *Watchdog* on Thomas's ass.

Thomas eventually returned to his warehouse full of now-unsellable, poisonous ingredients, and—furious—started to trash the lot. As he repeatedly punched a massive sack while shouting "NO!!!", it occurred to me that this was the first time I had ever seen a man fighting "some flour"—and I gave thanks, yet again, to the mad majesty of *Downton*.

But, in the end, Sunday's episode ended as it had begun: in Cousin Matthew's trousers. Post-Tinglegate, we were all on high alert for further developments in Matthew's pelvis—but were aware that the breakthrough he needed might come at a high cost. Previous cases of people in dramas "spontaneously" recovering from paraplegia seem to center around high drama—suddenly finding the power in their legs when a loved one is in danger, say, or when their own lives are at risk.

In the event, Matthew's miracle recovery didn't quite play out like that.

Joining Matthew in the drawing room, Lavinia—his current, wrongful fiancée—noticed something was seriously awry at Downton:

"Look!" she said, pointing to a table, with six cups and saucers on it. "They've forgotten to clear the tea things!"

Walking over to correct the servants' heinous mistake, Lavinia was given fair warning by Matthew.

"It's too heavy for you!" he said, as she picked up a tray.

But, too late! Lavinia had—inevitably—paid the price for the lower-orders' carelessness: tripping over an ornately-embroidered footstool, and having to steady herself by putting her hand on the marble fireplace, next to the ormulu clock.

"Heavens! That was a near thing!" she exclaimed, breathlessly—before they both realized that this moment of peril had jolted Matthew out of his paralysis: he was now standing next to her, broken spine a thing of the past, future now rosily re-filling with the possibility of rumpy.

On discovering the happy news about his heir, the Earl of Grantham rushed around Downton insisting everyone come and see Matthew in the drawing room at once. Really, he appeared one whisky away from ringing the bells in Downton chapel and shouting, "SEX WILL BE HAD! SEX WILL BE HAD!" to the entire cast.

I'm sure the staff were subsequently instructed to bring out the special "Heir's rediscovered sexual reflex" dinner service, as has been in the family for generations, in order that all of Downton might celebrate in the most Downton way it knows how—with the maximum of formality, oddness, and washing-up for the peasants.

We make a good team, Pete and I. Both journalists, both into carbohydrates, both agreed that the perfect babysitter for the children during the summer holidays is a man of dubious qualifications and reputation touting some massive see-through hamster balls, in which you can place your children.

Summer Is an Emergency

"THE THING ABOUT SUMMER is, if you work and you've got kids, it's an emergency," my husband says. "A total emergency."

Today is the worst day of August, so far: both of us are sitting next to a forty-foot paddling pool, on the seafront, in Brighton.

A cheerful, chainsmoking goblin from Manchester has set up some manner of novel amusement here: gigantic plastic "hamster balls," into which children can be inserted, then launched onto the paddling pool. Our children have taken to this activity with all the enthusiasm of genuine hamsters. They keep tumbling past us, upside down, screaming, "THIS IS AWESOME, DUDE!" and flashing peace signs.

Sitting at the picnic tables we wave, shout things like, "You look totally deranged! We're going to leave you here, and go home alone!", then go back to typing, furiously. My husband is trying to write the definitive overview of UB40's first, politically outraged, critically revered album. I am writing a stirring 4,000-word, pro-feminist refutation of waxing: both Brazilians, and Hollywoods.

Every so often, my husband stares at me blankly, and says "Dub."

I stare back at him, equally blankly, and say "Pubes."

The children wheel past in the background, screaming "COW-ABUNGA, MAN!"

Today—having run out of holiday allowance, two weeks into the summer holidays—this paddling pool is our office. An office with no ceiling, in which drizzle is falling onto our laptops. It's far more exciting than it sounds, though: for with Brighton council being inexplicably heel-draggy about providing free power outlets on any part of the seafront, we also have an thrilling, against-the-clock element of trying to finish writing before our batteries conk out.

"How long have you got left? I'm on thirty-seven minutes," I will say, anxiously checking the stats.

"I'm down to seventeen," my husband replies. "I've turned the 'Screen Brightness' down so low, it looks like a window onto eternal night."

It is like an episode of *24* centered on Jack Bauer sending a single, very important email.

Of course, to complain about this would be to suffer a gigantic loss of perspective. We are, by no stretch of the imagination, the most stressed parents this summer. We aren't even the most stressed parents on Brighton seafront—earlier, I had passed a child jack-knifing on the floor, wailing, "I don't WANT Nanna to be dead forever!"

At least, I tell myself, cheerfully, we're dandy, teleworking media nobs who *can* bring our work to a giant inflatable paddling pool in Brighton.

"Imagine having to bring your *lathe* down here," I keep thinking. "Or your *furnace*. Or the *mountain* you had to climb—because you are a professional mountaineer, like Chris Bonham. We are the lucky ones."

If you're working parents, the fact is simple: the holiday math doesn't add up. You, the parents, have four weeks of holiday a year. Your children, on the other hand, have thirteen. Ergo, you are about to lose your mind. It's not a system anyone would come up with now. It's a vexing remnant of the patriarchy—a society in complete denial that both a) MUMMY IS ON A DEADLINE TOO, NOW, and b) MOST CHILDREN DISLIKE GOING TO A THREE-WEEK-LONG DRAMA WORKSHOP WITH A LOAD OF RANDOMS AS MUCH AS YOU WOULD. The solution to two-parent-working families is *not* to get thousands of kids to learn the *Bugsy Malone* songbook—although, as I write that, I do realize how much my core beliefs have changed since I was twelve, and wanted to be Blousey Brown.

Two weeks later, it is the first day of autumn term. The school gates resemble the first assembly point after a plane crash. Slightly stunned parents stand around, waving goodbye to their children, with the auras of people who've recently spent so much money, and begged so many favors from Grandma and Grandpa, that they might now have to go home and lie very, very still for five days, before they can feel normal again.

"You got through, then?" one says.

"Yeah. Don't quite remember how, though. I appear to have spent over £6,000 on *Doctor Who* DVD box sets and bags of Mini Cheddars."

They then get on their mobiles, and start wearily arranging the transportation of their lathes, back from Polperro.

But you know what? Secretly, this is why I love the summer holidays. Unlike my husband, I get off on an emergency. In the summer, you can basically pretend it's the Second World War—running out into the street in your rollers, clutching a kettle, screaming, "THE GERMANS ARE COMING!", smoking black market fags.

Now it's autumn, however, you can't get away with that kind of stuff anymore. There's no more putting the kids to sleep in a cardboard box under the patio table. No more gin on the lawn at 2 AM. No more giving everyone Kit Kats and apples for breakfast. You just have to retrieve your shoes—from the lavendar bush, where you threw them, in July—put them back on, and go back to being normal, and sensible, again.

Until Christmas, anyway.

*Here is pretty much my entire life story in 830 words. Note a return to the jus-
tification of not going abroad. I don't know who I'm aiming all this "I will not
travel" ranting at, really. Maybe the Thomas Cook in my head.*

Time Travel in the Same Four Places

I'M NOT A GREAT believer in "traveling." Every holiday I've ever had
somewhere "novel" seemed to consist of repeatedly walking past much nicer
restaurants than the one we'd just eaten in, while crying, "Oh! That place
looks delightful! There's no feral one-eyed cats under the table *there*."

And that's ignoring the actual travel of "travel": a thing so awful it war-
rants its own insurance, sickness, and tiny hairdryers. Every time I think of
some distant wonder I might quite like to see—Sydney Harbour at night,
for instance; or Venice from a bridge—I ask myself, "Do I want to see it so
much that I would take my shoes off at Heathrow security at 6:55 AM?"

And every time the answer comes back, "No. I would rather keep my
shoes on and watch a documentary about them instead, thank you."

So instead of travelling, I just . . . go to places, instead. The same four
places, for the last twenty years: Aberystwyth, Brighton, Gower, Ullapool.
That's it. Nowhere else. Over and over, repeat and return. Like a casting-on
stitch done over and over in the same spot—but at slightly different angles.
When I go back to these places, I can see my ghosts from every previous
visit. When I go to these places, I don't travel in space—but in time, instead.

So when I go to Ullapool, in the Highlands, I walk the main street
seeing flickery, analogue broadcasts from earlier parts of my life. The time-
code on the oldest ghost is 1986. August—the August we bought a campervan. We've been driven off every other campsite in the area, as the owners
think—what with my seven siblings, and rainbow-colored wellies—that we

are travelers, displaced from Stonehenge. It's a miserable holiday: the rain is solid, cold. All we can do is eat sausage soup and read *Kidnapped* aloud to each other in increasingly risible Scottish accents. Everyone is angry. The dog nearly drowns. I want us to climb a mountain or swim in the sea, but we spend five days in a space the size of a wardrobe, staring at running windows, and then go home.

A decade later, and the ghosts from 1995 are of better quality—a brighter picture. I am nineteen, now. I've convinced a friend who has a car to drive me back to Ullapool, so I can finally see it in the sunshine—or at least through the rainy windows of somewhere more spacious, like a hotel. In the day, we both climb a mountain *and* swim in the sea, because I'm in charge of me now. At night, after drinking the most expensive wine we have ever ordered—£22!—we realize we're probably in love, and walk to the same bedroom without saying a word. Four years later we come back on our honeymoon, and spend the first night crying, even though we love each other, because. . . .

Here I am on the seafront in Brighton, in 1994. I have just told my best friend that we shouldn't go out with each other.

"We were meant to be just friends," I am saying. I have read about love in novels, and am sure I know all about it. This is one of the cleverest things I have ever done. I am eighteen. I exhale my cigarette, like a grown-up.

Here I am four years later, on the same stretch of seafront, with the same friend. We are on a bench. My head is in his lap. We are talking about what to call our baby in my belly. My wedding dress is in a bag at our feet. We get married in three days. Since we were last here, I have learned that I knew nothing at the age of eighteen. I know now that love can be a quiet, sure thing—like the first April sun on your arms—and not the pycroclastic blast I was waiting for.

In nineteen hours, we will find out the baby is dead. The grief that is coming for us has five blades on each hand: it will fall on us like a blizzard, and leave us on the floor.

We will weep on our honeymoon in Ullapool—so lost I could not tell you if it did rain at all, that time. At the time, I thought the deep sea pressure of sorrow was so great, it would crush my heart smaller, forever. I was sure I knew everything about it.

THIS MORNING, AT THE start of my holiday in Brighton, I watched our two daughters—eight and ten—on the beach.

"My heart is even bigger now," I thought. "And I know what love is, and I don't smoke, and the grief did not kill me, and I know I still no nothing, and I'm in charge of me, now."

A casting-on stitch done in the same place, over and over again, gets stronger. In Ullapool, Gower, Aberystwyth and Brighton, I don't travel to broaden the mind.

I return—something completely different.

Part **Four**

Enthusiasms, Advices, and Deaths

In which I meet Paul McCartney FROM THE BEATLES and ask him what would happen if—"Heaven forfend, Sir Paul"—his face got smashed up in an horrific car accident, mourn the deaths of Amy Winehouse and Elizabeth Taylor, open the "Nutters Letter Box," and offer a blow-by-blow of the Royal Wedding. But, first: back to a small domestic misunderstanding.

My French Dress

IT IS 7:48 PM. I am just about to leave the house for a night out with friends. I have checked I have a spare pair of tights in my handbag, ensured that the working remote is actually in the oldest child's hand—no more panicked, 10 PM "WE CANT FID [sic] THE CONTROLLS!!!" texts for *me*—and now, the last thing that needs to be done is to bid my husband adieu.

I walk into his "study," where he is listening to a reggae compilation while contemplating his new Fotheringay mug, which is full of tea. He has a happy look on his face.

"I'm off now, love," I say.

"Have a great night," he says, taking his headphones off, and beaming.

There is a pause. I kind of . . . stand at him a bit. Loom, maybe.

"I'm off now," I say, again, more purposefully. "Off into London. To see people."

"Make sure you've got your keys!" he says, cheerfully. "Have a great night. Send my love to . . . whichever bunch of arch, chain smoking homo sexuals you're on loan to tonight."

There is another pause. I stare at him quite intently. He stares back, confused. Pete can tell there is some manner of urgent business left unattended here—but he does not know what. I can sense his heart rate accelerating, like a panicked lab rat on sighting a speculum. The rat does not know exactly what is going to happen next—but it knows it's going to be bad.

"Do you . . . want a lift to Finsbury Park?" he asks, eventually.

"HOW DO YOU THINK I LOOK?" I shout.

Pete is immediately both contrite—"Sorry!"—but also back in charted territory again.

Twelve years ago, shortly before our wedding, I told him—with the kind of fearless honesty that lovers can afford—that I would only ever impose two rules on our marriage. 1) That he must never, ever throw me a surprise birthday party in our living room again. And 2) that every time I appear in front of him in a new outfit, he must say, without hesitation: "You look so thin in that!"

"You look so thin in that!" Pete says—delighted to be back on firm ground. He puts his headphones back on. He clearly thinks all the business has been concluded.

"Phew. Have a great night out," he says—going back to staring at his Fotheringay mug, which depicts the whole band as fifteenth-century minstrels. "I'll see you in the morning."

Unfortunately for Pete, "You look so thin in that" is *not* the droids I am looking for in this particular conversation. The dress I am in is a bit of a new development, in terms of my "fashion range." It's a 1950s tea-dress in shape—but in pattern, it's got an African-textile theme going on. I'm wearing it with zebra skin sandals, and a snakeskin clutch. Basically, I need to know if I look like some manner of "Lady Ace Ventura—Pet Detective" in it. I don't know if this "lysergic safari" thing is working.

Were I with any of my female friends or relationships, they would have understood this instantly. My sister Weena, for instance, would have greeted me with "You're perverting the assumed prejudices of post-war chicks, with some kind of 'demented gay Ghanian disco' vibe. It's *Mad Men* vs. Brixton Market. You're essentially saying you're a liberal—but with big tits. Nice. Catch that bus with confidence."

This is what women do—tell each other what story their outfits are projecting, by way of confirming that the wearer has got it right. The women who love you recite back to you the aspiration and impact of your "look"—hence a group of eight of us being able to greet our friend Hughes with, "Post-divorce slutty secretary—but with unexpected neon rave stilletos! You're a sexy lady who will not cling to one man tonight, but seek the communal ecstactic uprising of a room full of partygoers instead. In this Pizza Express we are having dinner in."

Women speak the language of clothes. Everything we wear is a sentence, a paragraph, a chapter—or, sometimes, just an exclamation mark.

Unfortunately, however, Pete does not speak the language of clothes. My dress and zebra sandals are essentially shouting at him in French. Unable to make out a word they are saying, he panics.

"It's a top-notch item," he says, staring at it. "Unusual. It's, ah, amazing that 'they' keep coming up with innovative things—even in 2012. That's . . . got to be good news for the fashion industry!"

There is a small pause—then he starts laughing so hysterically at the desperation of what he has just said that he slides off his chair, headphones still in hand, and kneels on the floor, red-faced, and weeping.

He's still there when I leave the house. Which is a bit annoying, because I did actually want a lift to Finsbury Park. My zebra skin sandals are chafing.

Sherlock Review 3:
As Good As Television Gets

IN MANY WAYS, SHERLOCK doesn't really come across as a TV show. The levels of fandom it inspires in the UK are what you'd more readily associate with a pop star, or a rock band. People queued at 5:30 AM to get tickets for the premiere screening at the BFI. There are whole websites devoted to fans' imagining of sexual encounters between Holmes and Dr Watson. There are women who cry when you say the words "Benedict Cumberbatch"—and not simply because they are trying to spell it in their heads, and failing.

And so to "A Scandal in Belgravia," the first of three new feature-length *Sherlock*s, charged with the tricky task of topping one of the most triumphant debut seasons of all time.

Within the first two minutes, writer Steven Moffat made it clear he wasn't intending to start things off quietly, while he found his feet: a pearly-arsed dominatrix known as "The Woman" entered a bedroom, holding a riding crop, asking: "Have you been wicked, Your Highness?"

"Yes, Miss Adler," a posh voice replied.

And then the opening title sequence rolled. Yeah. That's right. The first episode of the new season of *Sherlock* was about a Kate Middleton S&M blackmail scenario. In your face, *Waterloo Road*.

The next hour and a half were, to be scientific, as good as it's possible for television to be: other program makers must have been biting their wrists in a combination of jealousy and awe. Not only does *Sherlock* have the embarrassment of riches that is a cast list that reads "Benedict Cumberbatch, Martin Freeman, Lara Pulver, Rupert Graves," but its episode subject was the potent one of "Sherlock Holmes and love."

Having spent the first season setting Holmes up as one of the foremost men of the twenty-first century, "a man with an achieveable super-power"—all milk and ice and billion-dollar synapse blinking—this season seems to be about examining his weaknesses, instead. They've built him up—now they're going to knock him down. Or, in this case, blow up him, by throwing a fantastic pair of tits at him.

For Sherlock cannot fathom Irene Adler—"The Woman"—a high-class dominatrix with incriminating pictures of Middleton (it's hinted, anyway, if never made obvious) on her phone.

Played by Lara *True Blood* Pulver, Irene Adler lives in a beautiful house of monochrome damask, and her lipstick is as red as damask roses. On the orders of the Palace, Holmes is sent to the monochrome house to retrieve the pictures, and Adler prepares for his arrival.

"What will you wear?" her lover/assistant, Kate, asks.

"The Battle Suit," Adler replies.

When Holmes arrives—pretending to be a vicar, ridiculously; he's already acting like an idiot—she greets him naked. The Business Suit. He's pole-axed by her—not just by the quiet authority of her bare arse, swishing past him on the sofa; but her face, too. He cannot read her. Holmes, who can read everyone—he glances at Watson, for reassurance: notes his shoes mean he has a date tonight, his stubble that he used an electric shaver—cannot decipher a single thing about Adler. She can hide herself wholly, even when naked. Particularly when naked. After all, as she reminds Holmes, "However hard you try [with a disguise], it's always a self-portrait."

Holmes is so stupefied by the novelty of being outsmarted that he doesn't even realize he fancies her, at this point.

And Adler, against all her judgment and nature, fancies Holmes, too. Adler is as clever as Holmes, but also as damaged: she keeps blackmail material on her phone because she "makes her way in the world" with a series of deals and dodges; she has "friends" she regularly sedates with the syringes in her bedside cabinet. Nearly everything in the world bores her. Sex isn't fun—it's just a job. What really excites her is detectives, and detective stories. Despite being a lesbian, what ultimately excites her is Sherlock Holmes.

And so "A Scandal in Belgravia" was an hour and a half of two odd, fast, hot people being confused by each other: not quite knowing why they jangle when they're around each other; not quite knowing what to do with their feelings. Both have jobs that involve crushing their emotions: should they continue doing that—or actually trust each other?

In the end, their cataclysmic meeting results in a plane full of corpses rotting on a runway as Mycroft, the British government and the American government despair. "Holmes and Adler" really aren't the new "Hart to Hart." She's betrayed him, he's betrayed her, and all Holmes's suspicions about love—"The chemistry is terribly simple. And very destructive"—have been borne out. Love will never do for Holmes. He likes things to have conclusions, and endings. Love has no conclusion or ending at all. And, also, he fell in love with a mental. That was quite a big error.

From 8:10 PM to 9:40 PM, it was often hard to tell which part of you was being stimulated more by *Sherlock*: the eyes, or the brain. For while the script bounced along with a winning combination of screwball, rat-tat-tat dialogue and parkour-like plot leaps, Paul McGuigan's direction was of movie-like sumptuousness. You lost count of the moments that looked a million dollars. A shot from above of Mycroft (Mark Gatiss) closing his umbrella, and ducking into a café, out of the rain, had a sense of choreography to it; 221b Baker Street has never looked more sumptuous.

McGuigan seemed to particularly revel in the scene where Adler—trying to retrieve her phone—jammed a syringe into Sherlock's arm, and he floated off into a wiggy state of narcoleptic wooze. As Sherlock collapsed backwards, drugged, the camera rotated once, twice beside him—sometimes you couldn't tell if he were falling up, or down. As he finally came in to land, his face was the same color as the white-waxed floorboard he was bouncing off.

Here, in a dream, Holmes found himself on a moor—Adler beside him, on a chaise longue. They were two incongruous, pale, elegant town creatures in all this brutal, wet green. Holmes could still not speak: insensible on barbiturates, his bed rose up out of the moss like a benign tombstone, and Holmes fell upon it, winking out of consciousness, carried into the next scene.

It was as distractingly beautiful a piece of cinematography as you're ever likely to see, and—accompanied by David Arnold and Michael Price's lush, weeping soundtrack—left you walking away from the television after ninety minutes feeling like you'd just been fed lobsters, champagne and truffles through your brain.

The day after broadcast, an ill-tempered kerfuffle kicked off across a couple of blogs, accusing Moffat's script of misogyny. Irene Adler had ended up being rescued by Holmes, the argument went. She fell in love with him and then had to be rescued by him, like some courtesan Snow White. Obviously, as a strident feminist, my "Misogyny Alarm" is always on red-alert—but I have to say, it didn't ding once during *Sherlock;* save for a momentary sigh over just how many high class call girls I've seen on television over the years (approximately six million), compared to the amount I've actually met (none).

For *Sherlock* is a detective story, not a news show. It doesn't care about statistics, and nor should it. All I could see were two damaged people making a mess of each other's lives, while Martin Freeman did his patented "Martin Freeman eyebrows" from the sidelines. And, obviously, some of the best television this country has ever produced.

Two of the biggest-hitting columns in this book—on my hair.

I Wish to Copyright My Hair

I CANNOT, IN MY life, claim to have invented many things. No medicinal breakthrough. No plastic compounds. No movement in figure skating. True, I was part of a committee of fat children in the Midlands who conceived, in 1988, of the Cheese Lollipop—around 50g of cheap Cheddar speared on a fork, and sucked on during marathons of CBBC classic *Cities of Gold*—but I was just a cog, though a rather large cog, in amongst other equally gifted and gigantic cogs. It's also true that I was part of that same committee of fat children who, having all moved into their adolescence, came up with the Sherry Cappuccino one desperate Christmas. The curdled layers of Nescafe and Somerfield Ruby will live on in the minds of all those who experienced it. Indeed, they probably also live on in the cups we used. It was viscous stuff.

That aside, however, it's clear that, in a version of *It's a Wonderful Life* where I took the James Stewart role, and plunged suicidally off the bridge, Bedford Falls would simply shrug, and carry on with the eggnog, same as they always did. I haven't really contributed to mankind's magnificent struggle one iota.

However, there is one meager, paltry innovation I feel I can lay claim to in my otherwise uncreative life, and that is my hair. On Halloween 2003—note the date, hair historians, as I'm sure there must be, somewhere. Maybe at De Montford University, Leicester—I made drunkenly merry with a can of spray-in gray hair paint. On waking in the morning, I looked in the mirror, and was astonished at what I saw. What I saw was The Hair of My Life. The Hair of My Soul. I had one icy whoosh of hair over my left eye. A blue-gray streak. A frosted lock. It looked a bit Eleanor Bron, a bit Morticia, a bit the wise monkey elder in *The Lion King*. Clearly, this was the Recipe of Me. I went to the hairdressers, and got them to make me semi-gray permanently.

For the first three years, me and my hair were very happy. True, old people were apt to come up to me at bus stops and commiserate ("Ooooh, you're like me. I went completely gray at twenty-nine, after I had shingles. You want to get yourself one of those dye-jobbies from Boots."), but I felt I was on some kind of Hair Quest. I felt I was pushing the boundaries. I felt I was creative.

Then the bomb fell. Last summer, my brother Eddie—the maverick Cheese Lollipop committee member who, in 1988, had suggested we concentrate our cutlery research solely on the fork—rang me from Brighton.

"I've just seen a woman with your hair," he said. "In Peacocks," he added. "Buying leggings."

Initially, I was flattered. I visit Brighton quite a lot. It was not outside the realms of possibility that this woman had seen my hair, and simply been inspired. I couldn't blame her. I am in the possession of hair dynamite.

Then my sister, also in Brighton, rang a month later.

"I've seen FIVE WOMEN with your hair," she blurted out, immediately.

At this point, I must admit, I felt bad. These women had, fairly obviously, not copied their hair from me. They had copied it from the woman who copied me. They did not know their hair history.

The way things were going, there was every chance that my hair would go down in history as "origin unknown."

Then, a week before the end of the school term, things escalated dramatically, albeit mainly in my mind. Outside the school gates one morning—as startling as the sight of a polar bear—there was a mother *with my hair*. On my own territory! Bold as the slightly brassy gray tone her—clearly inferior—hairdresser had come up with!

While dealing with the fear of dying in hair-dying obscurity had been unpleasant, this new scenario was a different kettle of fish altogether. I think all women know what another woman stealing your signature style means. I recalled, from my teenage years, my friend Julie's fury on noting that a female classmate had appropriated her then-trademark—a Puffa jacket, worn with badges on the elasticated hem.

"It's war," she said, flatly, smoking a cigarette in Burger King, as you could, in those days.

And of course, this hair-stealing woman was, indeed, declaring war on me. For who would ever copy the hairstyle of someone they saw every day, if they thought they looked *worse* with it? The hair-stealing mother believed my hair looked *better* on her. That it was, by and large, a good hairdo, but *ruined by the addition of my face*. She was dissing me. This was clearly the act that would lead to the outbreak of war.

But just how does one fight a Hair War? Unsatisfyingly, this is the question I am currently stuck on, with another five weeks of the summer holidays to go, until I face my follicular nemesis again. The way I see it, I've got only three options. 1) Kill her—the sensible but possibly immoral option. 2) Kill myself—irresponsible, given my prominence in the pick-up rotation. 3) Get an entirely new do—frankly, I might as well be asked to traverse to Mordor to cast the One Ring into the Crack of Doom. I'm thirty-two. I'm too old for that kind of quest. This is the hair, for better or worse, I will die with.

So here I am, backed into a hair standoff I never asked for. I can't believe there aren't government guidelines on this kind of thing. I'm tearing my hair out.

Chicks With Big Hair Are My Chicks

UNTIL THE AGE OF twenty-five, the biggest fear in my life was that I would go bald. If I considered it for even one second, I had the kind of sweaty, spiralling panic that other people describe on being stuck in pot holes, or standing at the top of the Empire State Building.

My fear of hair loss was based in cool analysis of fact: as a teenage girl, I was quietly unappealing.

"You have a round, ruddy face, such as a peasant's," my sister told me, at one point, using her "helpful" voice. "Like a Halloween pumpkin—but not as sexy."

As we were also poor, I didn't have the resources—such as fashion, makeup, or cocaine—to increase my allure to the viewing eye. Simply, then, my hair was a precious commodity—as I could grow it very, very long. Long hair is pretty much the only beauty you can acquire if you have no money at all.

By the time I was thirteen, my hair was down to my hips. I had tended it assiduously. Nothing was too good for it. I would sit around, eating jam sandwiches, whispering, "Grow! Grow!" at my head, in what I deemed to be a voice encouraging to follicles.

At one point, I read in a nineteenth-century guide to beauty that rinsing with a beaten raw egg would add luster and shine. Consequently, I spent nearly two years walking around with an eggy, slightly sulphurous air. I was less "nymphette," and more "omelette."

Over these years of intense hair cultivation—I was essentially a "hair farmer," tending the hairfield on my head—my focus shifted, slowly but significantly, from having "long" hair, to wanting "big" hair.

"This is basically a 'hair cape,'" I realized, looking down, when I was around fifteen. "I look like Captain Caveman. I don't need *length*. What I need, is *width*. This hair needs to be predominantly based on my head. I'm going bouffy."

Turning, again, to my nineteenth-century guide to beauty, I noted that Victorian women would achieve their gigantic updos by padding out their hair with "rats": tiny pillows they would pin to their heads, and then arrange their own hair over, in a series of billows, knots and waves.

Keen to have my hair in an updo the size of a hat, I started to use "rats" myself. At the time, however, the only things I could find in the house that approximated "rats" were the tissue-paper liners for the terrycloth diapers my mother used on the babies.

While seeming, at first, to be securely fixed to my head, these liners would regularly fall out while I stood at bus stops, walked through parks, tried to purchase goods at a grocery store, etc. Then I, and anyone else around, would all stare at what appeared to be a giant sanitary napkin on the floor, which had just fallen out of my head.

"My rats," I would explain. It never seemed to make things better.

In the years since, I have, thank God, worked out how to satisfy my Hair Larging urges in a slightly more practical way—essentially by taking half the length off, then backcombing for ten minutes solidly every morning, in the way other people do yoga, or walk the dog.

As I joyfully embiggen myself into the vague silhouette of Chewbacca, I have time to reflect on just what it is about big hair that I find so elementally appealing.

Firstly, there is the obvious matter of perspective. By having big hair, it makes my body look smaller in comparison. As far as an aid to looking slimmer goes, this is the easiest one ever conceieved of. No fad diets, corsetry, optical illusion spray tanning, or artful couture: just a massive do.

Secondly, when it comes to wanting to look glamorous, there's something winningly practical about having huge hair. Heels cripple you; the bugle-beading on an expensive dress will chafe. Huge hair, on the other hand, can't fall off. You never leave you hair in the back of a cab. It's unbreakable, unstealable, and, most importantly of all, costs nothing. Aimed with a comb, you can whip your do up like egg-whites into a gigantic hair meringue, without it costing you a penny. Big hair is the party-do Marx would have backed, for sure.

And finally, while I am not prejudiced against people with small hair—as far as I know, there as never been any "small hair on big hair" violence recorded on "the streets"; we are not in conflict—there's something about big-haired chicks that makes me instantly inclined to like them. The iconography of big-haired women is compelling: cackling bar-maids in tight leopardskin; Rizzo in *Grease,* backcombing in the school toilets; Tracy in *Hairspray* wailing "But our First Lady, Jackie Kennedy, rats her hair!" when the teachers condemn her beehive. Dusty. Alexis Colby-Carrington. Winehouse.

It's the hair of the working-class girl on the make; on the town. A party helmet. A gigantic hair aura, indicating holy razziness—such as the Virgin Mary would have had, if she'd been in the Ronettes.

Hair takes us, naturally and easily, to the most famous hair of the twenty-first century. Not my own, alas—although it is something I am working on all the hours that God sends—but that of the Duchess of Cambridge, née Kate Middleton, our future Queen of England.

The Royal Wedding in March, 2011 was one of the big media events of the last ten years. Broadcasters and newspapers the world over wondered just how they could make their coverage truly reflect the grandeur, history and emotion of this occasion. On the one hand, this was something that would be included in encyclopedias, and be thought to reflect upon the age. On the other—two young, cheerful people in love. How best to report on this juddering disparity? How? HOW?

Thankfully, I knew: just write down everything Gary Kemp from Spandau Ballet said on Twitter throughout the ceremony.

The Best Royal Wedding Ever

IT MIGHT HAVE BEEN a Royal Wedding but, really, there was no pressure.

Should William and Kate have turned on ITV1's *Six O'Clock New*s the night before their wedding—perhaps in their bathrobes, in face packs, eating Shreddies—presenter Julie Etchingham would have soothed their nerves:

"This wedding," Etchingham said, standing outside Buckingham Palace, "is an opportunity for optimism about the future—in a moment when our history is marked by tough economic times at home, and DISAS-TER and DEATH *all around the world.*"

Well. That is quite an implication to take on board: that your wedding will, in some way, negate the effect of the Fukushima nuclear plant leak. However confident in your frock, finger buffet and vodka ice luge you may initially have been, it's got to be a bit of a jolt when *the news* tells you that your nuptials have the perceived ability to counteract radioactivity.

But the joy of something like a Royal Wedding, of course, is that everyone *does* go a little bit nuts around it. Last week *wasn't* a normal week. It was like the last day of the school year, or Friday at Glastonbury: everything upside down. Nothing usual. The shops ran out of bunting, lager and charcoal, the news disappeared from papers and TV, and what would normally be a workday turned into a holiday where it was perfectly acceptable to be sitting on the sofa at 11 AM, blind drunk, using an enormous foam rubber Union Jack hand to ferry peanuts to your mouth.

And so it was that the eve of the Royal Wedding had all the novelty of the day you move house—displacing all your usual objects and routines, and ending up with a supper of sardines and marmalade in the front garden, using only tablespoons. Odd conversations happened. On Thursday's episode of political show *This Week,* for instance, Richard Madeley claimed that the next day would see the marriage "consummated" at Westminster Abbey—an event inexplicably left out of *The Times*'s souvenir fourteen-page Order of Service.

Later in the show, presenter Andrew Neil asked him if he, Madeley, would "Get rid of Charles, and make William king?"

Madeley replied, "Well if he was gaga, obviously," with the kind of breezy certainty that suggested that, should our heir apparent actually "go gaga," Madeley would step up to the plate and finish Charles off with a spade, as if he were an old badger knocked down by a car.

As the sun set on April 28th, 2011, it was clear that this was a day that would live on in everyone's mind as the day Kerry Katona [@KerryKatona] tweeted, "Best of luck Kate and Wills. Hope it doesn't end like my last two," and Jeff Brazier [@JeffBrazier] (former boyfriend of the late Jade Goody, of *Big Brother* fame) made his big Royal Wedding statement: "Wills, I think your missus is fit. And for that reason, I just want to say, 'Well done.'"

Friday April 29, 2011

8:35 AM. It seemed that Kate Garraway had got the short straw: ITV1 had sent her out of London, away from the wedding, to Buckleberry—home of the Middletons. This is Middletonia. Middletonaria. Middletonton.

In a strapless dress and slightly incongruous furry bolero cardigan—it was colder than everyone thought it would be—Garraway was sitting outside Buckleberry's pub, surrounded by locals. One of them was holding a giant rabbit, which is wearing a Union Jack top hat.

"Buckleberry has become the center of the universe!" Garraway said—patently not true either in terms of the wedding (those international news crews aren't camped outside Westminster Abbey for nothing) or the composition of the universe (it has no observable center).

We cut away from Garraway to the crowds lining the Mall. A huge cheer had gone up, and the director clearly wished to see what it was. Alas—it was a huge Portapotty-emptying truck, at which the crowds were cheerfully and ironically waving their Union Jack flags. British crowds know exactly how to behave on a Big Day such as this, when the eyes of the world are upon them. You cheer the oomska-wagon with just as much fervor as you would cheer Princess Michael of Kent. It's one of the sly perks of being a subject.

Class-based bitchiness, meanwhile, is one of the sly perks of being a TV news anchor. Alistair Stewart had been outside the Goring Hotel since 6 AM, reporting on the nothing-happening emptiness that would, eventually, be stepped into by Kate Middleton on her way to the Abbey.

"The police presence is marvelously understated here," he smoothed. "Sometimes it's difficult to work out if it's a Middleton—or a member of staff."

ANOTHER ONE OF THE great things about this wedding is that it is happening so early. As a nation on a public holiday sets up the cafetiere and argues over the last Coco Pops variety pack, the King of Swaziland and Elton John are having to get into central London on a day with limited public transport options, then queue up for twenty minutes to get into Westminster Abbey.

Look—it is only 9:15 AM, and there is David Beckham, stuck in a celebrity-and-dignitaries traffic jam, and practicing his "staring into the distance looking noble" face while the crowd outside shouts, "Becks! Becks! Becks! Becks!"

Perhaps it is the sheer shock of the early hour, but Beckham's eyebrows appear to be verging just ever so slightly towards "Ming the Merciless." Next to him, his heavily pregnant wife, Victoria, stands in four-inch Louboutins, a ticking human time bomb. With the time currently 9:16 AM, and the service not due to end until 12:15, her pregnant bladder will be a matter of fretting concern to all the mothers watching on television.

"That poor cow still on that pew?" they will ask, as they themselves take advantage of their own, immediately-to-hand toilet facilities. "Let's hope she doesn't sneeze, or it is game over."

Last night, before the wedding began, there were a couple of things you would have felt incredibly confident in betting on. 1) The recurrence of the phrases "That dress," "Fairytale wedding," "What Britain does best," "The eyes of the world," "Diana's boys" and "Princess Beatrice, there, wearing a . . . thing."

2) Most women in the country crying quite heavily at some point during the ceremony.

And, finally, the most certain of all, 3) The BBC providing the definitive coverage of the event: solemn, reverent, knowing, stately, informed, and wholly befitting a royal occasion.

In the event, however, the BBC's coverage *is* solemn, reverent, knowing, stately and informed—and it doesn't befit this royal occasion at all. While the BBC gives us a thorough behind-the-scenes tour of the Household Cavalry's schedule today ("These boys have been shining their boots since 5 AM!") and thoughtful talking-heads in the studio, who marvel over the architecture of Westminster Abbey, ITV1 gets right in there: forcing milliner Stephen Jones to comment on other milliner's creations as they walk through the Abbey doors ("It's very . . . pretty," he offered, eventually, with a cat's bum mouth), giving us the money shots of Earl Spencer turning up ("There he is with his new fiancée—there's always a new one, isn't there?"), and zooming in on Prince Harry's girlfriend, Chelsy Davies, the minute she emerged from a car ("The wonderful thing about Kate is that she's so natural," Julie Etchingham mewed, as Chelsey's cheerfully bright orange face moved up the aisle).

In what was perhaps the definitive editorial decision of the day, at 9:30 AM, ITV1 cut from a live interview with David Cameron, who was being rather shiny and pious ("I know the whole nation wishes those young people a very great deal of luck") to show Tara Palmer-Tompkinson's arrival at Westminster Abbey instead.

The only possible reason for this newsflash-like urgency—Cameron was literally mid-sentence—was to see if Palmer-Tomkinson had, as had been speculated in the press, got her "new nose," following the recent collapse of her septum: thus making it abundantly clear that, for today at least, a minxy aristocrat's nasal integrity out-ranked anything the Prime Minister could say or do.

ITV1 had grasped what the BBC hadn't, or perhaps couldn't: that the way this country views the Royal Family has changed, and for the better. The ridiculous, childlike deference we had when Charles and Diana married—an era where there was the assumption that Diana would be a virgin, outrage at the creation of a *Spitting Image* puppet of the Queen Mother, and my father told me, in all seriousness, that I should never criticize the Queen in public "because you might get a punch in the face" (I was seven)—has gone, and it is better for all of us that it has. Opinions on what the national reaction to the life and death of Diana "meant" are two-a-penny, but I can't help but think that what we all learned, along the way, is that princes and princesses can be as lonely, hopeful, confused, unfaithful, devious, lost, simple, kindhearted, silly and breakable as the rest of us, and that demanding that they be anything other than fallible and human is apt to work out extremely badly for everyone involved.

The healthiest way William and Kate's future "subjects" could deal with watching their wedding, then, was to approach it as they would attending the wedding of a friend: i.e.: turning up in all good faith, having a couple of drinks, then cheerfully spend the rest of whole day taking the mick out of the décor, food, music, location and fellow-guests. Watch this just as they would watch *X Factor*—cheering the "good guys," slagging off the ridiculous or amusing elements on Twitter. And this, in the event, is just what ITV1 did.

By 10 AM, all the celebrities and dignitaries were assembled in the Abbey, and it was time to reflect on whose presence was sorely missed, due to the limited guest list. Personally, I yearned for Bill Clinton—old Big Dog. He was brilliant at the Olympic Bids—always in the background of a shot, mine-sweeping the room for poon and canapés. Tony Blair, similarly, would have been a good booking—or, failing him, Michael Sheen, who could have done the ceremony as Blair, then gone to the reception as either Brian Clough, or David Frost.

Guy Ritchie's arrival, meanwhile, underlined how awesome it would have been if he and Madonna had kept it together, and she was now stalking around the Abbey like Cruella de Ville with abs, making Nick Clegg cry with terror. And who didn't want George Michael there—a little bit stoned, having valet-parked his Jeep into a nearby tree? Thank goodness, then, that he could appear by proxy, via Twitter, while watching the ceremony from home—where, he informed us, he was wearing "Union Jack pants."

10:10 AM AND Huw Edwards on the BBC was getting very stressed about the day's schedule. "Prince William has *ten seconds* to appear," he said, making it all sound a bit like an episode of *24*.

10:11, and—a minute behind schedule—William finally emerged in the bright red uniform of the Irish Guards. As pop critic Tim Jonze [@timjonze] puts it on Twitter, "He's come dressed as Pete Doherty, circa 2003!"

Over CNN, horror instantly broke out amongst the American pundits with the advent of the minibuses, which were ferrying the wider royal family to the Abbey.

"These are airport shuttle buses!" one wailed—presumably laboring under the belief that the only way royalty and the aristocracy can be transported around is in a gigantic hollowed-out pumpkin, pulled by unicorns. What the American commentators failed to understand is that one of the things that Britain does best is putting loads of people on a bus. Look at *Summer Holiday.* Away-matches. Pakistani weddings in Wolverhampton. With this bus thing, we were playing to our strengths.

Martin Kemp [@realmartinkemp] from Spandau Ballet didn't think so, though: "Mini buses? Gimme a break," he snorted on Twitter. "Spandau or Duran wouldn't get in one of those. I bet Elton won't be going to the part in one. Off with the head of who organized that."

On the BBC, Kate Middleton had finally emerged from the Goring in a whiteout of flashbulbs. Even though we could not really see her, womankind had noticed one thing and was punching the air: the dress was sleeved! Yes! Finally the reign of evil sleevelessness is OVER! GOD BLESS YOU MIDDLETON! FASHION WILL NOW ALLOWS US TO HIDE OUR UPPER ARMS AGAIN, AS GOD INTENDED. Were the BBC to have a Body Dysmorphia-O-Meter, it would have registered an instant 40 percent drop across the nation. Our future Queen's biggest legacy had begun.

Sleeves aside, these first shots of Middleton in the car were not ideal. The framing of the telephoto lens was such that both her head, and her lower-torso, were cut off from view, and all we could see was Ms. Middleton's décolletage.

"It's a limited view, but a delightful view," Huw Edwards intoned, solemnly, as if he were now the BBC's Official State Perver. As the bride's father, Michael Middleton fussed around, placing the dress and train into the car, Edwards continued, "He is making sure everything is unsoiled, and undamaged"—an unfortunate narrative accompaniment to a man on his knees, half-buried under his daughter's dress, on the morning of her wedding.

11:05 AM, AND THE country's patriotism was peaking. This wedding looked *brilliant.* China must be *so jealous.* In your FACE, France. *No one* could do this better. America might have a funnier leader—Obama's take-down of Donald Trump involved clips from *The Lion King* and adroit political sideswipes; David Cameron does an impression of Michael Winner in a car insurance ad—but when it comes to doing the best-ever gigantic ceremony full of princesses, and people wearing uniforms, this wins. It's even better than the last scene in *Star Wars*.

William and a bedheaded Harry were joshing around at the altar like Luke and Han. The chief bridesmaid—Pippa Middleton—had a smokin' ass. The Archbishop of Canterbury's eyebrows were voluminous enough for him to be Chewie, and David Cameron and Nick Clegg could be C3PO and R2D2, if they wanted. This was amazing.

As if to confirm everyone's thoughts, Wayne Rooney [@WayneRooney] tweeted, "Congrats to prince William and Kate. Wow what a turnout." Rooney could appreciate the box office here as much as the next man.

As William pushed the ring onto Kate's finger, accompanied by an odd, squeaky sound—I think it was his shoes—and the couple tried not to giggle, one thing became pleasingly clear: this wasn't that much-touted thing, "a fairytale wedding," at all, thank God. It was just . . . human.

Because it's not just the public who have changed their view of the royals since the last wedding of an heir—the Royal Family itself has changed, too. Charles and Diana's wedding felt like something arranged by the elders and their advisers, into which Charles and Diana were parachuted, as the token meat in a vast machine. On that day, Diana—in her too-big dress—and Charles—with his heart somewhere else—looked like they were being eaten alive by St. Paul's Cathedral. In some ways, it's like they never came back out of there.

This wedding, however, feels like it's been imagined by a much younger and more confident generation: these glossy-haired girls and flush-cheeked, slightly awkward boys; this confederacy of tight-knit brothers and sisters and cousins. There is a sense of freedom, simplicity, camaraderie and fun here that one imagines Prince Charles watching from the pews in a slightly bittersweet way. These young royals seem to have a much better handle on being royal than their parents ever did.

Who would not enjoy this day?

Unexpectedly, the answer was: "Stephen Fry." Halfway through the ceremony—around the time of that hymn that sounded like the song the teapot sings on *Beauty and the Beast*—Fry [@stephenfry] incongruously tweets: "Ding's let Trump in. This twelfth frame is beginning to look huge. Nerve-wracking times."

At first, everyone presumed it was a joke—but when Fry followed it up with, "Mid-session interval and they go in 7-5 in Judd Trump's favor. No one yet pulling out in front, both these semis could go to the wire . . ." it became clear: Stephen Fry—friend of Prince Charles—really *was* tweeting the snooker during a Royal Wedding.

Someone needed to do something about this—and that someone was 1980s magician Paul Daniels: "WHO CARES?" Daniels [@ThePaulDaniels] asked Fry, as Twitter held its breath. Was Daniels about to take Jeeves into the Bunco Booth?

Daniels had been very passionate about this Royal Wedding: he had already castigated all the "snidey shits for coming out of the woodwork" who had dared criticize the day, definitively stated "WOW. That is what a Princess SHOULD look like" at Kate Middleton's arrival, and informed us that his wife, Debbie McGee, was "sobbing" from 10 AM onwards. And in his Musketeer-like defense of the Royals, Daniels found an unlikely ally: legendary 1980s puppet Roland Rat.

"I can't believe this English guy is so cynical!" Rat [@rolandrat] tweeted Daniels; presumably while wearing shades and a pink blouson bomber jacket.

"Off with his head!" Daniels agrees. The world's most unlikely Cavalier online militia had started to form.

Indeed, sorry to relate, in the interregnum between the ceremony and the kiss on the balcony, the mood had started to sour right across Twitter. A slightly boozy barroom belligerence had taken hold. One sensed that, across the country, there were a series of street parties at which celebrities were grudging participants—having been forced to "get out of the house and stop being such a miserable git" by non-famous spouses; only to spend the rest of the afternoon at a half-empty trestle-table, grimly downing multi-pack can after multi-pack can of Foster's and tweeting their distress to the world as their neighbors began a conga.

Pulp front-man—and recently divorced—Jarvis Cocker [@reallyjcocker] tweeted, rather dolorously, "10% of marriages end in divorce. Trust me—I know what I'm talking about."

George Michael [@GeorgeMichael] seemed a bit . . . hazy: "The greatest tragedy was Alexander McQueen not being around to make a fabulous creation for Kate," he tweeted—only to have to hastily clarify, minutes later, and presumably after some fairly irate replies, "Of course Diana's absence is the greatest tragedy—but it really goes without saying."

Things, however, had clearly degenerated most rapidly in the day of philosophical essayist Alain de Botton [@alaindebotton]. Having remained silent on Twitter all day, at 4 PM, de Botton suddenly weighed in with, "Women tend to miss the distinction between women who are beautiful, and women one would want to sleep with."

Ten seconds later, the follow-up tweet clarified what was on de Botton's mind: "Kate vs. Pippa."

As the world got its head around de Botton choosing to issue his Middleton Family Shag Order list on the day of the Royal Wedding, Jade Goody's widower, Jack Tweed [@JackTweed], finally issued his statement on this global event: "Not botherd about this wedding in the slightest everyone tweeting like they care is lying!!!"

He was wrong, of course—just like he was wrong that time he attacked that sixteen-year-old boy with a golf-club, and got sentenced to eighteen months in jail. People had cared a great deal. They cared about the idea of an event as big as the Olympics, or the inauguration of a President—and also about love, rather than sport or power. They cared about this rather serious young couple making their vows, in the way we care about all young people making vows. And they cared about the rather slash-fiction-ish idea of Pippa Middleton and Prince Harry getting it on. By 1:30 PM, the nation was roaring "Come on! KISS! KISS! You KNOW YOU WANT TO" at Pippa and Harry on the balcony as if this were *Seven Brides for Seven Brothers*, but with a much shorter cast list. And no beards.

As the new Duke and Duchess of Cambridge drove off in their Aston Martin to the reception—where they apparently danced to "You're the One That I Want" from *Grease,* and Prince Harry began his best man's speech with "Pippa—call me," before stage-diving off a windowsill into the crowd—you were given pause to reflect that—audience of two billion aside—they had given themselves just the wedding that they wanted.

And they had given us the wedding we wanted, too: heartfelt, worthy of a global audience, with David Beckham in it, and over early enough for everyone to get to the pub by 2 PM.

One of the reasons I'm too busy to get pregnant by a panda is because I spent the day with Paul McCartney. I SPENT THE DAY WITH PAUL McCARTNEY!

My Day with Paul McCartney.
From the Beatles.

I DIDN'T KNOW I was going to start crying until I started crying.

We're standing side of stage of the Mediolanum Forum in Milan. Outside, a fog as thick as snow has reduced visibility to fifteen feet. The hardcore McCartney fans—here, despite the earliness of the afternoon—stand in long queues at each of the Medioforum's twenty-five gates. The fog merges them into single, huge, lumpen entities.

Approaching the arena in a taxi, the Mediolanum Forum looks like it's under siege by a series of dragons, or slow-moving brontosauri. They are singing "She Loves You," damply, into the whiteout.

One particularly large, looming one is nearly fifty feet long. We drive past it, on our way to the backstage entrance.

"Yeah yeah yeah," the Loch Ness Monster sings, mournfully, as it recedes in our rear-view mirror. "Yeah yeah yeah."

Inside the Medioforum, and the whole building is also doing what the queues outside were doing: waiting. Waiting for Paul McCartney to arrive. He was expected at 4:30 PM, but it is now 6:30 PM—radios crackle with updates as to his location. His name is never really mentioned: it is just "He." Like when the animals talk of Aslan in *The Lion, the Witch and the Wardrobe:* "He's going to be another half-hour." "He's doing a radio interview." "He is on the move, towards Cair Paravel."

It is understood McCartney is the subject of all conversations. He is the purpose of everyone's presence here.

To while away the time while we wait for Him, John Hammel—McCartney's guitar tech for the last thirty-six years—takes me side of stage, to show me McCartney's guitars. Racked up at eye level, in a line, it feels less like looking at some musical instruments, and more like being introduced to dignitaries, or royalty. They have a quiet presence. They have life stories better than most human beings.

"This is the 'Yesterday' guitar," John says, taking a slightly battered-looking acoustic off the rack. There's some scratching, and chips, by the fingerboard. "This is the one Paul played 'Yesterday' for the first time on, on *The Ed Sullivan* show."

There's a Wings sticker on it, I note. "Yeah. Been there since 1973."

It's a remarkably pristine sticker for one that's been there since 1973. McCartney is clearly no nervous picker.

"That's the Casino—Paul bought it while they were recording *Revolver*," John continues, taking the next one off the rack with the air of a sommelier bringing out impossibly precious vintages from the cellar. "He played the solo to 'Taxman' on that. And wrote 'Paperback Writer' on it. That ukelele's from George. That Les Paul is from Linda—that's probably around £400,000. And this—is the Hofner bass."

We both fall momentarily silent as we look at it. This is one that looks like a gum-chewing, back-combing violin—the one that Paul got for the 1963 Royal Variety: "Rattle your jewellery," and neat bows to the Queen. The bass that started off making mono rock'n'pop'n'roll, and ended up on the roof at Apple. The McCartney Hofner bass.

"That is irreplaceable," John says, needlessly. "There was only one other like it and it was stolen to order—it'll be sitting in a private collection somewhere. It would never have been stolen on my watch," John says, with the quiet certainty of a man who would leave any potential thief crawling around on his hands and knees, looking for his severed legs under a chair. "I sleep with the Hofner in my bedroom. I put it in the wardrobe. I carry that, personally, with me everywhere."

"Paul uses them because they're the best," John says, simply. "He wants that sound on stage. He's not precious about them. He likes to throw them at me, headstock first, like an arrow. I've never dropped one yet." He pauses. "Yet."

I touch the Hofner bass with my forefinger. I imagine it left, carelessly, on the floor of Abbey Road as Paul and John sit next to it—smoking ciggies over it, scribbling the lyrics on a sheet of notebook paper. That's when I start crying.

In a way, I'm not really surprised I'm crying. As a godless hippy, The Beatles are the grid by which I understand the universe. When I was ten and I heard my nanna had died, I ate a whole Soreen malt loaf, in misery, and then vomited it out of the landing window, on the shed roof, while singing "Yesterday" in a mournful manner. Paul's words were the only thing I could turn to in that moment of childish sorrow.

In the next half hour, I could now, finally, be in a position where I could tell Paul McCartney this fact.

I must not tell Paul McCartney this fact.

I palm the tears off my face with my sleeve.

"He's coming. Stage left."

The radios crackle into action. A couple of phones beep. The attention of the entire arena is pulled to the access entrance, stage left, where a huge pair of double doors are opened up, and fog swirls up the ramp.

As this is lit up gold by car headlights, a half-joyful, half-mournful cry of "PAUL! PAUL!" comes from the serried Diplodoci outside. A car comes up the ramp, security opens the doors, and, there, now, here: McCartney emerges. McCartney. Straight-backed, swagged in a beautiful, long, mid-blue coat.

He looks like a straight line—a straight line that always moves in a straight line, unimpeded in his intended trajectory for decades. He walks into the arena. He greets his crew. He comes to me.

"What's your name?" he asks me. I tell him.

"I'm Paul," he says. He tells it like a joke. The idea of no one knowing who he is is absurd. Paul hasn't needed to give the actual information "I am Paul" since 1963.

"Being backstage at a McCartney gig is amazing," Stuart Bell, his PR, had been saying, earlier. "Because you'll find, say, Bill Clinton sitting in the corridor. Waiting! Waiting for Paul. They'll all wait for Paul."

Taking his coat off as he walks, McCartney walks straight onstage, where the band is waiting. Handed his guitar, he goes straight into sound-checking Carl Perkins's "Honey Don't."

For the next half hour, he plays to an audience of thirty Italian competition winners with a set that most people would pull out to headline a festival. "Something." "Penny Lane." "Things We Said Today."

Halfway through "Penny Lane" I think about how genuinely upset the world will be when Paul dies, and start crying again. We all want to believe in something we can regard with the awe and trust of a child. A Beatle is a man-made thing you can regard with the same astonishment you would the Moon.

"Oh, Paul!" I think, mournfully, as a perfectly hale and hearty McCartney bounds offstage, bidding the Italian competition winners "Ciao!" with a cheery wave, and exuding the energy of a man in his late-twenties. "Paul! I will vigil *hard* for you when you die."

AND, SO, TO PAUL'S dressing room. Here is his wardrobe, including six handmade, collarless Nehru jackets—the classic Beatle-suit—and six pairs of jet black, handmade Beatle boots. A brand new pair of Giorgio Armani socks sit next to them. A Beatle does *not* go on stage in pre-used socks. This is what we have learned today.

The room is in no way lavish—the walls are swagged with a few bright, Indian throws, a Diptyque Oyedo candle burns on the coffee-table. Four bamboo trees, in pots, add what I'm sure interior designers refer to as "room veg." A Pilates mat and ball sit under the gigantic TV, which is showing the Grand Prix. And that's it. The general vibe is "London middle-class comfort." We're basically in Islington.

"Hello!" Paul says, shaking my hand, and ushering us onto the sofa. He eats handfuls of chocolate-covered raisins, and occasionally glances up at the Grand Prix—"Who's winning?"—as I settle in to ask him the main thing that puzzles me. After playing over 3,000 gigs in your life (2,523 with the Beatles, 140 with Wings, 325 solo): What's still in this for you, Paul McCartney?

"I like . . . displaying the stuff," McCartney says, eating another chocolate-covered raisin. "I want to give people a good night out. I heard this story about Bob Dylan once—one of the guys in his band told me they were in the dressing room, going, 'That version of "Tambourine Man"— we're doing great, Bob!' and Bob said, 'Right, we're changing it tomorrow night.' Well I can see that, and that's cool, but I'm not like that.

"If I go to see Prince—I mean, I love his guitar playing, but I want him to play 'Purple Rain.' I'm probably going to be disappointed if he doesn't do it. If I went to see the Stones, I'd want them to do 'Ruby Tuesday,' 'Honky Tonk Woman' and 'Satisfaction.' So I'm basically talking hits. Why are hits hits? It's because we like them. They're the best ones."

McCartney explains that his soundchecks—attended only by competition winners—are where "I get to play the more obscure stuff; jam a bit. But I try to think about how I'd feel if I'd *paid* to see me jamming away. I think I'd think, 'You miserable sod,' and wouldn't want to see me again."

Paul then goes onto tell three stories that suggest—in marked contrast to the disconcerting, alpha, tribal elder of Earth vibe he emits—that he is still insecure, after all these years.

The first about how he only announces the first two dates of any tour, "to see how they sell," so that—when they sell out in six minutes, as happened with this week's 02 gig—he can sigh and say, "Well, people *do* still want to see me, after all." He pauses, then adds, in the interest of balance, "Although some of those would be to touts [scalpers], obviously."

The second is how he's only recently started playing a lot of lead guitar, "Because the first time we ever played—pre-Beatles—I totally screwed up on the first night. The Co-op Reform, Liverpool Broadway," he clarifies. "Above a shop. I totally blew it—the nerves got the better of me. So I never played lead guitar again."

"It's taken you this long to get your nerve back?" I ask, incredulously.

"Yeah," he replies. "I mean, I'm not really nervous now, but it was a big thing: when the Beatles did Wembley for the first time, I remember sitting on the Town Hall steps feeling physically sick. I thought, 'I've got to give this up.'"

He then goes to talk about how even Paul McCartney gets the occasional "tough gig."

"Occasionally there will be a corporate gig you have to play. We did a corporate gig for Lexus, and we thought, 'Oh my god, they're just standing there. They're so reserved.' So I turned to everyone and said, 'Hold your nerve! It's okay! Don't worry! We're good!' And we've learned to hold our nerve for the first few numbers because we get them. We always get them in the end. They always come back."

People need to go to the toilet, I say. They might have just been going to the toilet. Paul looks horrified.

"My recurring nightmare is that people are leaving. It always has been. I still dream I'm with the Beatles, and we're going [sings]: 'If there's anything that you want,' it's going great—and then people start getting up and leaving. And I turn to the others, and go, 'Oh God! "Long Tall Sally"! I always call out that one, in my dreams. 'Long Tall Sally'—that'll get them back."

Having established that Paul is still quite a nervous performer, I decide that this is the time to give him some friendly advice for his forthcoming UK dates. He's recently added "The Word" and "Give Peace a Chance" to his setlist, but there is still a glaring omission in a two-hour show that takes in "Maybe I'm Amazed," "Blackbird," "A Day In The Life," "Let It Be," "Live And Let Die," "Jet," "Hey Jude," "Let It Be," "Day Tripper," "Get Back," "Eleanor Rigby," "Penny Lane," "Yesterday," "Helter Skelter" and "Golden Slumbers."

"Paul," I say. "Do you know what I think people would go apeshit for now? The Frog Chorus. 'We All Stand Together' by the Frog Chorus."

He looks at me suspiciously.

"Seriously," I say. "There is a whole generation that will have a massive Proustian rush when they hear it."

"Oh my God," McCartney says, looking thoughtful. "Wow. I hadn't thought of that."

"Go frog! Go frog!" I encourage him. "Imagine when everyone starts singing 'Boom boom boom/Biya!'"

I am singing the Frog Chorus's "We All Stand Together" at Paul McCartney, in case he has forgotten it.

"You've planted a very dangerous idea there," he says, still looking unsure as to how serious I am. But I am in deadly earnest.

From the Frog Chorus we move on to McCartney's recent wedding, to businesswoman Nancy Shevell. The newspapers widely reported that McCartney had played at the wedding-reception at his house—"I didn't"—and that neighbors had complained to the police about the noise.

"Well our immediate neighbors were *at* the party," McCartney says, "and they loved it. But we did go on until 3 AM; it was Mark Ronson DJing loud rock 'n' roll music, and, if I'd been someone further down the street, *I* probably would have complained. Three in the morning? I would have been Aggrieved of Ealing."

I've only got three minutes left with McCartney, from my allotted twenty—I wasted five minutes trying to get his position on the current economic situation ("When the banks go bust, and we bail them out—okay, I can see that. But here's the bit I feel is missing—they didn't pay us back. I think everyone is like, 'Wait a minute—did I miss something?' I am with all those people [protestors] in that respect. Pay it back.") and whether the rumors of a forthcoming McCartney autobiography, or autobiographical documentary, are true ("Britney Spears has written hers aged, what, three? I've had Hewlett Packard digitize and index my entire collection of film and photographs, so I can find anything in seconds. Maybe I should, before I forget.")

"The other big news story of the year has been hacking," I remind him. "You were hacked?"

"Yes," McCartney says, looking serious. "There would be stories about how I was going on holiday to the Bahamas, or whatever—and I would know I hadn't told anyone. And the worst thing is that then, you suspect *everyone*. Your PA, who you thought was a great girl—'What if?' At the time of the divorce, I realized there was quite a possibility of many people hacking me, for *various* reasons . . ."

Paul raises his eyebrows here. Clearly he means Heather.

"So I just used to talk on the phone, and say, 'If you're taking this down, get a life.' It is a pity not to be able to talk freely on a private phone call. I tend not to say much on the phone now. If I leave a message, it's quite benign. You edit yourself according to the new circumstances of the new world. I think it really would be quite good to get some sort of laws. Actually," McCartney continues, lightening, "do you know what *really* annoys me? I'd like to be able to go on holiday and not have to hold my belly in for two whole weeks [in case of paparazzi]. I saw some guy on the beach the other week, playing in the sand, belly hanging out over his shorts, and I was so envious."

McCartney goes back to musing on hacking. "You know, I wouldn't mind a tabloid journalist's job. Obviously I've got the better job—but I like the idea of just . . . making up crap. David Beckham. You could go *anywhere* with David Beckham."

With McCartney's PR telling me my time is up, this the point where I ask Paul McCartney the question about what he'd do if his face got mashed up in an horrific accident.

"Paul. If you had a terrible accident and your face got all smashed up—heaven forbid, obviously—would you rebuild it to look like yourself: or would you change it, so you could finally become anonymous again?"

I think it's quite a good question. It touches on fame, beauty, identity, ego, and the idea of living two lives in one lifetime. But Paul's actual, current face suggests he doesn't think so.

"I would rebuild it to look like David Cameron," McCartney says, clearly thinking this is a shit question.

"Why?"

"Because I'm kidding. Silly girl."

"Sorry—it's just, Cameron? It seems like a uniquely horrible idea."

"I know. That's why it's funnier," McCartney says, patiently. "Imagine me singing 'Yesterday,' then people going 'Who is it? Cameron?' But, seriously, I'm from the 'Don't go there school.' I don't like visualizing stuff like that. I like to visualize myself living a wonderful life, being very happy, and all my family making a wonderful old age. I don't imagine things like that."

And that's it—my time is up with Paul McCartney, which I managed to end by bumming him out with visions of his face being mashed into a pulp. We have our picture taken together, then I go out into the corridor, where I make a low, sad roaring sound, such as Chewbacca makes in *Star Wars* when things have gone wrong. Why did I ask McCartney about his face being mashed up? Why? Why? I am the worst Beatles fan since Mark David Chapman.

AN HOUR BEFORE SHOWTIME, and the unmistakeable sound of an American tour manager balling someone out comes from just outside the catering area. Anyone who has seen *Spinal Tap* will know what this sounds like.

"I've told you before—if they don't have a laminate, you KICK THEIR ASSES OUT!"

It appears that someone has been sneaking local chancers into the venue. It's not clear who, exactly, is responsible for this—but it's notable the Chief of Police and his sidekick are standing there, in their shiny boots and slightly-too-large hats, with faces like smacked arses. No one in McCartney's entourage is talking to them.

"There's no reason for them to be here—but you just can't keep the local police out if they insist they want to come," someone explains.

When the shouting ends, the Chief of Police and his sidekick sit alone, in catering, and eat McCartney's tiramisu with that look on their faces which is specifically the face angry Italian policemen pull while eating creamy puddings on their own.

Showtime, and, on stage, McCartney looks twenty years younger than he did in his dressing room. It's not the lighting—it's the music. Singing "Penny Lane" is more effective than Botox or a facelift, if you are the person who wrote it in the first place. He piles into a two-and-a-half hour set with all the attack of a man in his late teens. This is a *ferocious* gig. There's a moment in "Jet" where he's playing that heavy, strobing, fuzz-edged bass with one hand, staring out at the crowd with a look that, for a moment, I can't place.

Then I recall an interview where he's asked, "Does going to see other bands make you feel competitive?"

And McCartney replies, "Actually, it works the other way. Without being too immodest, I tend to see shows and think, 'Well, we rock out pretty well.'"

And suddenly I know the answer to the question, "What's in this for Paul McCartney?" All that stuff about being an insecure performer—yes, that probably is one part of the motivation. But the combustion comes from combining insecurity with the fact that McCartney is the best in the world at this, he knows it, and the quietly aggressive part of him wants to go out there and, in the most elegant way possible, smash his competition to bits.

At root, McCartney is still the quiffed-up rock 'n' roll kid in the incongruous combination of black leather and cowboy boots in Hamburg in 1961, off his tits on speed at 4 AM, playing to sailors and whores. We might be in an arena that has spent all day waiting for a knighted global dignitary to turn up—but the set he blasts through is like the Death Star of rock'n'pop. Nothing can touch its fire power. This old man is in the middle of the greatest pop show on Earth. Just with the opening *"Aaaah"* of "Eleanor Rigby," he acclerates away from anyone who might come close.

As the gig comes to the end, I am confused as to why, joining us at the side of stage, is a whooping, dancing Kate Middleton, freaking out to "Helter Skelter." One always *presumes* everyone in the world is a McCartney fan—but I'm amazed at how little security the future Queen has. Then I realize this is, actually, Nancy Shevell—Lady McCartney—still-new wedding ring catching in the light. She has the extremely cheerful air of someone who came off honeymoon three weeks ago, and is really enjoying unwrapping all the diamonds off her John Lewis wedding list.

As Paul comes to the end of the "Golden Slumbers" medley, Shevell fetches a red terry cloth robe and, when he comes offstage, sweating, she wraps it around him, with a kiss.

McCartney exits down the ramp with her—out of the Medioforum, and into his tour bus. His private jet is waiting: he'll be in bed in St. John's

Wood by 3 AM. The crew line his route to the tour bus—whooping and clapping. He high-fives each one as he passes them.

"Thank you!" he shouts to everyone. "Thank you!"

And into the fog goes a blue-light flashing motorcade, over which can be heard the half-joyful, half-mournful cries of "PAUL! PAUL!"—the sound of his every entrance and exit since 1962.

I fly back to London with his plectrum in my purse.

And now onto celebrity weight-loss—a subject which, in Google returns, brings up more results than "potential nuclear holocaust" and "Charlie bit my finger" combined.

Celebrity Weight-Loss: The Truth

OVER THE YEARS I'VE been very fat (size 24—try getting *that* through the turnstiles at Regent's Park Zoo in a duffelcoat) and I've been very thin (actually I haven't, but all articles on weight have to start with this sentence, I have noticed)—and all through these vagaries of heftiness I have observed one thing: women have to lie about how they lost weight; and the more famous you are, the greater the lie.

If a non-famous person loses ten pounds and is asked to comment on it, they'll say, "Oh, I ate a bit more salad, and went running a couple of times," in a slightly awkward, "Let's drop this" manner.

The reality is, of course, that they've been running up hills at 8 AM in the morning with "Don't Stop Believin'" on repeat on their iPod, weeping with the searing pain that is manifesting, mysteriously, in one buttock only, only to return home to a great big plate of cold beetroot mash, and would rather die than tell you.

This reticence to fully disclose the reality of the endeavor stems from a) an unwillingness to become a Weight-Loss Bore (returning from the toilet: "Hey—everybody! Guys! Listen up! I lost an OUNCE!") and b) an awareness that if you—as is statistically likely—end up putting the weight back on, you don't want everyone casting pitying looks at you, and saying, "All that effort—and then she blew it all on ten-day holiday with an all-you-can-eat savory crepe-buffet. Oh, the humanity."

No—as regards the circumferance of your arse, as far as everyone else is concerned, you want them to think it's, "Easy come, easy go." An air of studied casualness about your weight is the aim. It's no biggie.

However. When it comes to celebrity weight-loss, this "studied casualness" is taken to absolutely absurd extremes. As someone who spends half their life reading glossy gossip mags—and therefore doesn't miss a single post-baby/new album/new boyfriend weight-loss story—I can confidently announce that we are currently living through an Imperial Phase of celebrity lies about weight-loss, and have duly collated my favorite ones here:

1. First post-baby photo-shoot: mom's looking HOT! She's at a premiere in a Herve Leger Bandage dress—just SIX WEEKS after pooing out a human-child! How, Celebrity—HOW?

"I've been so busy running around after the baby, the weight just dropped off!" celebrity mom reveals, giggling.

Whoah here, missy, whoah! "I've been so busy running around after the baby, the weight dropped off"? But how can that be? Your experience is so very dissimilar to mine! When *I* had babies, I seem to remember most of that time being spent pinned under a fractiously half-sleeping colicky infant: unable to move in order to carry out even the most basic of human functions, like breathing particularly deeply, or finding the TV remote.

The first nine months of a baby's life are an infamously non-mobile period. A baby's notable stasis has been the inspiration for a number of high-profile inventions—such as the stroller, and the sling. How—six weeks after birth—anyone could be "running around" after something with all the motility of an ancient tumulus is an absolute mystery to me. Perhaps celebrity dads strap the babies to remote-control helicopters, and get the celebrity moms to chase them around the house. Yes. That will be how Victoria Beckham lost all that weight after having Cruz.

1. "I've been so busy with work, I just forgot to eat!" Again, celebrities, your experience is so very different to mine. I work on the fringes of entertainment/media, and one thing that I have noticed

about entertainment/the media is that, in these fields, every single work-thing you could do—meetings, photo-shoots, aftershows, filming—is accompanied by AT LEAST three of the following: a plate of cheese and ham slices, brioche, potato chips, massive "platter" of assorted Pret sandwiches, miniature burgers, meat on a stick, selection of stupidly dandy cupcakes, spendy chocolate biscuits, twenty-four "deli-style" Scotch eggs, some salady shit that no one touches, and as many milky lattes as would take to fill a putative and revolving Lactose Hot Tub. You can't "forget" to eat in these conditions. Everyone *else* around you is medicating their constant, low-level media anxiety by troughing refined carbs, interspersed with fags smoked outside while texting their boyfriends about how everyone else they're working with today is a neurotic bitch. Just copy their behavior. You'll soon "remember" to eat again in no time!

2. "I went to see this amazing woman, and found out I am allergic to wheat/that my blood type means I can't eat cheese/that my face shape means bananas make me fat—and since I cut them out of my diet, I've never been more toned!" The truth: "As you can see, since I started mixing up all my prescription drugs in a big bowl by my bed and eating them like Dolly Mixtures, I've lost my mind* and I'm not terribly hungry. Life is GREAT!"

*Falls asleep for twenty-six hours straight.

Nearly the end of the book, now, and a couple of obituaries to finish things off. We will stumble toward the end piece through death, and loss. Black-veiled and attendant at the graveside, thoughtful. Thankful. Confused.

Two of my favorite women died in 2011—Amy Winehouse and Elizabeth Taylor. Two lush-lipped, hard-drinking British women—broads made of eyeliner, grace and balls.

In my dreams, as a fan, I would have been on casual, cheerful email terms with both—enjoying the very great pleasure of seeing their names in my inbox, in black pixel; when they're more usually up on billboards, in lights. Asking questions not for quote, but from curiosity. Trying, in some manner, to amuse a pair who—Cleopatra-eyed, both—had seen everything by the age of twenty-five.

In the end, the only thing I ever said to them was these obituaries—the worst letters, never sent; but posted up under headlines, instead.

Elizabeth Taylor: Heavy, Like Wet Roses

THEY WERE THE GREATEST eyes, and now they have ended: violet, violently beautiful and lush-lashed, Elizabeth Taylor's extraordinary eyes have passed from fact to artifact. Man, she was awesome—my favorite, my most-watched. The best of all the legends. A star in an era of dames and broads, Taylor out-damed and out-broaded them all—even fabulous Ava Gardner, who once, when her then-husband Frank Sinatra was described as "A 119-lb has-been," replied, "Yes. And 19 lbs of it is cock."

But Taylor topped that, effortlessly—with a private jet called *Elizabeth*, two Oscars, skin like milk and the ability to drink any man under the table, she could walk into any gathering like the commander of a star fleet. No one was superior to her—but then, no one was worthy enough to worship her properly until Richard Burton came along, for the first and then the second time, and kissed her right out of her shoes. Their relationship was like a bomb that kept going off: they were condemned for "erotic vagrancy" by the Vatican at the start of their affair, but carelessly racketed around the world collecting Van Goghs, Pissarros, Rembrandts and diamonds, arguing, drinking and trashing big beds.

Burton was lost the moment he met her—his description of their first meeting is one of the most astonishing declarations of love ever written. It twangs with holy lust, even forty years later.

"She was so extraordinarily beautiful that I nearly laughed out loud. Her body was a true miracle of construction—the work of an eningeer of genius. It needed nothing except itself. It was smitten by its own passion. She was unquestionably gorgeous. She was lavish. She was a dark, unyielding largesse. She was, in short, too bloody much."

In a world where women still worry that they are "too much"—too big, too loud, too demanding, too exuberant—Taylor was a reminder of what a delight it can be, for men and women alike, when a women really does take full possession of her powers. Burton's nickname for her was "Ocean." Sometimes, it seemed too small.

On my wall, I have a shot of Taylor in her late forties. She is with David Bowie—outdoors in LA, at a guess. Bowie is emaciated—at the height of his cocaine addiction, but still, clearly, both powerful and beautiful. He has his arms around Taylor's waist—a thicker, rounder waist than her corseted days in *Cat on a Hot Tin Roof*; she is heavy, like wet roses. She looks like a banquet. As she puts a cigarette to Bowie's mouth, her face is both lascivious and maternal—her lips are half-open; you can practically hear her coo, "Here you go, baby." In that one shot, she makes David Bowie—*David Bowie*—look like a helpless teenage boy.

She was a storm front of a woman, in sapphires. Tonight, I will drink cold, cold champagne in her memory. Then eat a diamond.

And Winehouse.

Winehouse—Jump on Your Voice, Like a Lion, and Run Away

IN A WAY NOT morbid or maudlin, all I can do is YouTube Amy Winehouse. I watch her in the kitchen, in the bedroom; in the garden, on the laptop, while I hack back gloomy loops of summer hops. Her voice seems unsuited for the outdoors, but I want her propped up on a garden chair. In the sunshine, now. In my head I call her "Winehouse," like a cartoon character or a punky kid: Winehouse with her tattoos and her stapled-on beehive; Winehouse with her long ankles, bottle in hand, tottery and roaring. A post-apocalyptic Marge Simpson; Betty Boop in charge of a pirate ship, Winehouse on *Never Mind the Buzzcocks*, shrugging off host Simon Amstell's joky, awkward concern, with the downbeat timing of Joan Rivers or Dennis Leary.

Would Amy like to collaborate with MOR chanteuse Katie Melua, Amstell wondered. (MOR is the genre otherwise known as "Middle of the Road," for its resolute determination in steering an unobjectionable, bland course right down the center of rock/pop. Melua was, at the time, skilled enough to have become Europe's biggest-selling artist, thanks to her ability to keep right in the central reservation for 200 miles of pop, without once ever deviating into anything memorable.)

"I'd rather get cat AIDS," Winehouse replied tartly, funnier than any comedian on the show, but still Winehouse—Amy Winehouse with the voice, with the astonishing voice, like Billie Holiday scared, angry, hot; tooling up. She wrote "Back to Black"—one of the best singles of the twenty-first century, a tendon-tight song that, halfway through, just dissolves into its own awfulness, leaving only the tolling of a church bell, and Winehouse singing "Black . . . /Black . . ." like it's the only direction she has left— when she was twenty-three. In the video, she dresses for a funeral. Sharp. Tight skirt. Eyeliner. She puts her gloves on, tearless. By the age of twenty-four, she has five Grammys. By twenty-seven, she's dead.

I can't stop watching her because I can't work out exactly how I feel about her dying. Her death is not something unexpected, after all—it had been coming down the tunnel for a long time. And yet it still rattled everyone—our preparedness is no preparation at all.

"This is how we will feel when polar bears finally become extinct," I think, "after all that sad waiting. Or when the last tiger dies."

We still won't quite understand why—even though we watched almost every minute of it happen. I'm not the only one puzzled—friends, particularly women, keep fretting over Winehouse's death. It's not some wailing, pent-up boo-hoo, like when Diana died. Rather, it's like when woodland animals circle another woodland animal who has died, uncomprehending as to why it has gone. How it could have gone.

Perhaps part of it is that we didn't see who Winehouse really was, at the time. Like everyone, I'd always thought her problem was alcohol and drugs: those years of being photographed in bloody shoes, bleakly marauding at 3 AM. When the Hawley Arms in Camden—epicenter of the drunken world at that time—burned down, everyone joked Winehouse had done it, by accident. Winehouse, with an unfortunate combination of crack pipe and Elnett hairspray.

But when a friend said, "What if her biggest problem wasn't drink or drugs, but her eating disorders?," the YouTube footage suddenly felt like it was being played again; but now, with new subtitles.

So here is Amy Winehouse at the Mercury Awards in 2007, coming on stage to gasps, the bright neons of her dress playing badly against the pint-sized hollows of her collarbone. Everyone thinks it's the crack—but she gives interviews where she says she spends all morning running on a treadmill. She wears hotpants and cut-off shirts, revealing that tiny, knotted belly—even in winter, even in snow. She cooks for everyone, but doesn't touch anything herself. "All she eats is Haribo," a friend reveals to the *Daily Mirror*. With an eating disorder like that, you'd have all the tolerance for drink and drugs of a newborn baby.

And because eating disorders are all about trying to regain control, it solves the biggest confusion I have had about Winehouse, since I heard she'd died: how you could have a talent—such a once-in-a-generation, seemingly gravityless, endless talent—and let it get so battered by your addictions that your big album, in 2006, is also your last. Surely you'd want to protect it as you would a child, serve it as you would an empress? Couldn't she discipline herself? To keep her very Winehouseness safe? Well, she was. She was very busy disciplining herself. She wasn't eating.

For anyone without a talent like Winehouse's—and that's all of us—we just stare, like unjealous Salieris, and wonder how someone could have something so astonishing move through them—yet not have it elevate them at the same time. We become like children. Couldn't that talent, somehow, have saved her? Couldn't a song as astonishing as *Back to Black* vouch for her against demons? Couldn't Amy Winehouse just climb on to her voice, like it was a lion, and jump out of the window, and ride far, far away?

But then, perhaps that's what she did.

This is the last piece in the book. Ending where we began—in bed, with my husband unwillingly dragging himself out of unconsciousness to deal with the kind of issue that looms large in the heads of women the world over, but seems like an outright declaration of insanity to all men.

My Tragically Early Death

IT IS 11:48 PM. We are just about to go to sleep. I can hear the dishwasher downstairs come to the end of its self-aggrandizingly-named Superwash. The house is silent.

Beside me, Pete's breathing changes down three gears—into early, stop-motion dreams. It has been a long day. He deserves his rest. Today is now ended. Sleep well, sweet prince, I think. Sleep well.

"Pete?"

"M."

"What would you miss most about me if I died tragically young?"

"Whrrr?"

"If I died—tomorrow—perhaps brutally—what would you miss most about me?"

"Not now. Please. So tired."

"When the sad, young policeman appeared at the door with his *Casualty* face on, and said, 'I'm so sorry—there's been an accident,' what would be the first thing that popped into your head, that started you crying?"

"This is happening? Oh God, this is happening."

Pete turns over. I sit up in bed.

"It's just, I know what upsets *me* most about me dying tragically young," I say. "Not being there for the girls the first time some fifth-form bitch is catty about their shoes. Never having learned French. Never having written that BAFTA-winning sitcom set in a lookalikes agency, called *Cher & Cher Alike*. But what about you? What would be making you feel utterly destroyed and helpless?"

Pete sighs. He is now totally awake. He does also look a bit sad. Talking about death in bed appears to be a bit of a downer. He finds my hand under the duvet, and takes hold of it.

"The total loss of companionship, love and sex," he says, with a squeeze.

Pause.

"That's a bit broad," I say.

"What?"

"I wanted more specific things."

"What?"

"I wanted to be able to imagine the exact points, during a day, you would suddenly go 'She's gone!' and collapse on the floor, sobbing."

"Why. On. *Earth*. Would you want to do that?"

I think this is a bit of an odd question.

"All women wonder it," I explained, patiently.

"Why?"

"We just do. It's a woman thing. It's a thing we do. You just have to accept it, as part of sharing the Earth with us—in the same way we accept you will come into the kitchen and show us a book on the history of service stations, from 1920 until the present day, going, 'Look at the pictures! Every single one is a gem!' while waving around a shot of three men in Sta-prest trousers smoking a fag outside a café on the A6. *You* do that. *We* like to imagine the after-effects of our tragic early deaths on our menfolk. So. What, *very specifically*, would leave you feeling hopeless and broken?"

"Splinters," Pete says.

"What?"

"Splinters. When the girls get splinters. You can go in there with the pin. Jesus. I can't do that. Splinters."

Pause.

"Okay," I say, "now you're being *too* specific. Can you take the focus of your Mourning Camera at some midway point between 'Total loss of companionship,' and 'splinters'? Something in the middle?"

Pete thinks. He thinks for quite a long time. His breathing catches a bit. Oh God! He's crying. I have a massive stab of love for him—crying for me, his dead wife, in the dark.

"Is it upsetting you?" I ask, squeezing his hand.

"Blarrrr. Fell asleep again," he says. "Did I start snoring? So tired."

"I'm DEAD," I say. "DEAD at thirty-six. Fucking tell me what the worst bits are! Now! Do it now! Now!"

"Okay," Pete says, totally awake now, sitting up in bed. "I would miss you when I wake up. I would miss you when I go to sleep. I'd miss you when I'm scared, and you say 'Everyone can screw themselves,' and it seems to make things better. I'd miss you every time our kids laughed, or cried. I'd miss you every time I looked at that tree at the end of the garden that you love, or smelled your perfume on a woman walking by, or saw someone laughing so much they made piggy snorting noises and lay on the floor, crying. I'd miss you all. The. Time."

It's a beautiful list. So full of love, and memory, and pride. I am a lucky woman.

"What about my bread and butter pudding?" I say. "No one else's bread and butter pudding is as good as my bread and butter pudding."

"Yes," Pete says, still emotional. "I would be sad to eat someone else's bread and butter pudding."

". . . and punning," I say. "Your second wife would never be as good at puns as I am."

"That is, also, true," Pete says, slightly brisker.

"And I think one of my real strong points has always been my ability to absorb a large amount of information, then render it down to the essential parts in a really easy-to-understand way. . . ."

"Just so you know," Pete says, turning over to sleep, "this is definitely another memory that will make me cry. A lot."

Acknowledgments

THIS BOOK WOULD HAVE nothing in it were it not for the fact that, over eighteen years at *The Times,* I have had a series of parodically clever and lovely editors, who made being a columnist for them a dream job, which I would willingly have done for free. Thank you, a million times, to Sarah Vine, Alex O'Connell, Emma Tucker, Shaun Philips, Mike Mulvihill, and particularly the properly demented and brilliant Nicola Jeal, for making my job something where I might, on occasion, find myself at 4 PM in February at Cliveden, in a massive wedding dress, wearing a Kate Middleton wig, and pretending to kiss a Prince William lookalike. And James Harding—you are the Gentleman Editor of Fleet Street, and I am proud to work for your paper. I know how lucky I am to deal with you all. Thank you.

At Ebury, I cannot spade enough appreciation onto the head dude, Jake Lingwood, who dreams BIG and then makes it all come true, and Liz Marvin, for being wholly indomitable. And there's a reason why Ebury's PR, Ed Griffiths, wins awards—he's scientifically and provably the best. I love you, Mr. Jeff Pigeon.

At my American publishers, Jennifer Barth insanely believed that *How to Be a Woman*—a book written by someone from Wolverhampton who once, while watching television with her family, sneezed a mouthful of sardines on the screen, then scraped it off and ate it again—could sell in the States, and got it in the *New York Times* Top Ten. This is an event which frankly I'm still lying on the floor about, having cold gin flicked at my face, trying to process.

And Gregory Henry, the US publicist for the book, wrangled an astonishing campaign—despite having to work around the massive disability of working with an author who says "lift" instead of elevator, and doesn't know who Diane Sawyer is. Or who those nice ladies we met on the *Today* show are. Who were they? They smelled of wine. I liked it. Thanks too to Jonathan Burnham, Erica Barmash, Amy Baker, David Watson, Dori Carlson, Lelia Mander, and all the other lovely people at HarperCollins.

Georgia Garrett—if you ever stop being my agent, I will end myself. You've got a mind for business, a body for sin, and the heart for long lunches.

To all the people who let me come and hang out with them for features—thank you. I hope I was reasonably accurate. It was a proper thrill to meet you all. Gareth Dorrian—thank you for replying to my panicked, anxious Tweet of "I AM THREE WEEKS OVER DEADLINE AND WILL GIVE CHAMPAGNE TO SOMEONE WHO CAN THINK OF A TITLE FOR MY BOOK" with the perfect, elegant, pun-ny and Beatle-ish "Moranthology." Enjoy your champagne. I've never been happier to put three first class stamps on a bottle of blanc de blanc.

As with the last book, I must thank all the people I hang around with all day on Twitter, in the saloon bar of my virtual "Cheers": @salihughes, @gracedent, @Martin_Carr, @DavidGArnold, @heawood, @Hemmo, @pgofton, @laurenlaverne, @traceythorn, @alexispetridis, @Dorianlynskey, @porksmith, @mydadisloaded, @mattpark, @nivenj1, @indiaknight, @victoriapeckham, @jennycolgan, @mrchrisaddison, @laurakirsop, @evawiseman, @emmafreud, @scouserachel, @julianstockton, @zoesqwilliams, @EosChater, @sophwilkinson and @stevefurst. Thank you for being my friends in my laptop.

To my daughters—Mummy lied. "The Man" has *not*, in fact, closed down Disney World, all the rides *didn't* get melted down to make more useful things, like school chairs—and YES! We *can* go there, now mummy's finished all the typing! The Guys—Caz, Weena, Eddie, Col, Henri, Gezmo, Jimmy and Jofish—BOOM!

And, finally, to my husband, Pete: thanks for letting me make up all those ridiculous conversations with you, over the years; just to fill up column space. We know I'd never *really* stay stuff like that—and your current silence on this issue is a legal acceptance that I really am *not* like that, and I am finishing the book now so you can't argue back yes yes thank you byeeeee.

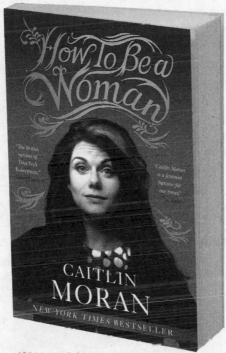